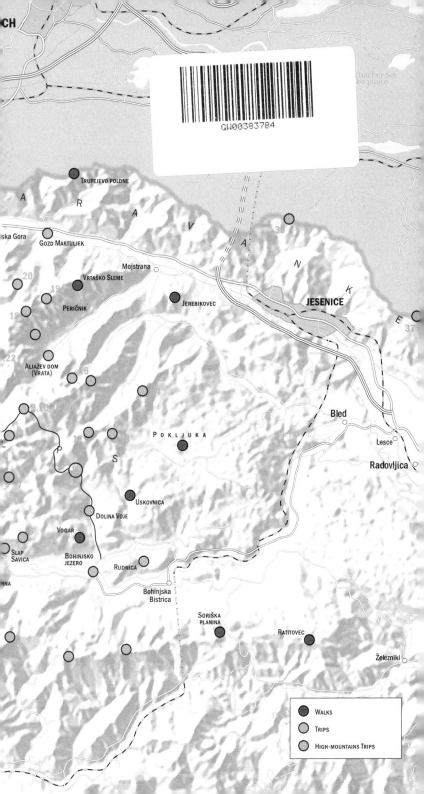

Mountaineering in Slovenia

The Julian Alps
The Kamnik-Savinja Alps
The Karavanke

SIDARTA

Mountaineering in Slovenia

Author
TINE MIHELIČ

Translation
MARGARET DAVIS

Editorial coordination
INES BOŽIČ SKOK

Sketches
DANILO CEDILNIK – DEN

Cartography
TADEJ MALIGOJ

DTP
JERNEJ HUDOLIN

Publisher
© SIDARTA, Ljubljana, 2003, 2007
e mail: office@sidarta.si
www.sidarta.si

Front cover: Stenar, Razor and Jalovec with the Western Julian Alps in the background
Photograph: Janez Skok

CIP – Kataložni zapis o publikaciji
Narodna in univerzitetna knjižnica, Ljubljana

796.52(497.4)(036)

MIHELIČ, Tine
        Mountaineering in Slovenia : the Julian Alps, the Kamnik-Savinja Alps, the Karavanke / Tine Mihelič ; [translation Margaret Davis ; sketches Danilo Cedilnik-Den ; cartography Tadej Maligoj]. – Ljubljana : Sidarta, 2003

ISBN 961-6027-36-0

121748480

Tine Mihelič

Mountaineering in Slovenia

The Julian Alps
The Kamnik-Savinja Alps
The Karavanke

Contents

Introduction

Slovenia is a mountainous country, a characteristic immediately noticed by every visitor. If you arrive by plane, just before you land at Brnik Airport you fly over wild mountain ridges. If you travel here from the north by road or railway you must cross a real alpine pass or take a tunnel under the Karavanke range. Other entrances to Slovenia also reveal this same mountainous character straightaway. Apart from the extreme northeast corner of the country, which belongs to the margin of the Pannonian Plain, hilly terrain predominates, often rising up to high-altitude ridges. These comprise the three Alpine groups of Slovenia. The biggest and also the highest one is the Julian Alps in the northwest, to which the major part of this book is dedicated. Northwards above central Slovenia and the upper basin of the River Savinja rise the Kamnik-Savinja Alps (Kamniško-Savinjske Alpe), while a good part of the northern border of Slovenia runs along the exceptionally long ridge of the Karavanke. The Slovene mountains even include the last outcrop of the Central Alps in the southeast – the gentle medium-high back of the Pohorje, to the south above the valley of the River Drava. This range represents the only granite hills in Slovenia, the other groups belong to the southern limestone Alps. South of the Ljubljana basin, i.e. in central Slovenia, the lower outlying parts of the Julian Alps touch the Dinaric Alps, which continue in ramified knots into the heart of the Balkan peninsula. Southern Slovenia is dominated by plateau-type terrain with a pronounced karst character, which then drops abruptly to the Adriatic shoreline.

This book is a mountaineers' guide, of course, and thus is devoted to the Slovene Alps. But for visitors to Slovenia it should be pointed out that there are beautiful and fascinating spots in regions where the influence of the high Alps does not reach, which also deserve your attention and time. Slovenia is a small country and you can cross it by car in a few hours. The tourist stationed in Bled at the foot of the Julian Alps, for instance, can organize with ease a one-day visit to attractive points even though they lie on the other side of the country. And these can include the marvellous subterranean caves and other places of interest in the Karst, marking out southern Slovenia, the soft, hilly world of Dolenjska along the River Krka or the gentle wine-growing area of Slovenske gorice in the heart of Štajerska (Styria).

The Slovene mountains cannot compare in altitude with the champions of the Central Alps, of course. A Slovene mountain counts as high if it exceeds 2000 metres. But there's a considerable number in this category, approximately 350. The highest summit is Triglav, which rises to 2864 m. But more than altitude, the Slovene mountains appeal with other charms. Their attraction lies precisely in the fact that they don't reach to extreme heights. Moreover, even at the greatest height, you are not surrounded by a lifeless wilderness, but a variegated world of flourishing life. Among the grey rocks you notice a tiny flower in a crevice, in some solitary cwm high up the whistle of a marmot takes you by surprise, and on pockets of grass among the bare rock you catch sight of the brown bodies of the most ancient inhabitants of these parts – chamois and ibex. If you are fortunate, you might see the peaceful flight of that ruler of the alpine sky – the golden eagle. The Slovene mountains are heavily forested on their lower slopes, while above that is an extensive area of grassland, individual larches and great swathes of

dwarf pine. These regions are also adorned by an incredible wealth of alpine flowers. Colourful gardens can reach up to the greatest heights, all the way to the ridges. Alpine meadows have been used for centuries by the inhabitants to pasture their herds at a higher altitude, as they migrate for the summer from village cowsheds to the "planine" (alps, i.e. mountain pastures). These are as plentiful as one could wish for and have become an important element in the folklore and ethnographic image of the Slovene landscape. With increasing height, naturally the rocks show through the greenness more and more, but they are so light-coloured here that they give the mountains a friendly look. The forms of summits and ridges are dynamic. Steep lines dominate, which is typical of limestone regions. Local climatic conditions have removed the last remnants of glaciers, though large snowfields are still part of the usual summer appearance of the Slovene mountains. Especially on the northern side there are magnificent rock faces, which often give the summits an air of inaccessibility and wildness.

However, the champions of the Slovene Alps are for the most part accessible to every experienced and well-equipped mountaineer. From early times the Slovenes have been very passionate mountaineers themselves, and their mountains are served by a network of well-maintained paths and staffed mountain huts, which is possibly the densest in the Alps generally. Each nation adapts its style of life to the region it inhabits and so it's no surprise that Slovene alpinists are among the best in the world. They got their motivation for supreme achievements in the most renowned mountain ranges of the world precisely in their own beautiful mountains at home, where they could hone their skills and expand their experience. The Slovene Alps in all their variety offer every possibility for activities in natural surroundings for visitors of whatever orientation. All the modern sports that engage people in the mountain realm find excellent opportunities here.

In this introductory section the characteristics of the Slovene mountains are sketched only in rough outline, more detail is given in individual descriptions. Precisely the Julian Alps play the main role in this book. For those who would like to have a complete picture of the Slovene mountain world, the other alpine groups are presented to a limited extent. This slender information might nevertheless give sufficient detail for you to visit these less well-known Slovene mountains, which in no way lag behind the famous Julian Alps for beauty and attractiveness.

pp. 2-3: The Peričnik waterfall in the Vrata valley
pp. 6-7: The Špik group seen from the Karavanke

Practical hints

MOUNTAIN HUTS

Mountain huts in the Julian Alps are quite abundant and well supplied (there are also some shelters and bivouacs without provision). Most of them can be reached by waymarked paths, some at lower altitudes can also be reached by road. The majority are open and staffed only during the summer season, though many have a winter room with basic sleeping accommodation which is available outside the season. The mountain huts offer beds, food, drink and information. The house rules differ from those in tourist accommodation down in the valley, since mountain huts aim at the visitor setting out early and feeling well rested. Visitors are required to observe the warden's instructions, and this is particularly important at "peak hours", when the most frequented huts are overflowing. If you are planning a mountain tour in the high season (August), it is recommendable to make a prior reservation by phone. All information about the open season for mountain huts and their telephone number is available in the office of the Planinska zveza Slovenije (i.e. the Alpine Association of Slovenia), Dvoržakova 9, 1000 Ljubljana, tel: +386-(0)1 430 74 10, fax: +386-(0)1 432 21 40, e-mail: info@pzs.si

The following is a list of mountain huts along the routes with basic data; access is given in the descriptions of individual tours:

THE BOHINJ MOUNTAINS

- Krekova koča na Ratitovcu, 1642m. Open in summer, otherwise at weekends.
- Koča na Soriški planini, 1306 m. Open in summer and the skiing period.
- Dom Zorka Jelinčiča na Črni prsti, 1835 m. Open in summer.
- Koča Merjasec na Voglu, 1540 m. Open all year.
- Dom na Komni, 1520 m. Open all year.
- Koča pod Bogatinom, 1513 m. Open in summer and the ski-touring period.
- Koča pri Triglavskih jezerih, 1683 m. Open in summer, winter room.
- Zasavska koča na Prehodavcih, 2071 m. Open in summer, winter room.
- Kosijev dom na Vogarju, 1054 m. Open in summer, later at weekends.
- Koča na Planini pri Jezeru, 1453 m. Open in summer, winter room.
- Koča na Uskovnici, 1154 m. Open in summer, otherwise at weekends.
- Vodnikov dom na Velem polju, 1805 m. Open in summer, winter room.
- Tržaška koča na Doliču, 2151 m. Open in summer, winter room.
- Dom Planika pod Triglavom, 2404 m. Open in summer, winter room.
- Triglavski dom na Kredarici, 2516 m. Open all year.
- Blejska koča na Lipanci, 1630 m. Open all year.

THE NORTHERN APPROACHES

- Dom Valentina Staniča pod Triglavom, 2332m. Open in summer, winter room.
- Triglavski dom na Kredarici, 2516 m. Open all year.

- Aljažev dom v Vratih, 21015 m. Open May-October, winter room in a little hut 200 m to the south.
- Koča na Gozdu, 1226 m. Open all year.
- Mihov dom, 1085 m. Open all year.
- Erjavčeva koča na Vršiču, 1525 m. Open all year.
- Tičarjev dom, 1620 m. Open in summer.
- Poštarski dom na Vršiču, 1688 m. Open in summer.
- Dom v Tamarju, 1108 m. Open all year.

THE MOUNTAINS ABOVE THE SOČA
- Dom Petra Skalarja na Kaninu, 2260 m. Open in summer.
- Koča na Mangartskem sedlu, 1906 m. Open in summer.
- Koča pri izviru Soče, 886 m. Open May-October.
- Zavetišče pod Špičkom, 2064 m. Open in summer, winter room.
- Tičarjev dom, 1620 m. Open in summer.
- Poštarski dom na Vršiču, 1688 m. Open in summer.
- Pogačnikov dom na Kriških podih, 2050 m. Open in summer, winter room.
- Tržaška koča na Doliču, 2151 m. Open in summer, winter room.
- Zasavska koča na Prehodavcih, 2071 m. Open in summer, winter room.
- Dom dr. Klementa Juga v Lepeni, 700 m. Open in summer.
- Planinski dom pri Krnskih jezerih, 1385 m. Open in summer, winter room.
- Gomiščkovo zavetišče na Krnu, 2182 m. Open in summer.
- Koča na planini Kuhinja pod Krnom, 991 m. Open at weekends.

THE KAMNIK-SAVINJA ALPS
- Dom v Kamniški Bistrici, 600 m. Open in summer, later at weekends.
- Cojzova koča na Kokrskem sedlu, 1793 m. Open in summer, winter room.
- Kamniška koča na Kamniškem sedlu, 1793 m. Open in summer, winter room.
- Kocbekov dom na Korošici, 1808 m. Open in summer, winter room.
- Češka koča na Spodnjih Ravneh, 1542 m. Open in summer, later at weekends, winter room.
- Planinski dom na Kališču, 1540 m. Open in summer, later at weekends.
- Dom pod Storžičem, 1123 m. Open in summer and occasionally at weekends.
- Dom planincev v Logarski dolini, 837 m. Open in summer and autumn.
- Koča na Klemenči jami pod Ojstrico, 1208 m. Open in summer.
- Frischaufov dom na Okrešlju, 1396 m. Open in summer.
- Koča na Grohatu pod Raduho, 1460 m. Open in summer.

THE KARAVANKE
- Koča na Golici, 1582 m. Open in summer.
- Valvasorjev dom pod Stolom, 1181 m. Open in summer, later at weekends.
- Prešernova koča na Stolu, 2174 m. Open in summer.
- Dom na Kofcah, 1488 m. Open in summer, later at weekends.
- Koča pod Olševo, 1232 m. Open all year.

ROUTES

Most of the trips and high mountain tours described here follow waymarked paths. The usual waymark in the Slovene mountains is a white circle with a red surround or a red arrow, often bent in the direction to be taken. Forks are indicated by signposts or easily visible writing on rocks. Steeper, exposed and dangerous places are often protected by iron pitons and wire ropes. The many frequented paths are generally well maintained, although in more solitary regions you might come across a less good path with faded waymarks or damaged security aids, which naturally demands extra caution. For the most part the wardens in mountain huts at the starting-point are acquainted with the state of the paths. If the number 1 is painted beside a waymark, this indicates the Slovene Mountain Way (Slovenska planinska pot), a route which leads one through most of the Slovene mountains and represents an appealing challenge for more demanding mountaineers. There are other connected routes with their own specific waymarks. Especially at lower altitudes you will often find unmarked paths, used by hunters, shepherds, foresters, or frequented by animals. These occur more rarely in the descriptions given here, since orientation on such paths is more difficult and the tours demand considerable experience. It is only exceptionally (two or three times) that you are invited to tackle a pathless area, but the tours in this category are some of the easiest and safest. They are indicated with suitable warnings.

MOUNTAIN GUIDES

Mountain guides in Slovenia are trained according to UIAA standards for guiding on paths, climbing routes and ski tours. The guides are registered at the PZS (Mountaineering Association of Slovenia), where you can obtain all the necessary information. Such services are also provided by tourist agencies in the more important places where mountain routes start from.

THE MOUNTAIN RESCUE SERVICE (GORSKA REŠEVALNA SLUŽBA – GRS)

The Mountain Rescue Service in the Slovene mountains is excellently organized, equipped and trained. The use of helicopters has greatly alleviated the extremely demanding work of rescuers and saved many lives. The international **SOS call** is six signals per minute. The audible or visible signal (shouting, using a whistle, torch, mirror, etc.) must be repeated at intervals of one minute until an answer is received. The answer to an SOS call is three signals per minute. Every person is obliged to respond to an SOS call and to relay the news to the nearest announcement post or rescue station. A mountaineering accident can be reported in all the mountain huts, to the police or to any information centre (tel: 112). Unfortunately, the Slovene mountain region is **not** completely covered for the purpose of using a mobile phone. For more information on the availability of a GSM signal see pp. 266-269.

EQUIPMENT

The description of trips and mountain tours will take you on safe valley walks as well as to the highest summits in the Slovene mountains. Of course, words need not be wasted on how to equip yourself for a walk around Lake Bohinj, but it is essential to say what sort of dangers can lurk in the high mountains and how to defend yourself against them. Here the greatest danger is caused by a sudden change in the weather, bringing cold, wetness, fog, lightning, falling stones, and the like. Even a snowstorm in the middle of summer is nothing unusual. The mountaineer avoids such dangers through prudent action and good equipment. One must find out about the weather situation before leaving for the mountains, and adapt the difficulty and length of the tour to those conditions. The climatic features of the Slovene mountains are such that you must never set off without reliable protection against rain and cold. Above 2000 metres **high-altitude equipment** is obligatory; this consists of good quality high mountaineering boots, warm clothing, rainproof anorak or windjacket, cap, gloves and spare underwear. It is also essential to carry in one's rucksack a torch, matches, first aid kit, penknife, map, compass, flask, an adequate supply of calories, etc. (and not least a bag for rubbish, which you take down to the valley). A sleeping bag can substitute for a mountain hut in remote areas, while an ice-axe is a necessary piece of equipment in early sumer. Demanding secured routes require special equipment for self-belaying on the steel ropes, and a climbing helmet is recommendable in exposed places. As for animals, only poisonous snakes represent a danger for mountaineers in the Julian Alps, but these are not rare, and ticks, whose bites can cause viral illnesses. Most of these dangers can be avoided, but avoidance is conditional on the mountaineer's experience, carefulness, knowledge of the mountains, good psychological form and accurate evaluation of his or her own capabilities. The sensible mountaineer will never venture on a tour that demands the utmost exertion.

SEASONS

This book describes the Slovene mountains and ascents to their summits in summer, i.e. snowless conditions. This concept, of course, is quite elastic, as it can change as regards the altitude, weather, and other phenomena that influence natural conditions. The most favourable period for going to the mountains is summer and early autumn. Lower and southern regions naturally lose their snow earlier than those that are higher and shady. The lower mountains offer summer conditions generally by May, but on Triglav the summer mountaineering season begins only in July. Even then you must quite often face crossing a snowfield. Especially when tackling the high mountains from the north, you need to carry an ice-axe until the end of July. And in autumn it is just the opposite. In September so much snow can fall in the high mountains that in shady places it will not melt away before winter. On the other hand, the sunny side can frequently be free of snow and warmly inviting right up to November. The way in which the mountain huts operate is similar. The highest ones, i.e. above 2000 m, are usually open from the beginning of July to the end of September. The period from 15 July to 15 September counts as the main summer mountaineering season. At that time the most important huts are generally very busy, sometimes even overflowing. It is therefore recommendable to reserve sleeping accommodation.

TRIGLAV NATIONAL PARK

Most of the Julian Alps lie within the Triglav National Park (Triglavski narodni park - TNP), which is protected by law. The points of entry into the park territory are indicated by signboards positioned beside the roads and pathways. In this area strict regulations apply which forbid all actions that are detrimental to nature, such as picking flowers, frightening animals, throwing away rubbish, lighting fires, camping and parking vehicles outside specified places. Observance of these and other regulations is checked by park wardens.

pp. 18-19: The Zajamniki alp with the Bohinj mountains in the background

The Julian Alps

The Julian Alps, as the highest and most extensive massif, are essentially the "Slovene Himalayas". Together with their foothills they occupy most of north-western Slovenia, and an important part also lies in the extreme northeastern corner of Italy. The northern neighbours of the Julian Alps are the long chains of the Karavanke and the Carnic Alps, to the west the mountain range sinks down beneath the soft fringes of Venetian Slovenia into the Furlanian plain (on clear mornings it is possible to see the Adriatic Sea from lofty summits), and to the east the Gorenjska plain broadens out. Across this plain the Julian giants flirt with the scarcely lower champions of the Kamnik-Savinja Alps. Southeastwards hills of medium height continue to the distant horizon, where the Alps touch upon the Dinaric mountain range. The Julian Alps are divided into the Eastern and Western sections, the meeting-point being the Predel pass between the Mangart and Kanin groups. This mountain range is built of Mesozoic marine sediments, with blocks of Dachstein limestone and dolomite predominating. Its pronounced karst character is very obvious. The Julian Alps include 200 summits above 2000 m, 25 summits that rise over 2500 m, while the highest peak is Triglav, at 2864 m. The range does not possess any regions with permanent glaciation; the modest remains of former glaciers are disappearing due to the increasingly meagre winters. However, earlier glaciation has left ineradicable traces in the typical shapes of the valleys and the abundance of glacial lakes. The waters flow north and east into the river basin of the Sava, south into the Soča and west mostly into the Tagliamento. Since the influences of the sea and the continental landmass mingle here, there is no lack of water. At higher altitudes there is an Alpine climate with long winters, thick snow cover and quick transitions to a short, hot summer. The summer mountaineering season lasts from July to September. The flora and fauna are exceptionally rich and varied. Most of the mountains in this area come under nature protection, since they lie within the Triglav National Park. The Julian Alps occupy the meeting-point of the three main European ethnic and language groups, and their inhabitants will greet people on mountain paths in four different languages: Slovene, Italian, Furlanian and German. The name Julian Alps was known to Roman writers and was linked with the imperial Roman family of the Julians. The part of the Julian Alps described in this book lies on the territory of the Republic of Slovenia.

These mountains are exceptionally diverse. The magnificent but cold and stern northern faces above the Upper Sava Valley (Zgornjesavska dolina) stand in sheer contrast to the sunny, friendly mountains of the Soča Basin, where the visitor can definitely feel the balmy influence of the nearby Adriatic Sea, along with no less magnificence! And then there is the serious yet dream-like world of the Bohinj mountains, where the greyness of the rocks is often enlivened by a sparkling blue tarn, and in green hollows below the bare mountain crests the music of cowbells is heard. The eastern fringe, where the Julians drop towards the Gorenjska plain is another special realm. Pokljuka, Mežakla and Jelovica are the names of enormous plateaus, covered with a practically uninterrupted green blanket of spruce forest. The backbone of the Julian Alps is the watershed ridge running from east to west. Here are the mighty champions: Triglav, Razor, Prisank, Jalovec and Mangart. North of Triglav and outside the major chain throng the wild and pinnacled dolomite peaks of the Martuljek and Škrlatica groups, while the Krn and Bavški Grintavec groups lying further south belong as a whole to the Soča Basin. The Western Julian Alps comprise three mountain groups dominated by the tremendous summits of Kanin, Jôf Fuart/Viš and Montasio/Montaž.

Thanks to their geological composition the Julian Alps form a decidedly bright mountain range, making a friendly and inviting impression. The views from the south of this extensive chain of lofty peaks, shimmering in the sun, are simply wonderful. On fine winter days the white ramparts of Kanin and Krn glitter like a blissful vision above the valleys' smoky haze as far as Venice. The panoramas of individual groups enjoy world fame. The view of the Martuljek group from the north has charmed great connoisseurs of the mountains of the world such as Tom Longstaff. There are unforgettable views from Sleme (not far from the Vršič road pass) down into the Planica valley and across to Jalovec, like a mountain crystal in its shape, or from Vogel across to the Triglav range, and so on. The panoramas from the summits themselves are majestic and superbly varied, as the Julian Alps are situated at the meeting-point of the Alps, the Mediterranean region and the distant eastern plains. Apart from the famous and often praised summits and viewpoints this mountain range still hides many a forgotten nook not to be captured on picture postcards. The beauty and diversity of the Julian Alps offer an inexhaustible wealth of ever new experiences.

There exist statistics that record the Slovenes are the most passionate and enthusiastic mountaineering nation, and this may well hold true. They say there isn't a Slovene who would not consider an ascent of Triglav his duty as a citizen, a sort of patriotic action. No wonder, since the Slovenes have made their highest mountain into a national shrine. This serves to explain how greatly visited the Julian Alps are. It would be difficult to find within the entire magnificent arc of the Alps a mountain group where the network of well-maintained, waymarked and, where necessary, secured paths is so dense as here, while the number of well-supplied mountain huts in the Slovene mountains probably establishes a record. All this points to the relatively easy accessibility of the Julian champions, which can be climbed by any walker of average training. Triglav, of course, has the biggest number of visitors; there can often be traffic-jams along its narrow ridge at "rush hours". But this ample chain still offers very many oases of peace and primeval mountain character. Lovers of this kind of mountaineering pleasure specially prefer the wild peaks above the valleys of Trenta and Bavšica. In the Julian Alps the Martuljek group occupies a virtually unique place, for much here has remained as in the earliest times and the extremely demanding ascents deter any mass invasion. As well as mountaineers, rock-climbers like to visit the Julian Alps, while in winter excellent possibilities are offered for ski touring. Their karst nature gives these mountains an especially honourable reputation among speleologists. Water sports and fishing are most at home in the Soča Basin. Additionally, some contemporary sports that choose mountains for their realization have grateful adherents in the Julians. In short, every visitor will find there his or her own appropriate goals. More detailed information is provided in the individual descriptions of mountain tours and trips. These are divided into three chapters dealing with the mountains around the sources of three rivers: the Sava Bohinjka, the Sava Dolinka and the Soča.

The mountaineering history of the Julian Alps ran parallel with the exploration of other parts of the Alps. The beginnings go back to the eighteenth century, when the spirit of the Enlightenment aroused interest in the "conquest of the useless". The year 1778 is regarded as the birthdate of Slovene alpinism, when four Bohinj men were the first to climb Triglav (eight years before the conquest of Mont Blanc!). The local people were familiar with most summits earlier than that through their work as shepherds and hunters; their training made them connoisseurs and guides. Thus in the nineteenth century they could offer valuable help to the majority of foreign explorers, who were drawn to the moutains firstly for scientific and only later for alpinist reasons. The most important of these was the alpinist and excellent mountain writer Julius Kugy (love for the *Julian* Alps was implanted in him even at his christening). In the company of Slovene and Furlanian guides he climbed most of these summits and enthusiastically showed to the world the beauty of the Julian Alps in the rich opus of his writings. Organized mountaineering began in 1893 with the founding of the Slovene Mountaineering Society (nowadays called the Mountaineering Association of Slovenia – Planinska zveza Slovenije - PZS), which has gradually built a more than generous network of mountain paths and huts. Today one Slovene in 20 is a member of the PZS, and at least as many as this regularly go off to the mountains. The first half of the twentieth century saw the classical period of climbing in the Julians. Here native alpinists naturally played the greatest role; they include such names as Henrik Tuma, Klement Jug, Mira Marko Debelak, Pavla Jesih, Joža Čop and Uroš Župančič. The importance and attractiveness of the Julian Alps is borne out by the names of famous foreign alpinists who were active here: Emilio Comici, Celso Gilberti, Ivano Dibona and Peter Aschenbrenner. It was on these foundations that later on contemporary Slovene alpinism was to be built; nowadays this occupies a top position internationally, for it has achieved outstanding results in every major mountain range in the world.

p. 23: Illustration from B. Hacquet: Oryctographia Carniolica, 1778

Hic ubi TERGLOVUS caput altis nubibus infert
Quanta laborantis naturæ munera cerno!
Quam stat sublimis! ventosque imbresque seren...
Despicit, atque simul raros ostentat honores,

The Bohinj mountains

Bohinj is like a tiny mountainous country at the heart of the Julian Alps. It comprises both flat ground and alpine terrain in the source area of the Sava Bohinjka River, which is fed by waters flowing down the southern slopes of the mighty Triglav group. The heart and indeed the greatest treasure of Bohinj is Lake Bohinj (Bohinjsko jezero), lying at an altitude of 525 m at the head of the valley. This inhabited valley is surrounded by a great circle of mountains with the highest Julian summit, Triglav, dominating all. Halfway between the valley and the mountain crests there stretches more level terrain, in places overgrown with forests and higher up with impenetrable swathes of dwarf pine. To the west and east the ridges touch upon the Soča Basin, while to the north they plunge headlong into the Upper Sava Valley. The beauty of this region and the relatively pristine character of its mountain environment cause Bohinj to be ranged among the loveliest corners in the Alps.

It's not all that long ago that Bohinj was considered a land at the back of beyond. This barely accessible alpine nook, surrounded with soaring ridges, remained for many centuries in its remoteness far from the big world. Because of their isolation, the inhabitants acquired a special identity, marked by the eternal struggle for survival among the mountains, where the forces of nature rule with a stronger hand than in the gentle lowlands. When a Slovene hears the word Bohinj, he inevitably thinks about the glitter of lofty summits, the keen winds blowing from the heights and the roar of foaming waters. From time immemorial the Bohinj people (*Bohinjci)* had to face the alpine world pressing everywhere on their farmsteads. But this was no enemy, for centuries of measuring their strength had led them to know it well and to love it. At times disasters did indeed come crashing down from the mountains: torrential streams swept over their fields and threatened their homes, avalanches often thundered right into the valley, destroying everything before them. But whoever knows the mountains also knows that the richest forests extend there, on open spaces the animals munch the juiciest alpine grass, and exploiting the mineral wealth connected with the iron industry (nowadays both are a matter of the past) was for centuries part of everyday life. And so the Bohinjci always respected their mountains and frequently dedicated their dreams to them as well. Up there, on the glowing ridges, among the grey crags and hidden hollows lies the world of Bohinj myths and legends. Hunters and shepherds experienced adventures in this alpine realm, honing their skills and coming to know every nook and cranny of their tiny kingdom, so that later they could reveal it to an incredulous public as mountain guides. Now Bohinj has long since changed from being a forgotten, distant corner; it is a well-known and popular tourist jewel, visited not only by Slovenes, but by holiday-makers from all over Europe.

Bohinj's "ground floor" is the inhabited lowland area. It is a long, winding valley with others branching off, where the action of glaciers long ago left a broad, flat bottom and steep, sometimes perpendicular slopes. The head of the Bohinj valley is called Ukanc (meaning 'at the end'). This wild region resounds with the roar of the foaming Savica river, which issues in the famous waterfall Savica from the mighty Komarča face. At the very heart of Bohinj lies its sparkling alpine jewel – Lake Bohinj. Below it the valley splits into two. The upper valley gradually climbs towards the outlying spurs of the Pokljuka plateau, while the lower one is the natural outlet of the lake, with the Sava Bohinjka River winding along it. Lower still the valley squeezes through a gorge between the Pokljuka and Jelovica plateaus and runs out into the Gorenjska plain. The administrative and economic centre of Bohinj is the village Bohinjska Bistrica, 512 m, in the lower valley, while the most important settlement in the upper valley is the former centre of Bohinj – Srednja vas, 620 m. Two bigger villages with important tourist attractions are Ribčev Laz and Stara Fužina near the eastern shore of the lake, otherwise many smaller villages and hamlets are scattered around this area. In some you can still observe the original character of old Bohinj. Apart from Bohinjska Bistrica, which has some industries, these are predominantly farming settlements, surrounded by lovely fields and hay-meadows.

Bohinj's middle "storey" consists of the plateaus that encircle the valley at an approximate altitude of 1300-1600 m. This region is also "inhabited", but only during the summer, when the air is filled with the clangour of cow-bells. The summer pasturing of animals on the *planine* (alps or mountain pastures) has a centuries-long tradition in the Slovene mountains and is one of the ethnographic specialities of the country. It is particularly at home in Bohinj. The plateaus begin on Vogel and extend across the wide spaces of Komna and the Triglav Lakes, but they flourish most of all on the broad Fužina alps that lie north of Lake Bohinj. Here the terrain in mighty sweeps climbs up to the topmost points. East of the deeply carved Voje valley stretches the somewhat lower lying and thus completely forested Pokljuka plateau. Above all these plateaus a glorious circle of lofty summits twists its way around Bohinj. The southern chain of this necklace comprises the ridges of the Spodnje Bohinjske gore (Lower Bohinj Mountains). In this area the ridge from its medium-high beginning on Ratitovec gradually climbs towards the west up to the first two-thousanders above Komna. The western chain surrounds the Komna plateau and the Triglav Lakes Valley and includes such fine mountains as Plaski Vogel and Lepa špica. Highest of all is the northern chain, where the monarch of Bohinj and all the Slovene mountains holds sway – Triglav, 2864 m. The ridge marking Bohinj's boundary then gradually descends towards the east and beyond the twin summits of Draški vrh (Veliki and Mali) disappears into the Pokljuka forests. Most of the Bohinj territory lies within the Triglav National Park (Triglavski narodni park) and therefore constitutes a conservation area with its own particular regime. Regulations relating to the national park are given on p. 17.

Bohinj is easily reached from central Slovenia by the Ljubljana – Bled – Bohinj main road (from Ljubljana to the lake approximately 80 km, from Bled 30 km), from the southern, Primorska side a rather winding road leads through the

Baška grapa and over Soriška planina. The Jesenice – Nova Gorica railway line also runs through Bohinj (the railway station is at Bohinjska Bistrica) and then burrows through the Lower Bohinj Mountains in a 6-km-long tunnel (a car-train is available). The network of local roads which give visitors access to the mountain realm will be detailed for individual trips and alpine tours.

This invitation to Bohinj is sent to a variety of addresses, embracing modest walkers as well as champions of the greatest heights. All will bring to their discovery of this lovely area their own particular approach, in keeping with their desires and capabilities. If you're interested in finding what place the Bohinj Mountains hold on the "scale of difficulty" presented in this book, then they are relatively easy and friendly – at least in comparison with the stern giants above the Upper Sava Valley or the steep, solitary mountains of the Soča Basin. And finally a personal comment from the author: this chapter on Bohinj is written by a native – a Bohinjec.

St. John's church beside Lake Bohinj

Walks

LAKE BOHINJ

is a precious jewel and the very heart of Bohinj. This 4-km-long glacial lake, up to 45 m deep, mirrors the shining image of its mountain giants as well as man and his attitude towards nature. Due to the crowds of visitors, the "health" of Lake Bohinj is very fragile. In summer the water is pleasantly warm and invites many swimmers, as well as adherents of other water sports. The lake is fed by pure alpine streams, mighty slopes plunge into it, while many routes to the summits start from its shore. Thus the lake is very closely linked with the world of mountains; together they create an indivisible whole and an aesthetically perfect image.

Whoever wishes to become acquainted with Lake Bohinj should simply walk around it. It is always pleasant by the water, whether the sun shines or you use your umbrella. The circuit can be completed in three hours though most are satisfied with an outing along the northern shore. This sunny side brings greater delight to nature lovers since the "gifts" of civilization have not reached here to the same extent as on the southern shore, where the road can be busy with traffic. It doesn't matter which direction you choose, but this description follows the anti-clockwise one. You begin the outing at Ribčev Laz, by the church of St John (cerkev sv. Janeza), which together with the stone bridge spanning the River Sava as it flows out of the lake, forms the best-known Bohinj view. A short walk along asphalt brings you to the parking place by the *gostilna* Kramar, and then a pleasant pathway follows to the end of the lake. This winds all the time right along the shoreline, first over the fields by the Fužina bay, then alternately through open sections and patches of forest at the foot of Pršivec, a high mountain above the northern edge of the lake. The path crosses numerous gullies, which display the action of mountain torrents during heavy rainfall. The mountainside grows ever steeper and in the last part huge rock boulders lean over the shore and the path. There are attractive natural spots for bathing along the shore, and no need to fear the way, even in the hottest summer. The route finally retreats away from the steep slopes onto a broad, grassy area at the end of the lake, which is also the "end of Bohinj", as its name, Ukanc, declares. By the bridge over the Savica stream, which supplies the lake, the path runs out onto asphalt near the Zlatorog Hotel (bus stop). From Ribčev Laz 1.30 h.

There is no need to tramp along asphalt on the southern side either. A raised pathway runs beside the road, and is pleasantly shaded all the way. It runs past the baroque church of the Holy Spirit (cerkev sv. Duha) and the Hotel pod Voglom, past the spot Pod skalco, which is a popular rock face for sports climbers, and your round trip of the lake is complete. From the Zlatorog Hotel a good hour. If you would like to avoid the petrol fumes on the south side too, we recommend a pleasant path about 100 m above the lake. It begins by the lower station of theVogel cableway, ascends to the height mentioned, then winds more or less horizontally through forest all the time and drops towards the lake shore by Pod skalco. This very twisting path is half an hour longer than the one previously described, and you need to watch out for the signs so you don't stray off into the network of forest tracks.

SLAP SAVICA

The Savica waterfall (slap Savica), together with the lake and Triglav, are the greatest natural sights in Bohinj. Its beauty and the epic poem "Krst pri Savici" (Baptism by the Savica) by the great poet France Prešeren have made this one of the natural symbols of the country for Slovenes. The waterfall plunges out of a cleft in the wildest corner of Bohinj – below the Komarča face. 80 m high, this marvellous waterfall is the natural outlet for the waters that gather deep underground from the Triglav Lakes Valley. A safely built pathway (over 500 steps!) leads you here in a good 15 minutes from the end of the road, marked by a large parking area and a café. (During the summer season regular buses drive up here and an entrance charge is made.) On a little promontory in front of the waterfall stands a tiny wooden construction, it is also possible to descend right to the deep green pool below the waterfall. (Be prepared for the spray when it is in full spate!) A recommendable alternative is to take the path from the Zlatorog Hotel through the forest at the foot of Pršivec; to the waterfall 1.30 h.

THE VOJE VALLEY

This is the name of a deeply carved valley of glacial origin which above the village of Stara Fužina cuts into the heart of the Triglav group. Here there are extensive hay-meadows scattered with cottages and hay-huts. Voje is enlivened by the Mostnica stream, with its source in a beautiful waterfall, which then flows placidly along the broad valley bottom, but at the lower end, cloaked with forest, it has hollowed out a picturesque canyon. The way into Voje is "classic", a recommendable Bohinj outing, finest done on foot, of course, although a road runs into the valley. Your starting-point is Stara Fužina. From here (or from the parking place to the west above the village) you aim first for the nearby Hudičev most (Devil's Bridge), which boldly spans the gorge above its deepest point, and then a safely built path winds just above the perpendicular edge. Between the second and third bridges the path is laid on both sides of this extremely picturesque canyon, full of "sculptural masterpieces" that the water has created through the millenia. Especially famous is Slonček (Baby Elephant), which thrusts its rock trunk into the wonderful aquamarine of a deep pool. Above the third bridge the path climbs steeply through the forest towards the left and soon reaches the mountain hut Koča v Vojah, 690 m, where the view of Voje's broad meadows opens out. To this point 1 h. (The road from Stara Fužina also comes here – a road toll is charged in the summer season.) You continue along the road, now closed to public use, to the fourth bridge, where you cross to the other side of the Mostnica (before the bridge a path branches off left towards Triglav). Now you can ramble over the lovely hay-meadows towards the end of the valley. As you approach the foot of the mighty Tosc mountain, which blots out your view of Triglav, you hear a rushing sound issuing from the forest. On your

right is a small café, and behind this a beautiful 30-metre-high waterfall soon greets you, gushing down a narrow gully. The path into Voje ends here, since by the waterfall you are confronted by the steep, nearly inaccessible world of the high mountains. From Koča v Vojah 40 minutes.

AROUND RUDNICA

You will soon become more closely acquainted with this forested hill that rises precisely in the middle of Bohinj, but this description takes you on a circular route around its base. On the way you'll see some of Bohinj's interesting sights that take us back to old times and the customs in this corner of the mountains. The route leads you into both valleys, with a traverse across the wonderful hay-meadows with their fine views named Senožeta (the name denotes hay-meadows). We suggest a clock-wise journey, beginning at the central Bohinj point, St John's church (cerkev sv. Janeza). Looking towards the upper valley, you take the footpath into Stara Fužina beside the main road. The village's name is reminiscent of the ancient Bohinj iron industry, which died out at the end of the nineteenth century. In the middle of the village is the well-arranged Dairy Museum (Planšarski muzej). You leave Stara Fužina by the church of St Paul (cerkev sv. Pavla) and look for a path at the foot of the hill on your left. After quarter of an hour a famous group of double hayracks greets you beside the road; these form a unique monument of folk architecture. Immediately afterwards you enter the village of Studor, pressed against the foot of the perpendicular face of a mountain with the same name. There are some beautifully preserved houses here of the traditional alpine type, one of which – the old Oplen homestead (Oplenova domačija) – has been arranged into a museum. The objects displayed and the ancient "black kitchen" offer a wonderful insight into the way of life of our ancestors. From Studor the village

A mountain and local architecture in harmony - Studor

road leads into Srednja vas, the former centre of Bohinj, but the coming of the railway meant it lost first place to Bistrica. Its former role is accentuated by the mighty church of St Martin (cerkev sv. Martina) high above the village (concerts of classical music are held here during the summer). You leave Srednja vas by a signpost near the "centre" and follow the cart-track across the fields. The next fifteen minutes takes you up leftwards across meadows and through copses and finally onto a farmers' lane running along the grassy ridge of Senožeta and affording a glorious view of the encircling Bohinj mountains. The track now bears southwest towards the lower valley, dropping through the forest into the village of Brod by the River Sava. Here you turn right, following first the road, then a cart-track that winds steadily on near the river's left bank. Small patches of forest and hay-meadows alternate, while here and there the path comes really close to the Sava, which is quite warm in high summer and invites you to a pleasantly refreshing dip. Higher up the river hides in a gorge but the path soon leads to the first farmhouses and beyond the bridge joins the main road near St John's church. The circular route takes a good 3 h.

p. 29: Voje - the Mostnica foams through rock troughs

Viewpoints

VODNIKOV RAZGLEDNIK

Vodnik's Viewpoint, 1017 m, is a small rise above the village of Koprivnik on the edge of the Pokljuka plateau, which just here plunges steeply down into the Bohinj valley. The hill stands exactly on the axis of the upper valley, the lake and Ukanc, so that Bohinj lies before you like an open book, while the great mountain chain glows above. The extensive view has something to teach in addition to its beauty, and the way to it is short and comfortable. The name reflects the Slovene poet Valentin Vodnik, who served as the village priest at Koprivnik at the end of the eighteenth century, and often visited this noble viewpoint. Koprivnik, 969 m, lies just north of the road that climbs from the Bohinj valley onto Pokljuka (from Bohinjska Bistrica 8 km, from the lake 10 km). There is a parking place by the church. Follow the direction sign southwards through the village (along the road), cross a forested hill by a footpath and then turn right past a solitary farmhouse. From here the forest path climbs to the nearby Vodnikov razglednik. From the church 20 minutes. A pleasant, shady footpath also leads here, branching off the main road immediately above the village of Jereka (1 h).

RUDNICA

The lower and upper Bohinj valleys are divided by a medium-high ridge with two forested tops, of which the western, higher one is called Rudnica, 946 m. Its name calls to mind the long bygone times of Bohinj iron-working. Its central position makes Rudnica a real "textbook" of Bohinj geography, but as it is

Rudnica (left) and Studor stand guard over the upper Bohinj valley

covered with forest, the whole horizon cannot be seen. Each forest glade surprises with a different view. You must piece the mosaic together yourself. From the west delightful hay-meadows reach almost to the top, but on the other side the mountain is steep, with sheer drops in places. Many paths and cart-tracks lead to Rudnica, so it can be hard to orientate yourself. Access from the village of Brod in the lower valley and from Senožeta (fine grassy slopes to the east below Rudnica) is very steep and can even be dangerous, so we recommend the comfortable route over Rudnica's western flank, starting from Stara Fužina. You branch off the main road near the church in the eastern part of the village (signpost) and follow the track across the fields to the foot of Rudnica, and then climb in long serpentine bends to the ridge just west below the summit (a good view!). Turn left as the gradually narrowing path twists towards the summit. A few more minutes through the forest and then take care: a sheer precipice yawns at your feet above the upper valley as you reach the top. From Stara Fužina 1.15 h.

The hilltop in the lower western ridge below Rudnica is called **Peč** (720 m) and offers a marvellous vista of the nearby Lake Bohinj. It can be easily reached by a waymarked path that begins by the concrete bridge halfway between St John's church and Stara Fužina. From the road 20 minutes.

"VOGEL"

Vogel, 1540 m, is the best known and most visited Bohinj viewpoint, which naturally must be attributed to the cableway. This popular point together with the ski centre has borrowed its name from the finely shaped mountain in the nearby ridge of the Lower Bohinj Mountains (hence the quotation marks). The true name of the sheer promontory where the Ski Hotel and the mountain hut koča Merjasec stand beside the cableway station is Rjava skala (Brown

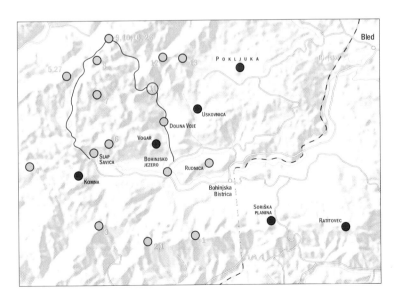

Rock). "Vogel" has gained its reputation especially with its high position, which allows a view of the "upper storeys" of the mountains. Here you can look the giants around the Bohinj valley in the eye. The first star in this panorama is, of course, Triglav, whose southern slopes fall in great steps from the high rocky wastes. Triglav is only the highest point of this extremely expansive range, made up of innumerable summits surrounding you on all sides. Below lurks a vertiginous abyss, and your gaze skims down to the dark surface of Lake Bohinj. Vogel is also an outstanding, well patronized starting-point for many alpine tours in the Lower Bohinj range; in winter it is a lively ski centre. Most visitors are brought here by the cable-car (the lower station is by the camp-site), but two waymarked routes are available to the more enterprising. The eastern approach is preferable: a good path leaves the asphalt road between the two hotels Jezero and Bellevue just below the latter one. You soon cross hay-meadows and then wind up quite steeply through the forest, which gradually changes from the lowland type into a highland one. As bushes of dwarf pine begin to mingle with the larches, the gradient eases and you walk over the undulating plateau to the Ski Hotel on Rjava skala. This pleasant, shady path takes 2.30 h. The western approach starts in Ukanc; the signpost is near the Zlatorog Hotel. Above the main road the path climbs steeply, crosses the forest road which comes from the lower cableway station, and in numerous bends gains the ski track of Žagarjev graben (Žagar's Gully) cut through the trees. Higher up you again bear left into the forest and ascend to the Ski Hotel on Rjava skala. From the Zlatorog Hotel 2.30 h. In some parts the route is rather difficult to follow.

On the ridge above Soriška planina, with Dravh and Ratitovec in the background

Trips

SORIŠKA PLANINA

On the broad saddle where Bohinj and the region above the valley Selška dolina meet, the sunlit pastures of Soriška planina are stretched out. This popular centre for outings and skiing is surrounded to the south by grassy, gently moulded slopes. The pastures extend to the ridge, from where the ground falls away into the valley Baška grapa. Across the ridge a taut wire fence is erected to prevent too bold a cow from rolling over into Primorska (the coastal region). Mountaineers aiming at just an outing like to come here so as to gaze from these gentle, modest hills upon the wild mountain giants displaying their grandeur on the other side of the valley. There are entrancing walks over the soft carpet covering all this area, especially in late summer when black bilberries are glimpsed among the greenery. Below, somewhat above the road, stands a mountain hut, 1306 m. The road from Bohinjska Bistrica runs over Soriška planina (Sorica alp) into Selška dolina or Baška grapa (from Bistrica 12 km). A pleasant footpath from Bohinjska Bistrica (branching off by the last houses along the road on the eastern edge of the village) winds past the village of Nemški Rovt and the solitary hay-meadows of Strmne (waymarks, 2.30 h).

The alp is surrounded by four easily accessible hills. The gentlest ascents are to **Dravh**, 1547 m, and **Lajnar**, 1549 m, on the left (the latter has been commandeered by skiers). The right side of the alp is dominated by **Slatnik**, 1589 m, and **Možic**, 1602 m, which already show some alpine features. Anyone can manage these short, easy climbs; the green idyll is disturbed only by memorials of the past in the form of decaying military fortifications. The Sorica quartet can be visited in one go even by an easy-going walker. The ascent to Dravh and Lajnar hardly needs to be described, for the grassy slopes can be crossed anywhere, but the well-trodden path in fact approaches both tops from the right. The easiest way to Slatnik is along the ridge from the left, and then you simply continue on to Možic, which you see in the north as the highest top in this little group. A waymarked path also leads directly from Soriška planina to the saddle between Slatnik and Možic, which is occupied by a large barracks. The summit of Možic is marked by an iron bunker that hides an interesting underground. It takes one hour to Lajnar, Dravh and Slatnik, and another half hour to Možic. You can choose your own combinations as you like.

RATITOVEC

On the eastern edge of Bohinj's alpine realm, the bare ridge of Ratitovec, 1678 m, rises above the tree-tops of the Jelovica plateau. This is a friendly hilly range, rich in flora, which does not belong to the high mountains. The pastures reach right to the tops and any child can reach them. The real mountains extend in their grandeur beyond the Bohinj valley. On the opposite (south) side the eye rests on the gentle foothills which in the distance fall to the plains and are lost in the haze. The unified Ratitovec ridge is gently undulating. Between **Tonderškofel** above the village of Sorica and **Kosmati vrh** in the east some of the tops have names, the highest being **Altemaver**, 1678 m. The frequent German names in this region recall the descendants of Tyrolian settlers long ago, who live on the Danje plateau south of Ratitovec. The mountain's steeply cut-away southern side is a real contrast to the gentle, open stretches on the north side that soon give way to the Jelovica forests. The mountain has plenty of visitors at all times of the year. Here we will describe the most attracive way to Ratitovec. Traversing the entire massif is a marvellous high walk along the undulating ridge. The path winds over colourful floral carpets, adorned here and there by shaggy dwarf trees.

The starting-point is Soriška planina, 1306 m, described in the previous section. Look for the signpost in the big parking place which directs you eastwards through the forest. You soon begin to climb towards the ridge-line. The forest gradually thins out as you reach the delightful grassy slopes you'll enjoy all the way. The first rounded top in the ridge is called Žbajnik, beyond a somewhat deeper dip rises the noticeable Kremant. You are now quite near the highest point of Ratitovec – Altemaver. The broad incline you've climbed so far changes into a somewhat narrow ridge, with veritable precipices falling to the south. From the summit you see in front of you the pleasant hut Krekova koča, 1642 m, while above it the last goal beckons you – Gladki vrh (Smooth Summit), 1667 m. From Soriška planina to Krekova koča takes 3 h. Naturally numerous paths head for the hut from all sides. If you'd prefer not to return the same way, we recommend the descent southwards by a steep path to the village of Torka, followed by an easy walk along the level road westwards through the hamlets of Zabrdo and Danje as far as the main road ascending to

Ratitovec is a popular destination in winter too

Soriška planina. These unusually beautiful parts were brilliantly immortalized by the Impressionist paintbrush of the great Slovene artist Ivan Grohar, who was born in Sorica. If you decide on this round tour, reckon on at least a 7-hour walk.

KOMNA

Above the steep slopes and precipices closing in the Bohinj valley on the west there lies the extensive alpine plateau of Komna, 1054 m. Its sombre landscape blends with the neighbouring Triglav Lakes Valley into an indivisible whole. This is the famous kingdom of Zlatorog ('Goldhorn', see p. 54). The summits, alps and valleys have unusual names, testifying to a very old folk tradition. The fairy tales and legends are a precious witness to the presence of ancient peoples, the predecessors of today's Bohinjci. They gently rock us into dreams about the early Celtic iron-workers, about the Fates (sojenice), and about the enchanting, flower-decked meadows uprooted by the offended Zlatorog in his anger.

The Komna plateau lies at an altitude of 1500 to 1700 m. Surely Zlatorog carried out a thorough work here with his horns; you will scarcely find anywhere else such a rugged relief. The plateau is covered by a carpet of dwarf pine, from which solitary larches protrude, dishevelled by storms and snow. These persistent fighters cling to their sentinel positions even when their life-sap has long since perished. The wind calls forth from their dead branches unique, melancholy songs. Above are ranged the westernmost summits of the Bohinj mountain chain. Their grey heads remind us of a company of old men, pondering wisely on far distant times. Zlatorog's kingdom is a poetic world of benumbed gravity.

But nowadays Komna is a lively place. Many come here for a pleasant trip, and it is also an excellent starting-point for many mountain tours, to be described later. The plateau has a special charm when winter changes it into a shining white sea. Gentle ridges enjoyed by skiers rise to the summits. Two mountain huts are available for visitors: Dom na Komni (1520 m, open all year) and Koča pod Bogatinom, 1513 m, close by.

The starting-point for Komna is "Savica", 653 m, the name for the area at the end of the Bohinj valley, reached by road and within sound of the famous waterfall. There are two restaurants by the car-park Three minutes above the road, by the little hut where you buy entrance tickets for the waterfall Savica, the path branches off for Komna. The comfortable, easy and completely safe path leads you in numerous serpentine bends through the steep beech forest. The upper, more level part of the route runs along a trough-like valley known as Pekel. You can see the mighty Dom na Komni from a considerable distance, standing on the fringe of Zlatorog's kingdom. The walk there lasts 2.30 h. Fifteen minutes further on Koča pod Bogatinom is situated in the heart of this plateau.

VOGAR

Among the destinations for Bohinj outings, the Vogar alp, 1054 m, counts as one of the most easily accessible. It's true the path there is stony and steep, but it's also pleasantly shady. The pasture lies to the west, on the edge of the plateau above the beginning of the Voje valley. This is where the great massif of Pršivec begins. In the middle of a grassy tract stands the mountain hut Kosijev dom, with the alp extending all around as far as the forest. Despite the road nearby, Vogar has remained a pleasant, peaceful place in the midst of the forests that you can retreat to from any "rush hour" complication down in the valley. The view is open towards the south with all the summits of the Lower Bohinj mountain range. And if you head for a prominence five minutes south of the hut, a wonderful bird's eye view of the lake opens up. An interesting feature of the alp is the abundant hummocks, a relic of glacial action in past ages. The starting-point is Stara Fužina, following the road that leads to Voje. Fifteen minutes' walk brings you to the signpost indicating the footpath branching off to the left. The track soon disappears into the forest. Three long, steep serpentines lead you in the next half hour to the edge of the plateau, and the rest of the way to Kosijev dom is gentle and easy. (To the left of the path is an invitingly fine viewpoint by a metal memorial, a spot where paragliders like to jump off and float into the valley.) From the road 1 h.

You can also come to Vogar by car along a macadam forest road, which climbs from Voje through the steep side valley of Suha dolina. The road, which is well signposted at the forks, takes you over the northern edge of the alp, where there is a car-park with an indication for Kosijev dom - 10 minutes. In the summer a road-toll is charged. Vogar is then the starting-point for walks in the Fužina alps region and the ascent of Pršivec, 1761 m.

FUŽINSKE PLANINE

Northwards above Lake Bohinj, between the valleys of Voje and the Triglav lakes, lies the mysterious world of the Fužina alps. This is a high plateau with rugged karst relief, covered with forest, and higher up with carpets of dwarf pine. The landscape is wrapped in sombreness, the parental faces of the mountains in the background are grey and stern. Rough slopes, riven crags, hunched larches … no merry, playful shape anywhere. Nevertheless, this solitary land conceals more life than you might expect. A splash in the lake amidst the forest betrays lively goings-on beneath the surface, on a tiny path twisting through the dwarf-pine you can be startled by a big capercaillie suddenly taking off, up on the rock edges you'll notice the brown bodies of chamois – prehistoric inhabitants of these parts. But life is liveliest in the hollows, where cowbells jangle across the lush grass. This is the home of Bohinj highland dairy farming, which for centuries has made good use of the favourable natural conditions in the local mountains. For mountain lovers the Fužina alps represent a precious world miles removed from noisy highways. On these solitary pastures you will feel nature breathing - often a completely untouched nature. But if you wish to know this small region better, then a difficult task awaits you. The territory above the pastures is pathless and almost impenetrable, only experienced masters of the high mountains can attempt these summits. In the following description we will be content with the easily accessible "ground floor" of the Fužina alps, and admire the giants from below.

Trips into this region start from the Blato alp 1147 m, lying in a deep basin in the middle of the forests above (and west of) the Voje valley. It is reached by a forest road from Stara Fužina – which branches off from the Voje road about one kilometer above the village – via the Suha valley (10 km, road-toll in summer). If you decide to go on foot, it's best to take the route over Vogar.

Planina pri Jezeru (Alp by the Lake), 1450 m, does not belong to the high mountains. Its pastures are encircled by deep forests, which are reflected in the mirror of a large lake lying amidst the most popular parts of the Fužinske planine. Above the tree-tops the distant ridges shine out, with the great bulk of Debeli vrh dominating the landscape. The big mountain hut here is the only one of its kind in the heartland of the Fužina alps. The approach from Blato along a fairly rutted forest track lasts a good hour. Planina pri Jezeru marks an important intersection of mountain paths: to the left is the steep ascent past the Viševnik alp to Pršivec, in the direction from which you have come, the route continues past the alps of Dedno polje and Ovčarija to the Triglav Lakes, while to the right another path winds off to Planina v Lazu.

Planina v Lazu, 1560 m, lies in a broad basin in the centre of the Fužina mountains. The shepherds' huts crouch under the ample hips of Debeli vrh and Ogradi like chickens clustering under the mother hen. The alp in these impressive surroundings is refreshed by a permanent spring. But better than cold water, the excellent sour milk the herdsmen prepare during the grazing season will tempt your palate. You can reach Laz directly from Blato: follow the path to Planina pri Jezeru for 10 minutes, and a signpost will direct you right onto a pretty steep path, and you arrive in 1.30 h. More recommendable is the route via Planina pri Jezeru. Here you turn right along a pleasant, mostly gentle and extremely picturesque path and again you reach Planina v Lazu in 1.30 h. The route continues eastwards in a gentle ascent to Krstenica, while to the north another way climbs steeply over the saddle Lazovški preval towards Velo polje.

A living alp: Dedno polje

Planina Krstenica, 1655 m, lies on the eastern margin of the plateau, which here falls abruptly into the Voje valley. Due to its location on an open ridge the alp offers a superb view. On Krstenica, too, you can refresh yourself in the grazing season with dairy products. Starting from Blato, you'll walk an hour and a half to reach Krstenica. From the end of the road a rutted track leads up steeply to your right, and after 20 minutes an unmarked path branches off to the left. A short steep section is followed by easy walking to the lower edge of the alp, but the Krstenica buildings are considerably higher up. It's highly recommendable to make a round tour: start at Blato, continue to Planina pri Jezeru and on to Laz, and finally to Krstenica. The route from Laz to Krstenica takes 1.30 hours, passing through very picturesque forest that covers the undulating plateau at the foot of Ogradi. The descent from Krstenica to Blato involves rather demanding orientation: from the herdsmen's huts drop straight down over grassy slopes for about 10 minutes to a small flat area on the edge of the forest. A well-trodden path delves southwards into the forest and by the nearby hunters' hut turns left. A pleasant half hour's walk is followed by a short steep slope, below which another rutted track runs on to Blato. From Krstenica 1 h. The round tour delineated here takes 5-6 h.

USKOVNICA – KONJŠČICA

Uskovnica, 1154 m, is an exceptionally expansive alp on the western edge of the Pokljuka plateau, which drops here to the out-of-sight Voje valley. On these green pastures amidst the Pokljuka forests and overlooked by the mountains, you can forget about the valley for a time. That does you good. For centuries the alp gave Bohinj dairy farming its specific tone, but nowadays the road there has had the usual effect, driving that idyll away. The former herdsmen's cottages have taken on the contemporary appearance of weekend

The Konjščica alp at the foot of Viševnik

homes. Of course the local people still use the broad meadows, but day trippers and mountaineers keep them company in ever increasing numbers. This is a marvellous starting-point for the high mountains, which shine so invitingly above the forests. The view embraces the whole alpine necklace around Bohinj; only Triglav is missing, as the corpulent bulk of Tosc presumptuously hides it. Uskovnica has no dead season, since skiers also value it highly. The large mountain hut offers everything needed. Plenty of paths and cart-tracks bring you here, not to mention the two roads from Pokljuka and the valley. The shortest way on foot is from Stara Fužina via the hay-meadows of Blatca (2 h). The road leads from Srednja vas in the upper valley; it is allowed for public use as far as Lom on the edge of the alp (from the valley about 5 km, 15 minutes on to the hut). The waymarked path from Voje is very recommendable; the route begins a little below the waterfall (signpost). All the time it climbs through the forest before swinging right to traverse level ground and so reach Uskovnica. From Voje 1.30 h.

An hour's walk above Uskovnica you come to another broad alp, **Konjščica**, 1437 m, lying in a dell scooped out below soaring summits. Compared with the lordly Uskovnica, open on all sides, this is a modest little chamber. In summer hordes of Triglav candidates march past Konjščica, but this planina is also the popular destination of a pleasant excursion from Pokljuka or Uskovnica. It comes alive in the summer months, when the cheese dairy has good things to offer. Konjščica is hemmed in all around by rough, steep slopes ripped by wild gullies. This alpine environment forms a self-contained unit, dominated behind by the two Draški vrh summits, and with the rocky ridges of Viševnik (on the right) and Sleme filling the side wings. This region is held in high honour by skiers; in particular the descent from Veliki Draški vrh is one of the most beautiful in the Slovene mountains. You reach Konjščica from Uskovnica by a comfortable, gently ascending track in an hour's walk (signpost by the water-trough 5 minutes to the north from the mountain hut). There is a still shorter route from the end of the road coming from Pokljuka (3 km on from the end of the asphalt at Rudno polje, then half an hour's walk).

POKLJUKA

On their eastern side the high Julians drop towards the lowlands in a very hesitant manner; their hesitation has a concrete name and image: Pokljuka. This ample plateau, covered with spruce forest, rolls along between 1200 and 1400 m. Its economically important wealth of timber is also an attraction for visitors desiring relaxation and healthy air. They come in great numbers, and in all seasons of the year – as mountaineers, trippers, skiers, mushroom pickers, and so on. Indeed these mighty forests, with big mountains bending over them, provide an ideal place for a break. Pokljuka is full of natural beauties and points of interest; it is one of the most appealing regions within the Slovene mountains. The plateau cannot be seen from the Bohinj valley, just its margin softly undulates on the northeastern horizon. Two good roads lead here from Bohinj and Bled, joining a wide-flung network of roads on the plateau itself. Pokljuka serves as starting-point for numerous alpine tours, including the shortest route to Triglav. A circular journey will be explained that highlights some of Pokljuka's attractive features. Unfortunately the route can't be recommended without the use of four (or at least two) wheels, as it mostly involves roads.

The road from Bohinj to Pokljuka turns uphill at the little village of Jereka in the upper valley, and passes through the villages of Koprivnik and Gorjuše as it climbs onto the Pokljuka plateau. From the level saddle you first catch sight of its great expanse and the surrounding mountains. Quite soon an open area appears on your left. This is the large Šijec peatbog, a natural sight with unique flora. By Mrzli Studenec you join the Bled road and follow it left to the Šport Hotel (from Bohinjska Bistrica 20 km). The asphalt road passes over a low ridge to reach the **Goreljek** alp, 1250 m, which is the tourist centre of Pokljuka. You leave the asphalt by the signpost "Zajamniki" on the southern edge of the alp (a road also comes here direct from Koprivnik). The rather rutted road turns up right into lovely forest. Four kilometres from Šport Hotel you notice down on your left the wide basin of the Jelje alp, and the road immediately afterwards winds round a forested ridge.

Leave your car here, since to the right a path starts for the nearby **Javorov vrh**, 1482 m. You mustn't miss the ascent to this excellent viewpoint! A modestly waymarked path winds along the gentle ridge and in half an hour brings you to an overgrown summit. The viewpoint is just a little further, on an open rocky promontory, below which yawns quite a precipice. A broad view opens up to the north and west, at your feet is the rolling expanse of Pokljuka, surrounded in a mighty arc by the Julian giants. You return by the same path.

The road then leads past the alps of Konjska dolina and **Zajamniki** to Praprotnica (from here it's a short way to Uskovnica). (Zajamniki with its often photographed "street" of cowherds' huts is extremely picturesque. It is possible to reach it by a pleasant footpath from the little village of Podjelje above the

The Šijec peatbog in the midst of the Pokljuka forests

upper valley.)   Now follow the signpost for Rudno polje, where you regain the asphalt road in front of a large military barracks. From Šport Hotel to here 15 km. You return by the asphalt road to Mrzli Studenec and your starting-point. This description will seem more like some rally than an excursion around mountain pastures. But the directions serve only as a rough orientation. You'll make your own decisions as to what to do on Pokljuka, nor will that be difficult. When you notice some mysterious nook, stop the car and take a stroll among the mighty spruces. The solitary glades, pastures and peatbogs invitingly call you to take a look, and the soft carpet of moss beckons you to take a rest. And if you bring no noise into this forest seclusion, your respectful attitude will be acknowledged by a concert from a feathered orchestra high among the branches. In this way you will pass a fine day on Pokljuka.

pp. 44-45: Črna prst seen from the south, with Triglav dominating to the right

1

Črna prst

Alpine botanical garden

ALTITUDE: 1844 m
STARTING ALTITUDE: 512-804 m
HEIGHT DIFFERENCE: 1300-1040 m

This famous mountain above Bohinjska Bistrica represents the beginning of the alpine realm in the wreath of mountains around Bohinj. Perhaps it is precisely the gentle influence of the neighbouring foothills that created the conditions here among the grey rocks for such beautiful gardens to appear, full of diverse mountain flowers, including rare and endemic species – some of the latter grow only on these slopes. Together with Golica in the Karavanke, which each spring is white with drifts of narcissi, Črna prst enjoys the greatest botanical fame. This is an easily accessible mountain, and just a few metres below the summit stands the mountain hut Dom Zorka Jelinčiča. The many visitors are attracted by the wonderful views, which are typical of all the summits in the Spodnje Bohinjske gore. This finely shaped, steep mountain

Primorska hamlets bask in sunshine below Črna prst

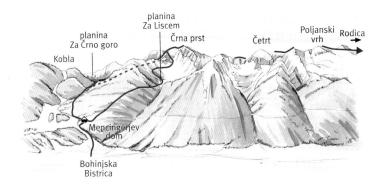

got its name from the black stratum a little below the top (Črna prst means 'black soil'.) The rocky Bohinj side is in striking contrast with the steep grassy slopes of the Primorska (the Littoral) side, where in former times the local people wore crampons to mow the grass. Črna prst will also feature in the next section, where the ridge route from Rodica will be described. The route given here directly from the valley is the normal access. If you want to experience these brightly coloured gardens in peak profusion, visit Črna prst in early summer, best of all in June.

STARTING-POINT:
Bohinjska Bistrica; most people begin their tour from the mountain hut Mencingerjev dom on Rovti near the village of Ravne; distance by road 3 km.

DESCRIPTION:
The signpost Črna prst directs you from the crossroads in the middle of Bohinjska Bistrica southwards through the village streets and then along a cart-track to the hill Rebro. The path climbs an disused ski-track to Mencingerjev dom (45 min). Just to the right below the hut a waymarked path leaves the road and climbs steeply into the forest. The steep rough path soon eases, and the route becomes really pleasant. Half an hour later you reach the upper road and follow it for 5 minutes to the right (raspberries in August!). The next steep incline similarly lasts half an hour, bringing you to the alp Za Liscem, 1350 m, with its fine view. Here Črna prst appears in its mighty character, with steep, grassy Lisec on the right and forested Črna gora on the left. From this point the old path leads along the open valley, the new one bears left through the forest. On a fine little terrace at the foot of Črna prst you enter the real high-altitude world, which is where the marvellous gardens also begin. The path climbs the slope among numerous boulders. Below a smooth crag, where the crevices are full of Zois' bellflower (Zoisove zvončice), the path turns left and gains the main ridge on the saddle Čez Suho by making a long traverse. Now a short ascent towards the right leads you to the hut and the summit, through the luxuriant flowers and with the views widening out all the time.

DESCENT:

Unless you wish to return the same way, we suggest an alternative, more easterly variant across the alp Za Črno goro. You retrace your steps as far as the saddle Čez Suho, where immediately below a path branches off to the right, which beyond a gash in the ridge of Črna gora, drops down a steep gully and crosses overgrown terrain to the alp Za Črno goro, which lies in an extensive basin enlivened by a stream. The route then enters the forest, descending to the upper road and on over haymeadows to Mencingerjev dom.

DIFFICULTY:

Caution is needed along the summit ridge, as the path leads over steep, grassy slopes, otherwise the tour is easy and safe.

TIMES:

Bohinjska Bistrica – Mencingerjev dom 45 min
Mencingerjev dom – Črna prst 2.30 h
Descent to Bohinjska Bistrica 2.30 h
Total 6 h

2

Rodica – Črna prst

View of Triglav and the smell of the sea

ALTITUDE: 1966 m
STARTING ALTITUDE: 1540 m
HEIGHT DIFFERENCE: 426 m

The Lower Bohinj Mountains form a powerful and high barrier between Bohinj and Primorska (the Littoral). From Ratitovec to Bogatin the ridge contains many summits that project only a little above the level line. This gives the group the appearance of a monolithic solid wall. The Primorska side is steeper, more bare and angular than the Bohinj side, where forests reach high up towards the edges. This form of mountain ridge is thus particularly inviting for a traverse. But crossing the entire ridge is a strenuous adventure lasting some days, and demanding in the western part, whereas the ridge between Rodica and Črna prst provides a pleasant one-day tour along a moderately demanding waymarked path. It is described in this direction so as not to forego the comfortable access by the Vogel cable-car. Unlike the summits in the western

The Črna prst ridges are renowned for their rich flora

49

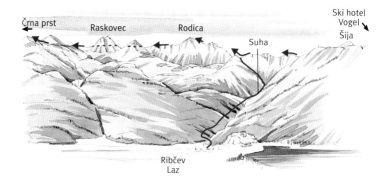

Črna prst — Raskovec — Rodica — Suha — Ski hotel Vogel — Šija

Ribčev Laz

section of the chain, those between Rodica and Črna prst seem to have been created for a leisurely hike. The undulating ridge is only occasionally bristly, and is mostly covered with soft beds of flowers. The individual tops in such a ridge walk are not even important, because you're "on the top" all the time. However, at least the first summit Rodica should be presented. This is a shapely pyramid in the central part of the ridge southeast of the Vogel ski centre. It has a particularly honourable place among skiers. The Suha alp lies in a basin to the north below the summit.

STARTING-POINT:
The Vogel cable-car station, 1540 m.
DESCRIPTION:
From the Ski Hotel two chairlifts take you high below the summit of Šija, but in summer only the lower one operates (at times). Otherwise a comfortable waymarked path goes along by the chairlift, trying to avoid the unpleasantly rough ski route. The rise of Orlov rob (Eagles' Edge), 1800 m, reached by the upper chairlift, is bypassed on the right by this path, which then leads to the saddle at the foot of Šija. Somewhat higher a level path marked with the number 1 winds across the slopes, this is the Slovenska planinska pot (Slovene Mountain Route). (**Šija,** 1880 m, the summit in the main ridge nearest the chairlift, is accessible from here across the grassy slope, though without a footpath; 20 min.) You turn left along the path and climb to the main ridge. Here the Primorska expanses are spread out, and together with the Julian fortresses beyond Bohinj they will accompany you all the way. Above the saddle of Čez Suho the slope gently ascends to the top of **Rodica**.
(It is, of course, possible to reach Rodica on foot from the valley; the starting-point is Ribčev Laz. The asphalt road between the hotels Jezero and Bellevue is left by the signpost Rodica, beckoning you left into the forest. The level walk ends on the forest road, above which the route climbs steeply through the forest. Higher up the gradient eases, and the path intertwines with the serpentine bends of the road (pay attention to the waymarks!). Above the upper road the path runs through a gently sloping valley, interrupted by a

steep section. Soon you reach the planina Suha, 1400 m (a good 2 h to here), where in summer numerous cows are jangling their bells. Now you cross the high-altitude threshold; from here on the path twists among dwarf pine and rocks. Lush grass gives way to cushions sprinkled with tiny mountain flowers. Beyond this steep section you can get your breath back in a deep hollow, as the path continues through a gentle valley and gains the ridge to the right below the summit of Rodica. From Ribčev Laz 3.30 h.)

The ridge from Rodica to the east is at first sharp and precipitous. In places the path retreats to the slopes, either to the Bohinj or Primorska side. This most demanding part of the tour requires concentration and caution, as the terrain is exposed and drops away sharply. When the ridge broadens, you catch sight of **Raskovec**, 1967 m, a mountain very like Rodica in shape. Here the route veers to the Primorska side, but a detour to its grassy top (no path) will only detain you for 15 minutes. The path now becomes increasingly straightforward. In fact, crossing Matajurski vrh, Poljanski vrh, Konjski vrh and Četrt constitutes the most pleasant part of the tour, as the comfortable path lets you devote all your attention to enjoying the views. The route actually bypasses the summits, but they represent no difficulties whatsoever. Beyond Četrt you drop into a deep notch affording a fine view of the Primorska village of Stržišče, and then the (again somewhat narrower) ridge ascends to **Črna prst**, 1844 m, where the mountain hut Dom Zorka Jelinčiča invites you from a distance.

DESCENT:

Continue a short way on along the ridge and at the first saddle turn left towards the valley. The left path over the alp Za Liscem is shorter, the right one goes via the alp Za Črno goro. The two paths join at the mountain hut Mencingerjev dom half an hour's walk above Bohinjska Bistrica.

DIFFICULTY:

The ridge Rodica - Raskovec demands careful walking, elsewhere the path is easy. You should attempt the ridge only in reliable weather; do not let a storm catch you up here because of the danger of being struck by lightning.

TIMES:

Vogel cable-car station – Rodica 2.30 h (the lower chairlift shortens the way by 15 minutes)
Rodica – Črna prst 3.30 h
Descent to Bohinjska Bistrica a good 2 h
Total 8-9 h

3

Vogel

God-parent of alps and a ski centre

ALTITUDE: 1922 m
STARTING ALTITUDE: 1540 m
HEIGHT DIFFERENCE: 382 m

West of Šija the ridge of the Spodnje Bohinjske gore falls to its deepest notch and then with a mighty upthrust rises towards the highest, 2000-metre peaks. The herald of this upward leap is the lovely pyramid of Vogel. The mountain lent its name to the well-known ski and tourist centre, and in so doing lost some of its identity, since "Vogel" (the ski centre) is much better known than the real Vogel. Thanks to the short and easy access, made possible by the cable-car, the mountain has plenty of visitors at all seasons of the year – even from the Primorska side, where the mountain hut Koča na planini Razor stands one hour below the summit. The invitation to visit Vogel has the same content as other summits in this range: an easy, comfortable path leads through beautiful gardens to an exceptionally fine viewpoint. And still another advantage: you can go to Vogel,

Šija's steep southern (Primorska) slopes, with Vogel in the background

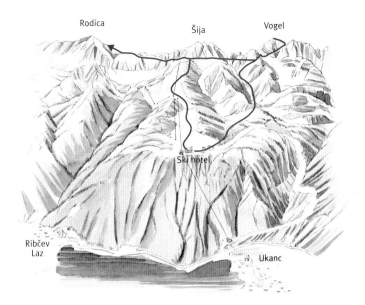

even though you may have slept on in the morning.

STARTING-POINT: The Vogel cable-car station, 1540 m

DESCRIPTION: Leading to the alp Zadnji Vogel, where the ascent begins, is a slightly unpleasant path (signpost Komna), which in a gradual descent follows the rough ski route, but occasionally escapes from it into the deliverance of the forest. From the alp (half an hour from the cable-car station) you set out along a gentle valley southwards, but soon leave it by a path over a steep incline to the right. Above a small plateau this path climbs to a notch in the main ridge, where you momentarily glimpse Primorska, and returns to the Bohinj side. Then once more the southern horizon is spread out - for a slightly longer time – before the route bears right for the last time at the foot of the summit section of Vogel. It winds on almost horizontally, but beyond the summit fall-line, a signpost on the rock sends you upwards towards the nearby summit, and you gain the main ridge just right of the highest point. I would like just to mention the possibility of climbing from the valley. The waymarks begin at the Zlatorog Hotel, and direct you over the main road, and soon after over the forest road, then steeply up through the forest to the end of the broad gully Žagarjev graben. Here you reach the ski route and follow it to the alp Zadnji Vogel (2.5 h), where you join the above-described path.

DESCENT: Return by the same route to Zadnji Vogel and then back to the cable-car station or else down by Žagarjev graben.

DIFFICULTY: The tour is easy, indeed very comfortable if you use the cable-car.

TIMES:

Ski Hotel (cable-car station) – Vogel 2 h

Descent 1.30 h

Total 4 h

From the valley to Vogel 4 h

4

Bogatin

Zlatorog's throne

ALTITUDE: 1977 m
STARTING ALTITUDE: 1520 m
HEIGHT DIFFERENCE: 457 m

The most eminent mountain above the Komna plateau is Bogatin (meaning 'the rich one'), although neither in height nor in appearance is it anything special. Slovenes simply like this mountain, just as they like their most beautiful alpine fairytale. The story of Zlatorog (the mythical white chamois with golden horns, guardian of the treasure under Bogatin) derives from the precious folk tradition of Trenta, that small land in the upper Soča Basin, Bohinj's neighbour, which was always very closely linked with its mountains. Bogatin has the main role in the story, as the treasure was hidden in its bosom. The whole tale revolves around it, symbolizing in its tragic dimension the centuries-long stubborn struggle of the Trenta people for survival in that cruel mountain world. For mountain lovers the tale of Zlatorog is especially close to their hearts, since the search for treasure in the mountains is an exquisite image for that

The Spodnje Bohinjske gore chain forms a background to Koča pod Bogatinom

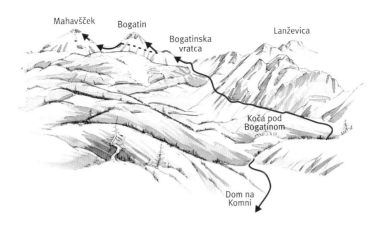

Mahavšček Bogatin Lanževica

Bogatinska vratca

Koča pod Bogatinom

Dom na Komni

mysterious and uncontrollable force which drives them into the realm of "useless" summits. It is not only Bogatin that hides treasures, but usually a kinder fate awaits today's seekers than the unfortunate Trenta hunter.

Bogatin belongs to the ridge of Spodnje Bohinjske gore as their last summit in the west. It is quite shapely, although not a mighty figure. The much used route from Komna towards Krn passes by it. This easily accessible top is the most frequented of all the summits above Komna, as it is the nearest as well as being famous. Bogatin stands in the midst of a marvellous skiing paradise.

STARTING-POINT:

The Komna plateau, 1520 m (p. 37); from Savica 2.30 h; the tour can be made in one day from the valley.

DESCRIPTION:

The first part of the way to Bogatin heads westwards along the comfortable "mulatiera" (a former miltary route) that leads from the mountain hut Dom na Komni past the nearby hut Koča pod Bogatinom. This gentle ascent leads to the Gracija valley at the foot of Bogatin. The path avoids the valley via the steep slope on the right and then rises to the broad pass of Bogatinska vratca, 1803 m, to the right below the summit. Here the route turns left and climbs steeply to a small grassy platform under the rocky summit section of Bogatin. A fairly steep ridge leads towards the top, and here and there you need to hold on to the rock. The summit is narrow and exposed. Your gaze glides across the broad expanses of "Zlatorog's kingdom". If you wish to see the soft Primorska panorama as well, you must expend some more effort to reach the neighbouring Mahavšček, 2008 m, enticing also because it figures among the two-thousanders. From Bogatin to Mahavšček is a good half hour's walk.

DESCENT:

By the same route; but you can make a pleasant curve to the saddle below Mahavšček, from where a gentle traverse path leads back to Bogatinska vratca.

DIFFICULTY:

The summit ridge requires some caution, otherwise the tour is easy.

TIME:

Komna – Bogatin 2 h

5

Lepa špica

A mountain mirrored in the Triglav lakes

ALTITUDE: 2398 m
STARTING ALTITUDE: 1683 m
HEIGHT DIFFERENCE: 715 m

The western flank of the Triglav Lakes Valley is dominated by a great and beautiful mountain. Officially it is *veliko* – 'great' (Veliko špičje), but according to its local name it has long been *lepa* – 'beautiful' (Lepa špica). In this the Bohinjci and the Trentarji are united, for they do not exactly lack great and still greater mountains. Lepa špica shows the Trentarji an expansive rock face, composed of mighty pillars, which glow so beautifully in the evening sunlight. The Bohinj side of the mountain, however, belongs to the marvellous world of the Triglav lakes, where green tongues of vegetation with brightly coloured decoration stretch high up into the rocky edges, often grazed by a small herd of ibex. This pleasant and alive mountain is quite different from the grey Fužina recluses, which gloomily stare across the valley. This showy beauty prefers

Koča pri Triglavskih jezerih stands beside Dvojno jezero; Veliko špičje rises behind

most to appear in the bright mirrors of the Triglav Lakes. Not so long ago Lepa
špica was a completely pathless mountain, but nowadays two attractive routes
take you there, which can be combined into a round tour, here described in
the clockwise direction. The ascent to this proud summit is one of the most
beautiful in the Julian Alps.

STARTING-POINT:
The mountain hut Koča pri Triglavskih jezerih, 1683 m (tour no. 10, from Savica
via the Komarča cliff 3-3.30 h, from Blato via the alps Planina pri Jezeru, Dedno
polje, Ovčarija and the Štapce pass 3 h)

DESCRIPTION:
Follow the lakes highway – the path up the Triglav Lakes Valley – for half an
hour, and by the signpost bear left along a gentle waymarked path towards
Lepa špica. You walk through luxuriant gardens to the foot of the steep slopes,
which you negotiate to the right of the summit fall-line. A steel rope helps you
up the crags, above a green head the path winds over patches of turf, which
increasingly disappear among the rocks. The summit ridge is gained
somewhat right of the top. The view is magnificent. Deep below you flows
the River Soča, with the wonderful world of the Trenta mountains revealed
above it. On the opposite side sparkle the little emerald eyes of the Triglav
Lakes; behind, the company of Bohinj patriarchs rests in wise contemplation.

DESCENT:
Walking along the ridge to Prehodavci is the most beautiful part of the tour.
In places the path winds along the ridge above the vertiginous Trenta
precipices, but the sharply cut towers are avoided on the lake side. Some
spots are really exposed, and iron aids are encountered here and there. While

Dvojno jezero (Double Lake)

Lepa špica

Prehodavci

Koča pri Triglavskih jezerih

taking in the wealth of views, you cross some tops in the ridge and in between you play hide-and-seek with ibex. From the last small peak, the path drops onto the picturesque karst plateau (*podi*) on the edge of Prehodavci, a broad saddle where the Triglav Lakes Valley plunges deeply and abruptly into Trenta. The mountain hut Zasavska koča invites you from a distance. From here descend to the Zeleno jezero (Green Lake), where you again join the "lakes highway", leading you down to the starting-point.

DIFFICULTY:
A demanding waymarked, partly secured route, exposed. Reliable weather is essential for the ridge (danger of lightning).

TIMES:
Koča pri Triglavskih jezerih – Lepa špica 2.30 h
Lepa špica – Prehodavci 2.30 h
Prehodavci – Koča pri Triglavskih jezerih 2 h
Total 7-8 h

6

Pršivec

ALTITUDE: 1761 m
STARTING ALTITUDE: 546 m
HEIGHT DIFFERENCE: 1215 m

I won't say that Pršivec is not lovely at any time, but nevertheless this *is* an autumn mountain. You must go there at the season of golden larches and valley mists. If you are fortunate enough to be on Pršivec when the fog covering the lake below begins to tear apart, you will gaze in astonishment at the tumultuous boiling from the witches' cauldron. The wide open view always has some wild, twisted larch in the foreground. The closer you come to the summit, the more the troops of these alpine fighters with the storms thin out. But the most resilient have still managed to anchor themselves among the rugged rocks right on the top. The relief is like a whirlpool; highly reminiscent of the karst orgies of the Komna plateau. If you miss the path on Pršivec, you'll get into a pretty pickle, but otherwise the approach is easy and extremely beautiful. Without any doubt, it's one of the finest Bohinj tours.

Bohinj seen from Pršivec: Rudnica divides the lower (right) and upper valleys

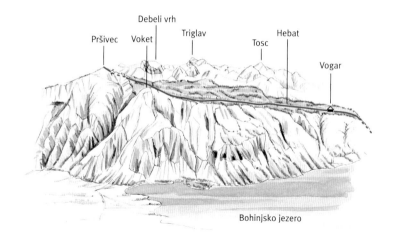

Debeli vrh
Pršivec Voket Triglav Hebat
Tosc
Vogar

Bohinjsko jezero

Pršivec is that mighty mountain which dominates the northern side of Lake Bohinj like a spreading chestnut tree. It stands a solitary individual, with something defiant and mysterious in its character. That latter feature especially applies to Pršivec's karst underground. Will anyone ever explain the secret paths of the waters which disappear in the clefts and abysses on the summit plateau? Far below they crash out with tremendous force, especially in storms. Whoever has seen the Govic waterfall bursting out of its cave at the foot of the southern face of Pršivec will never forget that spine-tingling scene.

STARTING-POINT:
Stara Fužina
DESCRIPTION:
The usual route to Pršivec leads over Vogar (see p. 38). Above the mountain hut there, the cart-track soon changes into a waymarked path. The first steep stretch is followed by a pleasant 15-minute walk along the forest path to a little stream below the alp Hebat. The next steep interval is slightly longer, but then the route runs along a panoramic edge above the wild southern cliffs. The smooth surface of Lake Bohinj shines far below. The path climbs gently, the hike is sheer enjoyment. Higher up you bear further right into the forest. The plateau around you is called Voket. Here the walking comes to an end, as the path thrusts into the steepness of the summit structure. The spruce forest recedes as the larches, heralds of the high mountains, become increasingly numerous. On a small saddle a wild view of Ukanc, glimpsed through a precipitous gash, takes you by surprise. The last steep section is avoided by the path on the right. (on the left is a demanding variant along the ridge). The terrain becomes ever more rugged – the real alpine karst of Pršivec. As the path turns onto the ridge, the only exposed place awaits you in the passage across a smooth crag. The view from here into the perpendicular depths is magnificent. Soon the ridge flattens and broadens out, so that the last few minutes of the ascent mean enjoyment at your leisure. On the summit is a

tempting patch of green and it goes without saying, the gathered company of Bohinj stalwarts literally encompasses you.

DESCENT:

Descending in the same direction can be replaced by a pleasant journey via the alp Planina pri Jezeru. The waymarks drop away from the summit towards the north. The tiny path leads past grassy hollows (on the left is one of the entrances to the Pršivec underworld – Majska jama) and further on to the Viševnik alp, 1615 m. On this picturesque and panoramic alp one of the alpine dairies is arranged into the Zavetišče Draga Bregarja, which offers modest refreshments in the summer season. The path then winds rightwards into the forest and passing by mighty bellies of rock drops steeply to Planina pri Jezeru, 1450 m, with its mountain hut. A rutted cart-track leads towards Vogar, but is actually headed for Blato. So you need to watch out, so as not to miss the turning for Vogar (right) after half an hour's walk.

DIFFICULTY:

An undemanding tour with one exposed place.

TIMES:

Stara Fužina – Vogar 1.30 h
Vogar – Pršivec 2.30 h
Pršivec – Planina pri Jezeru 1 h
Planina pri Jezeru – Vogar 1 h
Vogar – Stara Fužina 1 h
Total 7-8 h

7

Debeli vrh

The champion of the Fužina mountains

ALTITUDE: 2390 m
STARTING ALTITUDE: 1147 m
HEIGHT DIFFERENCE: 1243 m

Of the summits that rise above the Fužinske planine, Debeli vrh (Bulky Summit) is undeniably the most prominent, showing itself to the Bohinjci like a kind of upturned bowl, surrounded by steep rock faces. It vies with Tosc for top place among Bohinj's corpulent giants. Along with Triglav and Mišelj vrh, its rounded summit is an unmistakeable character in the northern Bohinj panorama. The mountain is inseparably linked with Planina v Lazu, which spreads its grassy tongues high into its flanks. Among mountaineers Debeli vrh is a highly regarded goal, and not only because of its mighty, authoritative figure. The way to this pathless mountain is long and tiring, one of the elite Bohinj tours. Just below the summit you must even do a bit of rock climbing. The mountain is alluring for rock-climbers and ski tourers as well. The easiest approach leads eastwards

Debeli vrh above Planina v Lazu

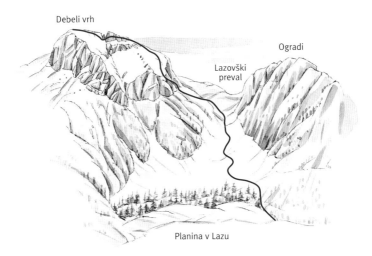

Debeli vrh

Ogradi

Lazovški
preval

Planina v Lazu

under the summit from the saddle Lazovški preval (across which runs a waymarked path), but the terrain up there is pathless.

STARTING-POINT:

The mountain hut Koča na Planini pri Jezeru, 1453 m, where an overnight stay before the tour is recommendable. If you wish to accomplish the tour in one day, then Blato, 1147 m, at the end of the road from Stara Fužina, serves as starting-point. From here you ascend straight up to Planina v Lazu. All these routes are described in the trip to the Fužinske planine on pp. 38-43.

DESCRIPTION:

From Planina pri Jezeru walk for 1.30 hours along the gentle path to Planina v Lazu, 1560 m. Then there follows a steep ascent northwards to the saddle Lazovški preval, 1966 m, between Debeli vrh and its eastern neighbour Ogradi. It is best to leave this waymarked route somewhat below the saddle, where a passage along a rocky gully presents itself, heading for the rounded eastern ridge of Debeli vrh. When you have successfully resolved the orientation puzzle, sheer enjoyment awaits you along the ridge with its wonderful views. The easy ascent along this grassy backbone is interrupted just below the summit by a sharp notch, which demands some metres of exposed climbing. The terrain is mostly bare and barren, so the lush grass covering the roomy top of Debeli vrh is a pleasant surprise. The luxury of a soft armchair is disturbed only by the countless "chocolate sweeties" – a proof that chamois like to occupy this spot. The view from this lofty place is stupendous. You descend the same way to Planina v Lazu, and then on as you wish.

DIFFICULTY:

A very demanding, and in the top section pathless tour, with a short climbing intermezzo. Difficult orientation. Only for experienced mountaineers. A guide is recommended.

TIMES:

Koča na Planini pri Jezeru – Laz 1.30 h   Debeli vrh – Laz – Blato 3 h
Laz – Debeli vrh 3 h   Total 8-9 h

8

Kanjavec

The dream mountain for ski tourers

ALTITUDE: 2568 m
STARTING ALTITUDE: 1453 m
HEIGHT DIFFERENCE: 1115 m

Kanjavec is the second highest Bohinj mountain after Triglav. Despite this, mountaineers do not aim for it so often, although they hurry in crowds over its flanks towards the Triglav sanctuary. The mountain is the central knot of all the ridges between Velo polje and the Trenta valley, and primarily the ruler of a stony kingdom – the bare wastes of the Hribarice with their snowfilled sinkholes and wind-whipped ridges. Scarcely a blade of grass appears among the rough rocks. However, it displays its significant position among the Julian giants more to the Trentarji than to the Bohinjci with its majestic north face. In summer this overlooked champion waits calmly for its great days, when covered by a deep blanket of snow. The summer visitor would barely recognize it, for then it looks like a bride in shimmering white. The numerous wedding guests with skis on their feet can hardly wait for the festivities to begin. Kanjavec basks in its reputation as the most marvellous ski summit of the Julian Alps. From here as many as seven super ski routes descend into the Bohinj valley. But in summer, too, the mountain is worth visiting, for its great height affords a generous view. Not a few take in Kanjavec on the way from the Lakes Valley to Triglav. However, this description will lead you to Kanjavec by a solitary route crossing the Fužinske planine.

STARTING-POINT:
The mountain hut Koča na Planini pri Jezeru, 1453 m (p. 39); from Blato 1 h, from Stara Fužina via Vogar 3 h, an overnight stay will be essential.

DESCRIPTION:
The half-hour walk to the alp Dedno polje is a pleasant morning warming-up session. Here you choose the northwest direction and follow the waymarks over a steep drop into the valley Za Kopico, squeezed betweeen the ridge of the Vogels (on the right) and Kopica and the two Zelnaricas. This gentle valley seems to have died, but after all you are on the way to the stony kingdom. On the pass Vrata, 2192 m, your gaze can rest on the bright jewels of the Triglav lakes, but the path winds high above them across the screes under the lonely ridge of the Vršaki. Soon you join the route from the lakes towards Triglav

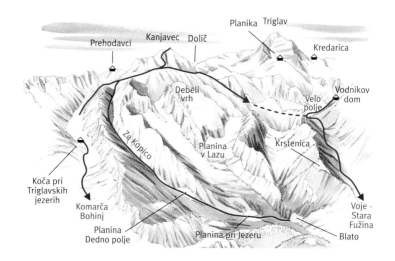

and ascend to the Hribarice plateau. It's now only half an hour's walk northwards over these lifeless, stony slopes. On the summit the view sweeps into the great depth of Trenta with its forests and greenery and then all around to embrace most of the stalwarts of the Julian Alps.

DESCENT:

If there is no vehicle waiting for you on Blato, meaning that you don't have to return the same way, you can enrich the tour by descending through the valley Velska dolina into the Voje valley or towards the Pokljuka plateau, or via the Triglav Lakes and down the Komarča cliff to Savica.

DIFFICULTY:

An easy, but strenuous two-day tour, which should be postponed in poor visibility (fog).

TIMES:

Planina pri Jezeru – Kanjavec 4-5 h
Descent 3 h
Kanjavec – Velo polje – Stara Fužina 5 h
Kanjavec – the Triglav Lakes – Komarča – Savica 5 h

p. 65: Mišelj vrh with Kanjavec in the background

Triglav

Triglav, 2864 m, is the highest summit of Bohinj, Gorenjska, Primorska, the Julian Alps and indeed Slovenia. Its name is generally interpreted as 'mountain with three heads'. This "king" represents for the Slovenes an eternal symbol of national consciousness. It would be difficult to find another nation that honoured its highest mountain with such zeal and in such unison. As if in their subconscious there remained some sediment of beliefs inherited from their distant ancestors, who sensed that Triglav was the abode of the gods. In truth Triglav is a majestic and beautiful mountain, seen from far around. Among the ranks of famous Alpine peaks it holds a place of honour and enjoys its merited reputation. It is no mere coincidence that it was one of the first to be conquered (eight years before Mont Blanc!), although by no means an easy mountain. The south side of Triglav belongs to the alpine world of Bohinj. This is its kind, friendly face, unburdened by the wild majesty of the North Face or the soaring heights seen from Trenta. Here, too, the three-headed image can be observed in its fairest light. So it comes as no surprise that the pioneers first climbed Triglav from this side. The Bohinjci take no little pride in their renowned compatriots. "The four bold men", who in 1778 first overcame the fear of the unknown, untamed lofty peaks were the first Slovene alpinists. Today an ascent of Triglav counts as the fervent wish and "duty" of every Slovene, as well as many a guest. For an experienced mountaineer Triglav is a completely safe mountain to approach. Life reaches high up its ramparts, while easy, comfortable paths rise to the foot of its rocky crown. Steel ropes are strung along its steep summit crags. Large mountain huts offer protection and care for your needs - many people up there take pains to make the route to the desired mountain as pleasant as possible. Nevertheless, for an ascent of Triglav it is essential to equip yourself with due deliberation and forethought, since particular weather laws rule at these altitudes. You must reckon with the possibility of sudden and violent changes in the weather; snow and ice in the height of summer are a frequent and perfectly normal occurrence. Two routes (with plenty of variants) lead to Triglav from Bohinj, and these can be combined into a large-scale traverse, with opportunity to get acquainted with several other local jewels as well as the mountain itself. Combinations with routes described elsewhere in the book will be left to the imagination of the individual mountaineer.

9

To Triglav from Pokljuka

The shortest route to the patriarch

ALTITUDE: 2864 m
STARTING ALTITUDE: 1340 m
HEIGHT DIFFERENCE: 1524 m

The shortest and naturally the most frequented route to Triglav runs from the Pokljuka plateau. Many mountaineers make this tour in one day, but the majority still prefer to sleep somewhat below the summit so as to experience the charm of early morning high in the mountains; the view from the summit is also at its best just then. Staying overnight in the Triglav huts during the summer season can be less than enjoyable, though, since candidates for the top generally outnumber the beds available, but most don't let this bother them. The way itself is beautiful and intriguing, there is something kind and friendly in the very nature of the tour. Many people sense a gentle smile in Triglav's expression above Velo polje.

The view of Triglav from Velo polje

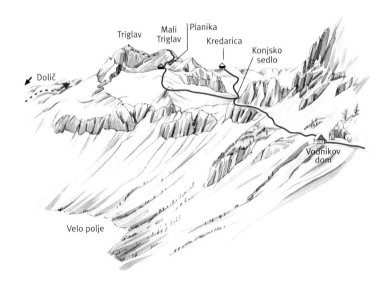

Triglav Mali Planika
        Triglav Kredarica
                          Konjsko
                          sedlo
Dolič

                                    Vodnikov
                                    dom

Velo polje

STARTING-POINT:

Rudno polje, 1340 m, is the Pokljuka alp at the foot of Viševnik, reached by an asphalt road (from Bohinjska Bistrica 23 km, from Bled 22 km). The "Triglav highway" begins by the army barracks. You can shorten the way by half an hour if you use the forest road that continues from Rudno polje another 3 km to the parking place 30 minutes below Konjščica.

DESCRIPTION:

Immediately beyond the army barracks a gentle forest road turns right. A little beyond the foresters' hut (10 minutes from Rudno polje) the waymarks head left into the forest. After half an hour's steep climb the path turns left and crosses the slopes above the Konjščica alp. Then at the foot of the wild gully under Viševnik a new ascent begins that soon leads into the lovely alpine cwm of Jezerce in the heart of the Draški vrh group. Somewhat before that it is joined by the path from Konjščica, if you decided on the above-mentioned shortcut. In Jezerce turn left and past a permanent spring climb through the valley to the saddle Studorski preval, 1892 m (to your right rises Veliki Draški vrh, tour no. 12). A fine view of the Bohinj valley and the Spodnje Bohinjske gore accompanies the following pleasant part of the tour, i.e. walking across the protruding belly of Tosc. Here the path goes almost horizontally over the steep slope, richly decked with alpine flowers. Beyond the exposed but safe passage over an artificially carved out ledge, the path climbs over the threshold of Velo polje. Here Triglav first displays himself in full glory. But you shouldn't neglect the truly beautiful vista of Velo polje's entire surroundings, dominated by the commanding figure of Mišelj vrh in addition to Triglav. In the west the tops of the Fužina mountains keep to themselves, with bulging Debeli vrh at their head. A herd of ibex quite often grazes here. Before long you find yourself at the mountain hut Vodnikov dom, 1817 m, situated on the flank of Tosc and overlooking the broad valley of Velo polje, from where the sound of distant cowbells may come floating up. (Many Triglav candidates also come here from Stara Fužina along the Voje valley, a route partly described on pp. 28-30. This approach is steep and strenuous, as it involves tackling the mountain from its very foot.) Beyond Vodnikov dom the path gently ascends across the base of steep Vernar. Two secured rocky passages are then encountered before you reach the saddle Konjsko sedlo, 2020 m, where you finally come under the real Triglav massif. Here two routes for Triglav branch off – for Kredarica (right) and Dom Planika. This description follows the former and uses the other for the descent, but the order is not obligatory; the other way round is just as good.

Above the saddle the Kredarica path slants up to the right across bare slopes. Its monotony is enlivened by a steeper section with a steel rope. On the protruding nose of Kalvarija it is joined from the right by the route from the Krma valley before you tackle the final climb along a stony back. The serried ranks of numerous mountain chains seen on the northern and western horizons come as a fine surprise before you cross the threshold of the enormous mountain hut Triglavski dom na Kredarici, 2516 m.

All this long journey is just an introduction to the proper ascent of Triglav. Its steep faces now stand challengingly right in front of you. The first goal is Mali Triglav (Little Triglav), which rises directly above Kredarica. A short drop to the small saddle is followed by crumbly ground as far as the first rocks, with a huge waymark and the beginning of the secured route. Many a newcomer holds his breath at the sight of the gaping precipice behind the first edge. But if the steepness and great depths cause you no difficulties, it's a pleasant, airy climb to the top of Mali Triglav, as the route winds

The secured route above Kredarica

through natural passages which are abundantly secured. A narrow ridge links this summit with the main one. This exposed bridge caused fear and trembling to the pioneers of long ago, but now it is so well secured there's no need for fright at all. The only problem is if people accumulate here. Towards the summit it is gradually easier as the ever grander view rejoices your heart. Soon the well-known form of the Aljaž turret (Aljažev stolp) slices into that view and when your gaze floats down into the fathomless depth of the Trenta valley, your achievement is complete – this is the highest point of Slovenia!

DESCENT:

If you have decided to descend on the same side, return to Mali Triglav by the same way. On the southern side, above the mountain hut Dom Planika, the rocks are less steep than those above Kredarica, and thus recommendable for the descent. At first you go over open rock by a carefully secured route, then though a narrow gully to reach the crumbly terrain above Planika. This large hut stands on the Ledine plateau lying at the Bohinj base of the summit structure of Triglav. Barely an hour's walk further down you find yourself on the saddle Konjsko sedlo, and follow the previously described route back to the starting-point.

DIFFICULTY:

As far as Kredarica (or Planika) this is an easy tour, followed by a well-secured but quite demanding and exposed route, which calls for some skill and courage. The rocks, which have been polished to a high degree (by countless boots), also require additional attention. If a storm should threaten, drop any idea of attempting the summit with its iron fetters!

TIMES:

Rudno polje - Vodnikov dom 3 h
(from Stara Fužina through Voje 4-5 h
Vodnikov dom – Kredarica 2.30 h
Kredarica – Triglav 1.30 h
Total ascent 7-8 h
(the route via Dom Planika is about 1 h shorter)
Descent to Rudno polje 5-6 h
Total 12-14 h

10

To Triglav via the lakes

The way through Zlatorog's kingdom

ALTITUDE: 2864 m
STARTING ALTITUDE: 653 m
HEIGHT DIFFERENCE: 2211 m

The longest Bohinj route to Triglav is at the same time the most beautiful. Its exceptional character derives from the journey through that jewel of Zlatorog's kingdom, the Valley of the Triglav Lakes. On the lifeless wastes of the Hribarice and Triglavski podi you will come to know the sombre, petrified aspect of the Alps, and on the ledges of Kanjavec's north face the most majestic wildness. The summit climb will be the brilliant finale to this dreamworld journey. Take your time for this tour – Triglav is finest of all when traversed in three days. Do not hurry past the beauties and panoramic spots where you can establish friendship with the mountains while pleasantly resting!

STARTING-POINT:
Savica, 653 m, the parking area in front of the restaurant and mountain hut; from the Zlatorog Hotel at Ukanc beside Lake Bohinj 4 km (regular bus service during the summer).
DESCRIPTION:
The Pokljuka approach hands you some difficulties only at the end, but choosing this way, you must immediately reckon with the demanding steepness of the Komarča cliff. From the carpark cross the wooden bridge over the Savica stream, continue for a minute or two along the forest road, and a signpost will direct you uphill. At first the going is still gentle, but the rock face above the path on the right announces the commencement of Komarča's stiff gradient. After the first serpentine bend a path branches off left for the source of the Savica waterfall. (You must make this 5-minute detour, for the Savica's birth is dramatic. The water spumes from a dark cleft into a small pool and immediately leaps down foaming into the abyss.) The path then twists up the ever steepening slope in numerous serpentines, traversing narrow little ledges between the perpendicular cliffs, and in places is decidedly exposed. However, such sections are made easier by steel ropes. A good hour later, you reach a wonderful viewpoint on the edge of the Komarča face – this signals the end of the difficulties. Five minutes after you leave Komarča, the smooth waters of Črno jezero (Black Lake), 1294 m, gleam through the trees. This wild yet

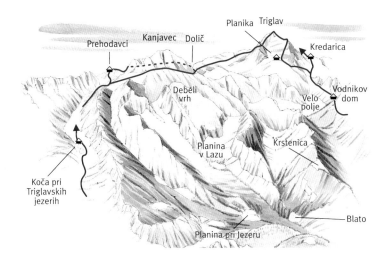

picturesque place at the foot of the mighty face of Stador is dark indeed, as emphasized by the tall spruces and the dark overhangs just above the lake. As the path continues to the Lakes mountain hut, it leads you through an attractive "virgin forest" of spruce. At first you ascend below great overhangs, but before Bela skala (White Rock) you come one storey higher. The spruce forest gives way to larch, a sign that you are entering the high-altitude realm. The big mountain hut Koča pri Triglavskih jezerih, 1683 m, stands on the shore of Dvojno jezero (Double Lake), in which Lepa špica is mirrored (see tour no. 5). The upper part of the valley is simply one sumptuous flower garden, here you are truly in the very heart of Zlatorog's kingdom. The easy path winds between little hills and enormous boulders, which have long since broken off from the rock faces. Now the larches thin out, while above the biggest lake, Ledvička (Kidney Lake), the cruel alpine climate has subdued even the most resilient warriors. Here begins the "kingdom of stone", which pronounces the proximity of the Triglav heights. On your right the reddish rock faces of Tičarica, Kopica and Zelnarica lean over the valley.

By the shallow Zeleno jezero (Green Lake) the path forks. The less experienced will choose the righthand path, which leads over the lifeless Hribarice plateau, 2358 m, under Kanjavec (see tour no. 8). From here the waymarks drop to the head of the valley Velska dolina and bear left to the mountain hut Tržaška koča na Doliču, 2151 m. But pastmasters are advised to turn left at Zeleno jezero and head for the nearby mountain hut Zasavska koča na Prehodavcih, 2071 m. From here there is an extremely attractive, bold and, naturally, demanding route along the ledges of the Kanjavec north face to the saddle Dolič at the foot of Triglav. This path first scrambles over the tame back of Vršac, and then advances through the middle of the stupendous abyss above the Trenta side valley of Zadnjica. The small, giddily exposed ledges are well-secured so that a mountaineer accustomed to bold routes can traverse this indescribably wild face with enjoyment and in safety. The path leaves the

73

frowning precipices somewhat below the Dolič saddle with the hut Tržaška koča, 2151 m.

The last stage begins comfortably. The "mulatiera" (a former Italian military transport route) ascends in easy bends across the lifeless wastes to the upper Triglav plateaus. Even at a distance you can spot a large construction situated on a saddle left of the path – the remains of the former Italian army barracks known as Morbegno, 2520 m. (It should be explained that between the two World Wars the Soča Basin – and consequently the western side of Triglav – was under Italian rule.) From here the route aims across rough scree for the rocks of Triglav's west face. Follow exposed but reliably secured ledges towards the right, then a crumbly gully leads to the notch Triglavska škrbina, 2659 m. The path now zigzags over the summit section. The climbing is easier than along the way from Kredarica, though there's no shortage of exposed places here either. On the final ridge more and more new horizons open up before you. Except for the distant frozen three-thousanders far to the north, everything lies deep below you. Any moment now and you'll see the long-awaited Aljaž turret.

DESCENT:

This very beautiful but nevertheless long approach you'll probably do in one direction only. For the descent you can choose the route described above, past the hut Vodnikov dom to Pokljuka, or straight on down into the Voje valley and finally to Stara Fužina.

DIFFICULTY:

Technically the Lakes approach is somewhat easier than that from Pokljuka (that is, if you go via the Hribarice, since the Kanjavec ledges are very demanding), but on the other hand it's much longer and more strenuous. On the summit crags there is also the danger of falling stones. Before climbing to the summit itself, check the sky for any threat of a storm!

TIMES:

Savica – Koča pri Triglavskih jezerih 3 h
Triglavska jezera – Hribarice – Dolič 3.30 h
Triglavska jezera – Prehodavci – Kanjavec ledges – Dolič 4.30 h
Dolič – Triglav 2.30 h
Total for the ascent 10-11 h
Triglav – Vodnikov dom 2-2.30 h
Vodnikov dom – Voje – Stara Fužina 3-3.30 h
Total for the descent 5-7 h
Total 15-18 h

This tour takes at least two days. The majority stay overnight on Dolič, which is sensible and recommendable.

pp. 74-75: The Triglav panorama from Rodica

11

Around Bohinj

Over saddles and alps – at the foot of the giants

A vertical cross-section of Bohinj clearly shows its storeyed structure. The ground floor is represented by the inhabited valleys and Lake Bohinj, whereas the roof is the high-altitude world of ridges and summits. Sandwiched in between there lies a varied and expansive medium-height region, consisting of plateaus, hollows with pastures and small valleys with lakes. This virtually uninterrupted green ring surrounds the Bohinj valley at an average altitude of 1500 m. It begins in the forests of Jelovica, narrows into a succession of basins under the Lower Bohinj Mountains (Spodnje Bohinjske gore) and then swings out into the mighty plateaus of Vogel and Komna. In the Triglav Lakes Valley it thrusts high up among the giants, spills over into the broad expanses of Fužinske planine, overleaps the Voje valley and dies away in the forests of Pokljuka. The unity and interlinkage of these parts invites the visitor to make combined tours, where you can ramble from alp to alp, crossing a series of passes, relaxing on lake shores, and admiring the lofty summits from the soft world at their foot. On every saddle a new view opens up, quite often with a complete change of landscape. At these altitudes where life is exuberant, the

The magnificence of autumn colours around the Triglav lakes

ancient tradition of alpine dairy farming naturally fits in with the indigenous flora and fauna. As you go there in search of beauty, happiness and enjoyment, remember that you are only on a visit. We owe this alpine world a due measure of respect, best expressed by leaving no traces behind.

This Bohinj region will be traversed in a clockwise direction, starting the tour comfortably by cable-car to reach Vogel. The tour described lasts at least two days. Since plenty of variations are possible, each person can choose their own section as their imagination dictates.

STARTING-POINT:
The upper Vogel cable-car station (Rjava skala), 1540 m
DESCRIPTION:
The first stage leads from Vogel to Komna, which itself is a popular tour. The "Vogel" area is described on pp. 33-34, while the way towards Komna as far as the foot of the true Vogel is given in tour no. 3. This traverse route (from which you can branch off to climb Vogel) is one of the most beautiful Bohinj walks. You won't believe who built it: border guards during the period when the border between Yugoslavia and Italy ran here. You walk along it without the least exertion over the panoramic flanks of mountain tops between Vogel and Meja as far as the saddle Konjsko sedlo, 1782 m, under the side ridge with its rocky summit Migovec, 1901 m. From the saddle you drop into the basin beneath the mighty Vrh nad Škrbino, and then the path turns right into the mouth of the valley Ražnova Suha. At first you descend steeply on overgrown terrain but soon go uphill again. As you reach the nearby saddle, the green sea of Komna laps below you. The path winds in a complex slalom amidst the dwarf pine and finally leads to the mountain hut Dom na Komni, 1520 m, visible from a great distance (see also p. 37).

The second stage links together the two main areas of Zlatorog's kingdom – Komna and the Triglav lakes. From Dom na Komni you descend somewhat along the "main road" towards the valley, but then the path veers left, venturing into a karst labyrinth. Soon you enter the steplike Razor valley and follow it to the foot of the bulky Kal, 2001 m. A sharp bend to the right takes you onto a broad plateau, across which you gently descend into the Lopučnica valley. For quite some time the Dolina Triglavskih jezer is finely spread in front of you; it's a half-hour climb from Lopučnica to Dvojno jezero (Double Lake) with its mountain hut. From Vogel to the hut Koča pri Triglavskih jezerih, 1683 m, is a really good one-day journey. (Direct access from the valley is described in tour no. 10)

The climb to the Štapce pass to the east above Dvojno jezero will involve you in some quite lively morning exercise. (From Štapce it is only half an hour further on to the fine, panoramic summit of Tičarica, 2071 m, northwards above the saddle; recommendable.) But your exertions will soon slip into oblivion, for now a pleasant journey awaits you across the plateau of the Fužinske planine. This mysterious little land is described on pp. 38-40. A gentle descent runs out into the extremely extensive alp Ovčarija, 1660 m, where you turn left and drop over a saddle to the lively Dedno polje, 1560 m. Once again you choose the leftward path, which winds around Kreda, 2025 m, and leads to the alp Planina v Lazu, 1560 m, at the foot of mighty Debeli vrh, 2390 m. The last strenuous ascent leads northwards to the pass Lazovški preval, 1966 m to the east below Debeli vrh. Then there follows the most alpine section of the tour, as you keep to the contour line across the plateaus between Debeli vrh and Škednjovec. The rocky surface of this landscape is a sure sign that barren stretches of the high mountains lie close at hand. On the pass Mišeljski preval, 1996 m, you achieve the "summit" of this tour. In front of you lies an expansive hollow with the alp Velo polje and its magnificent surroundings, dominated by Tosc, 2275 m (on the right), Mišelj vrh, 2350 m (in the centre) and of course Triglav. The route drops steeply into the valley Mišeljska dolina and passes the alp bearing the same name before running out into Velo polje. If you're in a hurry to reach the valley, you can turn right here down into Voje, otherwise you have a half-hour climb up to the mountain hut Vodnikov dom, 1817 m.

DIFFICULTY:

This technically perfectly easy tour requires persistence and ability in orientation. In some places the path is rather difficult to make out, and if you miss it, you'll find yourself in a tight corner. In particular, the passage from Laz to Velo polje is very complicated in poor visibility, so fine weather is essential. One of the most beautiful tours in the Julian Alps.

TIMES:

Vogel – Komna 4-5 h

Komna – Triglavska jezera 2.30 h (overnight stay)

Triglavska jezera – Laz 3 h

Laz – Vodnikov dom 4 h (possible overnight stay)

Vodnikov dom – Voje – Stara Fužina 3 h

12

Veliki Draški vrh

A Bohinj mountain beauty

ALTITUDE: 2243 m
STARTING ALTITUDE: 1438 m
HEIGHT DIFFERENCE: 805 m

Draški vrh is a fine and distinctive mountain. From Bohinj it is seen as a veritable pyramid in the mountain chain on the right below Triglav. Together with its western neighbour Tosc, the two form an inseparable yet totally contrasting pair. Tosc (colloquially 'Fatty') all bloated and clumsy, Draški vrh youthfully slim and bold. A true pyramid with its sharply pointed peak is the shape that brings the greatest number of points in a mountain beauty competition, so Draški vrh beyond the shadow of a doubt deserves the appellation of the subtitle above. Naturally this beautiful mountain is a real magnet for visitors. Although waymarks have not reached it, there's no need to be afraid of climbing it, since it is easily accessible in all directions from the Bohinj side. It is quite different on the north side: here Draški vrh boasts a majestic face, one of the

Tosc, Draški vrh and Ablanca; Triglav is veiled in cloud

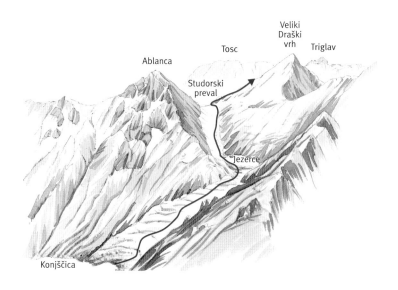

mightiest in the Julian Alps. Veliki (Great) Draški vrh is "a man for all seasons": in addition to mountaineers and rock-climbers, it makes skiers enthusiastic as they revel in its smooth Bohinj slopes without precipitous faces. Consequently it knows no dead season, and rewards visitors who come with whatever motivation still further with an outstanding view. Of course it is Triglav that draws the greatest admiration, as it reaches for the sky beyond the giddy depths of the Krma valley. Precisely in this direction the Slovene alpine champion shows his three-headed form most clearly. Together with its younger brother, Mali (Small) Draški vrh, 2132 m, to the east, its southern neighbour Viševnik, 2050m, and the finely pointed Ablanca, 2004 m, to the south, Veliki Draški vrh comprises a beautiful mountain group that surrounds the Konjščica alp in a horseshoe shape.

STARTING-POINT:
Konjščica, 1437 m (see p. 41, 1 h from Uskovnica, 30 minutes from the end of the road from Rudno polje on the Pokljuka plateau).
DESCRIPTION:
From the alp you follow the waymarks up along the valley. As you leave the pastures behind, the path twists among dwarf pine, and above a steepish section the path from Pokljuka joins this one from the right. Half an hour above Konjščica you enter the lovely cwm of Jezerce, which lies at the heart of the Draški vrh group. From here a valley leads gently up towards the left. Passing by a permanent spring, you gain the saddle Studorski preval, 1892 m, offering a good view towards the south. Now you leave the waymarks and set off to the right without any path along the ridge towards Draški vrh. The only problem is the gradient at the foot, where a plantation of dwarf pine first of all gets in your way (a route has been cut through it), and above that a rocky barrier some metres high. (If this passage seems too

demanding, it's possible to skirt it all along a trodden little path over the slopes on the right.) The gradient soon eases off and the rest of the walk along the wide open ridge is sheer enjoyment. The horizon grows broader with every step, more and more new summits spring up across the nearby ridges. The summit of Veliki Draški vrh is surprisingly capacious but beware: an enormous precipice yawns above the Krma valley.

DESCENT:
The quickest descent is by the same route. But it's recommendable to descend over the eastern slope to the saddle between Veliki and Mali Draški vrh. For the first metres go back along the ridge you've ascended by, and then left over the grass. Continue to drop down over easy ground along the edge of the north face. The saddle is a real green luxury where, lying on your stomach, you can delight in the deep vistas into the Krma valley. A trodden path leads back to Jezerce down to the left across the steep grassy slopes at the foot of Mali Draški vrh.

DIFFICULTY:
A technically easy yet pathless tour, requiring independence from waymarks and a basic understanding of orientation in the high mountains.

TIMES:
Konjščica – Veliki Draški vrh 2.30 h
Descent 2 h

p. 81: Hidden in the midst of forests and mountains: the Konjščica alp

View of Mali Draški vrh, Viševnik, Veliki Draški vrh and Tosc from Planika

13

Višcvnik

ALTITUDE: 2050 m
STARTING ALTITUDE: 1340 m
HEIGHT DIFFERENCE: 710 m

In the Julian Alps the term "high" means that the summit in question is over 2000 m. Višcvnik exceeds this magical boundary only by some metres, but nevertheless we are obliged to count it as one of the stalwarts. As mentioned in the subtitle, it is the nearest Bohinj two-thousander, which you can treat yourself to (naturally with the aid of a car) even after lunch. The "non-selective" access (excuse the expression) inevitably renders the mountain vulnerable to mass visits. On Višcvnik you can meet mountaineers, Pokljuka trippers, parachute jumpers, the odd shepherd searching for sheep or even a whole troop of soldiers from the nearby army barracks. Certainly this is the most frequented Slovene two-thousander in winter time, for it is particularly valued by skiers. All this throng of visitors have something in common: on the top their faces beam with joy. When all is said and done, that's what propels us into the mountains!
All the same, Višcvnik is not so mild as the above paragraph tried to present it. From Pokljuka it can be seen as a steep, sharply pointed summit, while its furrowed western flanks above Konjščica present real alpine wildness. The view from the top first bumps against the ridges around Konjščica, and then floats freely towards the Triglav heights. The mountain rises steep and high above the Pokljuka forests and so offers an especially fine view of this green, undulating expanse.

STARTING-POINT:
Rudno polje, 1340 m (25 km by road from Bohinjska Bistrica, 22 km from Bled). Here numerous forest roads scatter in various directions. Immediately beyond the army barracks (an asphalt surface to here) the road turns right towards Višcvnik. The path to the mountain starts about one kilometre higher, where a ski route with tow-lift cuts across the road.

DESCRIPTION:
The path, indicated by sparse waymarks, at first follows the ski-lift, but then continues along the steep valley to a small flat area at the foot of the steep summit structure of Višcvnik. Here you bear left and ascend onto the broad

Viševnik

Selišnik

Rudno
polje

ridge, where a marvellous view opens up towards the south. The path is now set for the summit; at first winding amidst dwarf pine, and then over grass. A narrow ridge leads to the top and demands some attention.

DESCENT:

If you don't want to descend by the same way, you can make a fine round tour by descending towards the north into the basin of Jezerce. Set off by following the waymarks along the northern ridge. The path twists among rock towers as far as the saddle Srenjski preval below Mali Draški vrh, which here shows its rocky, inaccessible face. Descend through a valley of rough scree into the lovely alpine cwm of Jezerce. You can return to Rudno polje by a direct route (the lefthand path) or past the dairy huts dotting the Konjščica alp (slightly longer).

DIFFICULTY:

When there is no snow, this is a completely easy tour (i.e. no great exertion is needed).

TIMES:

Rudno polje – Viševnik 2 h
Viševnik – Jezerce 1 h
Jezerce – Rudno polje 1.15 h
Total 5 h

p. 85: Viševnik is popular especially for ski-touring

14

Debela peč and its neighbours

The summits above Lipanca

ALTITUDE: 2014 m
STARTING ALTITUDE: c. 1300 m
HEIGHT DIFFERENCE: c. 700 m

The mountain chain which forms the northern rim of the Pokljuka plateau extends from the Draški vrh group far to the east. Its last high summit is the well-rounded Debela peč (Corpulent Crag). By this point the rugged alpine world has lost much of its sharpness and the summits are easily accessible. The forest roads and good paths enable everyone, really, to indulge in visiting these tops with their exceptionally panoramic vistas. Consequently the small mountain group of Debela peč has long been a favourite goal for family trips with less demanding mountaineers, who nevertheless can enter the real high mountain world up here and free of danger can enjoy its intoxication. An excellent starting-point is offered by the friendly mountain hut Blejska koča na Lipanci, 1630 m, which is open almost all the year round; above it rise four easily accessible summits. But – be warned! These gently rounded mountains are abruptly sliced off on the opposite side, high above the Krma valley, and if you have children with you, you must hold their hands.

The alpine quartet above Lipanca bears the names **Mrežce**, 1966 m, **Lipanski vrh**, 1968 m, **Brda**, 2009 m, and **Debela peč**, 2014 m, going from left to right. Mrežce is the nearest, Brda provides the finest viewpoint, Debela peč is the highest, and Lipanski vrh is the godparent giving a name to the group. Many excursionists treat themselves only as far as Lipanca, but it's worth mentioning that the gentle slopes of this group offer a compelling invitation to visitors during the winter as well.

STARTING-POINT:

Blejska koča na Lipanci, 1630 m. A waymarked route leads here from Pokljuka, branching off from the asphalt road by the signpost about 50 metres from the lefthand turning for the Šport Hotel. From here it takes you first along a forest road northwards to the fine, open alp of Javornik, 1295 m, in the next half hour it crosses two forest roads, then climbs through the forest into a grassy valley and so reaches the hut. 1.30 h. An even shorter way is possible if you drive along the forest road from Mrzli Studenec (by the intersection of the Bohinj and Bled roads; the forks are clearly indicated). This comes to an end in the forest half an hour below Lipanca.

DESCRIPTIONS:

Mrežce

Mrežce has already been mentioned as the nearest summit above Lipanca. From the mountain hut the path ascends towards the left onto a small forested flat area. At the signposted fork, where the left (long!) path heads towards Triglav, you bear right. There are some steep stretches as you climb towards the summit slope. A pleasant walk awaits you over gentle grassy patches and on top a prize in the form of a tremendously extensive view. The descent is by the same route, though experienced mountaineers can tackle the demanding ridge eastwards to the neighbouring

Lipanski vrh

This is generally easily reached from the east. You follow the path to Debela peč to the top of a steep gully, then veer left and ascend along a gentle valley to the pass Lipanska vrata in the main ridge above the Krma valley. From here a pleasant path follows the undulating ridge westwards to Lipanski vrh.

Debela peč – Brda

This pair of two-thousanders above Lipanca provides a round tour which is the very best mountain ascent in this region. The path to Debela peč first leads through a lovely larch forest, and then up a steep gully onto plateauish terrain where you notice on the right the interesting, neatly rounded top of Okroglež. A pretty long but not overly steep slope brings you to the summit ridge, where the distant northern ridges sail into view. (At this point on the way back you turn towards Brda.) From here the path runs to the right, partly downhill to the

The Lipanca alp

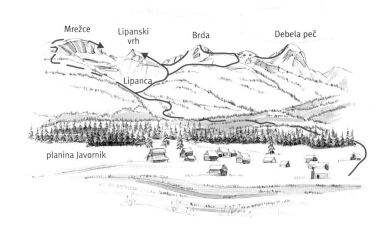

Mrežce
Lipanski vrh
Brda
Debela peč
Lipanca
planina Javornik

foot of the grassy summit slope of Debela peč. Another 15 minutes and the top is reached. Take care that those snug soft cushions on the summit don't lead you astray into lightmindedness: the mountain on the north suddenly drops away into a dizzying abyss!

When you return to the little saddle where the path branches off for Brda, you must accept the more restrained use of waymarks, since this is not a fashionable mountain. But the terrain is easy, softly shaped. Don't rush upwards too quickly or you'll drown in dwarf pine! The transverse path needs to be followed quite some way. Only by the edge does a good route present itself towards the nearby summit. Here luxuriant greenness greets you as you step onto the spot where the most beautiful view of the mountains around Krma crowns the tour.

Descend from the summit westwards, but from the small saddle in the vicinity you drop down to the left to reach the continuation of the transverse path. Descend further without any difficulty over grass into a small valley and on to Lipanca.

DIFFICULTY:
The tour is recommendable for children of all ages. Progress is easy everywhere.

TIMES:
Pokljuka – Lipanca 1.30 h
Lipanca – Mrežce 1 h
Lipanca – Lipanski vrh 1.30 h
Lipanca – Debela peč 2 h
Debela peč – Brda 45 minutes
Brda – Lipanca 1 h
Lipanca – Pokljuka 1 h

Northern approaches

In our hemisphere the northern side is naturally shady. In the Slovene mountains and in the Alps generally, this term (northern approaches) carries a further meaning, conditioned by the geomorphological composition and the appearance of the mountain range. Tectonic forces have fashioned the largest European mountain chain in such a way that the sunny sides are mostly friendly and more gentle, while the northern sides are steep and dark. This feature is particularly marked in the Julian Alps. It is no coincidence that the term "north face" is firmly embedded in the very concept of alpinism. Immensely steep slopes, normally linked with wildness and magnificence as well, naturally involve difficulties and dangers. Thus the northern routes to Alpine summits are understood to be more demanding than those enjoying sunshine.

However, it is precisely this characteristic that produces the allure of the ascents described in this chapter. Many mountain lovers turn from the gentle slopes where they learnt their moutaineering ABC to tackle ever more demanding routes. The desire for more impressive experiences draws them into a world of precipitous abysses, wild nature and utmost effort, since the greatest labour yields the most precious fruit. This chapter reveals such choice northern ascents. But of course there is no intention of scaring more modest ramblers and driving them away, for even the shady side of the Julian Alps offers lovely sunlit nooks where the fear of wildness is removed to a safe distance.

To the north of the Julian Alps the waters flow into the Sava Dolinka River, which flows through the Upper Sava Valley (Zgornjesavska dolina) towards the Gorenjska plain. In comparison with the winding valleys of the Sava Bohinjka and the Soča rivers, the Upper Sava Valley exemplifies regularity with its straight bottom, and wide open glacial shape, gradually sloping up towards Rateče. This valley is inhabited to a greater altitude than any other in Slovenia. Since it lies in the shadow of the highest peaks, it is cool here even in summer and in winter often shiveringly cold. It's not surprising that some of the oldest Slovene ski centres are to be found here. The valley shows its more friendly aspect along the sunny slopes of the Karavanke.

The Upper Sava Valley with its mountain giants is one of the most beautiful alpine places anywhere. Well-deserved praise was bestowed on it by the great discoverers and alpinists of the pioneer age while equal admiration is aroused among present-day visitors from all over the world. Triglav, Špik and Jalovec figure among the summits known throughout the ranks of mountaineers and their north faces (as well as others) hold a venerable place within European alpinism. Thus the image of the northern side of the Julian Alps has become Slovenia's most glorious alpine visiting card.

Thus the ascents described in this chapter have their starting-points in the Upper Sava Valley, though most climbers set off from the side (transverse) valleys, which are not inhabited and at their furthest point reach to the foot of the mountain faces. These valleys and basins are called Krma, Kot, Vrata, Beli potok, Za Akom, Pod Srcem, Pišnica and Planica. Above them the giants rise in majestic splendour. To the east begins the high range of Debela peč, which with its long ridge above the Krma valley abuts the Triglav massif. Apart from the monarch himself, Rjavina makes a great impression. Between the Vrata and Pišnica valleys the chain reaches its greatest height; here the Martuljek and Škrlatica groups boast of the boldest peaks and the most difficult access, with Špik dominating. To the west, above the head of the Pišnica valley, the splendid peaks of Razor and Prisank rub shoulders with the chain. Beyond the busy pass of Vršič (reached by road) there begins the long ridge of the Mojstrovka summits, with their precipitous north faces, which in the company of Travnik, the famed Jalovec and the Ponca chain surrounds the Planica valley. Between the tame Mežakla above Jesenice and Ciprnik above Planica a series of pleasant tops, reaching less than 2000 m, is ranged just above the valley. Their gentle nature invites the walker to attempt less demanding ascents.

The most important settlement in the Upper Sava Valley is the industrial town of Jesenice; numerous villages are dotted further up along the valley, the most significant as departure-points for the mountains being Mojstrana, Gozd - Martuljek, Kranjska Gora and Rateče. These are quiet places where the most important activities for the economy are agriculture and stock-breeding, alongside the tourist activities. The Upper Sava Valley is easily reached from central Slovenia by the main road Ljubljana – Jesenice – Rateče (90 km from Ljubljana), and from the Posočje region over the Vršič pass (Bovec – Kranjska Gora 46 km). From Austria a main road leads over the Koren pass (Würzelpass) or through the Karavanke tunnel (toll), while from Italy one easily passes over the Rateče/Fusine border crossing. Jesenice lies on an international rail route.

pp. 90-91: Triglavski dom na Kredarici is the highest meteorological station and mountain hut in Slovenia. It offers accommodation all the year round.

Walks

VRATA

Five valleys cut in towards the base of Triglav: the wildly romantic Zadnjica in Trenta, the sunny Voje on the Bohinj side, Krma, like a long street through a double row of skyscrapers, the solitary Kot and – Vrata (which means 'door', 'gate'). Each has its own charm and each provides a unique view of the Slovene monarch, but nevertheless Slovene mountaineers have chosen Vrata as the most "Triglavian" valley. Above it Triglav reveals himself in the most majestic form. The head of the valley is closed in by the famous North Face, which with its architectonic and aesthetic perfection, and especially its magnificent, soaring pillars, takes away every visitor's breath. Vrata is not dominated by Triglav alone. As many as six among the ten highest Slovene summits are gathered above Vrata, if we mention only the "top league". Their exceptional character and easy accessibility draw the crowds into this valley, so that mountaineers are generally in the minority.

Along the Vrata valley runs a road that ends at the mountain hut Aljažev dom (10 km from Mojstrana, parking area 5 minutes from the hut). The footpath partly avoids the road, but it must be admitted that nowadays you hardly meet anyone walking through the valley. However, if you plan only a trip into Vrata, then walking is highly recommendable, along its pleasant and shady path. The route begins in the village of **Mojstrana**, 650 m, halfway between Jesenice and Kranjska Gora. At first both road and footpath wind just above the cascades of the Triglavska Bistrica River, which is a youthfully energetic,

Triglav's mighty North Face towers above the Vrata valley

pleasantly rippling companion. Right here, of course, you are not in the mountains, the peaks are infinitely high and distant, and the first to call forth most admiration is the mighty yet elegant Stenar, 2501 m. The first natural attraction along the way is the **Peričnik** waterfall, which spumes over such tremendous conglomerate overhangs that a tourist path has been constructed actually behind the pounding column of water. To the left a steep path leads from the 52-metre-high main waterfall to the upper fall, which is a half-sized copy of the lower one. Below, by the road, you can get refreshments at the little hut Koča pri Peričniku. If you visit both waterfalls, the detour will take about one hour. Beyond Peričnik the road and footpath join for a time but above the steep incline (Kreda) the path again bears left into the forest, winding past solitary meadows and under galleries of conglomerate rock. Above on the right the angular pyramid of Kukova špica, 2427 m, temporarily overshadows the other mountain giants. When the footpath again joins the road (for the rest of the way), something immensely high and majestic begins to soar into view behind the outline of Cmir. Every gaze naturally quickens towards the holy temple where the most glorious sight in the Slovene mountains is gradually revealed in its splendour. The Triglav North Face! Here words fail. In front of the mountain hut **Aljažev dom**, 1015 m, (10 km from Mojstrana, 2.30 hours on foot), which stands on a slight rise at the edge of a lovely forest glade, cast your gaze to the other side as well; especially to the right, where the towers of the Škrlatica and Rokav groups project into the sky. If the grandeur of the Triglav pillars seems cold and heavy, then here high up among the sunlit towers you sense a breath of playful dynamics. If you add on the other parts of the panorama, including the velvet green around the foot of these mountains, you really feel an unsurpassable perfection in this wreath of peaks above the Vrata valley.

To the right of Aljažev dom you notice a neat chapel, while above it in the forest the huge rock boulder of Mali Triglav (Little Triglav), studded with pitons, invites the more courageous ones to try some pleasant gymnastics. But you simply must spare a hour or two for a walk up the valley. Soon you will catch sight of the biggest piton and karabiner in the world: a memorial to Partisan – mountaineers who fell in the war. Beyond some patches of beech forest you'll find yourself beside the youthful Bistrica River, and if you continue still further, you'll soon reach its source. Now you are really near the first strata of the soaring North Face; if anywhere at all, it's here that you recognize your human smallness. The Triglav paths and climbing routes now launch into the rocks and declare the end of a simple walk. Perhaps on another occasion, equipped and well-trained, you'll continue your way and experience the heady excitement of the Triglav heights.

MARTULJEK

"Is there anythinge else in all the Alps, including the whole range of the Julians, comparable to the hidden mystery of Martuljek?" wrote one of the greatest classic alpinists and a connoisseur of most of the world's mountain ranges, the Englishman Dr Tom Longstaff. The name Martuljek denotes the mountain group between the Vrata and Pišnica valleys, which with its magnificent peaks like

Gothic spires throws down its challenge immediately above the Upper Sava Valley to the east of Kranjska Gora. In its appearance – the perpendicular faces, the reddish tinge of the rock and the dynamic show of its numerous turrets and towers – this wild crest is reminiscent of the Dolomites. The two great stars of Martuljek are the accordion-like, reddish Široka peč (Broad Crag), 2497 m, in the eastern wing and of course the sheer pyramid of Špik (Spear), 2472 m. Snow lies all year round in the high basins at the foot of these majestic faces and feeds the Martuljek stream. This leaps over two precipices in beautiful cascades and below at the village of Gozd - Martuljek (the old name is Rute) flows into the Sava Dolinka. This region is one of the most solitary, untouched and inaccessible areas in all the Julian Alps. Here from the north not a single path leads to the summits, only experienced alpinists can attempt an ascent. The trip to be described allows us just to humbly admire the untamed giants from their gentle base.

As an introduction to Martuljek we suggest a trip to the small village of **Srednji Vrh**, 960 m, situated on a sunny terrace in the middle of the Karavanke slopes opposite Špik (from the village of Gozd - Martuljek 4 km along a steep and narrow asphalt road, 1 hour on foot). From here you can enjoy one of the most splendid views in the country. The Martuljek peaks stand before you as if on exhibition and confirm the praises conferred by the honourable Englishman. To reach the foot of these mountains you similarly need to start in the village of Gozd - Martuljek, 750 m, leaving the main road by the Špik guest house. After a few hundred metres the forest road comes near the Martuljek stream and the first banks where the water has carved a deep gorge, with a comfortable tourist path leading through it. After you have crossed two small bridges, the waterfall **Spodnji slap** (Lower Fall) comes thundering down on

Mojstrana nestles at the foot of Rjavina, Triglav and Stenar

96

the left. Below it the path winds to the right into the forest and climbs up to a broad cart-track. Turn left here. Soon after a path branches off right under Špik, but the cart-track drops gently leftwards to the stream, which here flows peacefully across flat forest ground. The waymarks for the path to the Zgornji slap (Upper Fall) stay on the west bank, but a small bridge invites you to make a necessary turn across the stream to find the indescribably lovely haymeadows of **Jasenje**, 930 m, spread out before you. Here you'll think that the vertiginous pyramid of Špik pierces the sky. During the summer season you can replenish your energy with good homemade refreshments in the Brunarica (Log Cabin) pri Ingotu. The walk from Gozd - Martuljek so far takes 45 minutes.

If you would also like to see the **Zgornji slap**, return to the west bank of the stream, where the waymarked path gently slopes upwards, with a pleasant carpet of spruce needles underfoot. The path ascends in several stages, but at the foot of high steep slopes a signpost points you left towards the waterfall. This 10-minute section leads across a steep slope where you should take care not to slip into the stream foaming down below. Compared with the lower waterfall, this one is higher, slender and more alpine in character. From the valley 1.30 h. The return is by the same route.

ZELENCI

Unlike the Sava Bohinjka River, which bursts forth dramatically in the mighty Savica waterfall, the birth of the Dolinka is hidden away like a mysterious fairytale. No thunderous roar of falling waters or rapids. In blue-green pools among the reeds one can detect the bubbling of the water springing up. On a dewy morning only the splash of a trout enlivens the motionless surface of the water. When the Ponca summits high above glow in the sun, their picture is

The Martuljek summits in splendid array; the view from Srednji Vrh

mirrored on that smooth surface in shades of dawn pink. Zelenci (Green Waters) – as the source of the Sava Dolinka is named - lies between the villages of Podkoren and Rateče near the extreme northwest corner of Slovenia. Due to its beauty and natural particularities Zelenci is protected by law as a nature reserve. Together with the marshes, which here and there turn into peat bogs, and the first meanders of the Sava River, Zelenci represents a tiny, very sensitive ecosystem that is continually threatened by the proximity of human settlements and busy roads. Much plant and animal life is to be found there, typical of an aquatic and marshy environment, including rare and endangered species. Surrounded by wonderful countryside, Zelenci is a truly precious natural attraction, which requires a nature-friendly approach from the visitor. One of the first to announce the beauty of Zelenci to the world, even 200 years ago, was the famous English scientist Humphrey Davy.

Most visitors come to Zelenci by walking a few minutes from the main road (between Podkoren and Rateče is a large parking area, with a small café). But you will more fully experience this natural jewel if you begin your trip at the foot of the ski slopes below the village of Podkoren. You can walk along the southern river bank westwards, following the disused railway track; immediately around are the typical features of marsh and peatbog. Later you take the marked tourist path, which runs around Zelenci among the reedbeds and over small bridges, leading you to the northern bank of the lake. The tour can be rounded off by returning on this side. The round trip will last an hour. Walking is permitted only on the marked pathway.

PLANICA – TAMAR

Of the transverse Upper Sava valleys, Planica is the most western and the

Zelenci, the Planica valley and the Ponca chain

highest. It branches off the main valley towards the south by the village of Rateče, 865 m, near the state border. The name of Planica resounds especially among Slovenes and winter sports lovers around the world. Its fame has (literally) leapt across Slovenia's borders for one of the most attractive sports was born precisely here – ski flying. Today Planica is the world metropolis of bold fliers; it possesses all the historical landmarks of this sport (breaking the 100 m record, the 200 m record, ...). There is no other place where so many Slovenes suddenly throng together as the Planica arena at the time of the major competitions. The ski jumps stand at the foot of the Ponca range, rising on the west side of the valley. And what about Tamar? This name denotes the head of the Planica valley, wedged between two mighty mountain chains. On the left stand the precipitous faces of Mojstrovka, Travnik and Šite, a challenge for rock-climbers, while on the right stretches the long chain of the Poncas. The aesthetic culmination of the Tamar wreath of mountains is set right back at the end of the valley, where these two ridges meet. Jalovec, that noble obelisk of crystal shape, can vie with Triglav and Špik in any alpine "beauty competition". Tamar is greatly cherished by mountaineers, and even more so by rock-climbers; in particular the north faces of Travnik and Šite belong to the "alpinists' cream" of the Julian Alps. Lovers of ski touring also deeply admire this valley. The mountain hut **Dom v Tamarju**, 1108 m, open all year round, makes an attractive destination for an easy trip.

From Rateče a road leads to Tamar, but beyond the ski jumps it is open for public use only between 18.00 and 8.00. You can reach the ski jumps by the road from Rateče (2 km) or by a marked footpath which gently winds through the forest near the foot of the Poncas. In winter a popular cross-country ski route is laid out here. After an hour's walk the trees give way and the alpine giants are revealed in all their glory. The wide open forest glade lies before you like an enticing carpet, at the far end you notice the mountain hut, and just look, its architecture tries to imitate the famous Jalovec. To the right tumbles the waterfall **Nadiža**, which bursts forth from the Poncas' flanks, cascading over rocks, and yet this flood of water disappears in no time into the gravel. A path which anyone can manage (10 minutes from the valley) leads to its source. If the seductive grassy carpet has not induced too lazy a mood, carry on further up the valley. The goal isn't important. Beyond the first patch of forest the voices of the valley die away and you are face to face with the mountains. Perhaps you will hear that mysterious call which draws you another time to venture still higher.

Trips

JEREBIKOVEC

Mežakla is a medium-high forested plateau on the northwestern edge of the Julian Alps, which the deeply cut Radovna valley separates from the true mountain range. To the north it falls steeply into the Upper Sava Valley above Jesenice. The highest point, Jerebikovec, 1593 m, rises on the northern edge of the plateau above the village of Mojstrana. This bald eminence counts as one of the most beautiful viewpoints in the Julian Alps. Wild strawberries grow on the very top while beneath a nearby spruce a colossal antheap teems with life. So you are not really in the high mountains here, but they shimmer all around in a mighty semi-circle.

The starting-point for an ascent of Jerebikovec is the village of Mojstrana, 650 m. From here follow the road towards the Radovna valley for a good kilometre to the top of the second incline. Near the Triglavski narodni park board you notice a signpost for Mežakla and turn left up the slope by a forest path. For more than 30 minutes this is very steep, but higher up more gentle serpentine bends begin. A good hour's walk from the road the gradient suddenly eases, the trees stand back and reveal a friendly forest clearing. The dilapidated huts indicate that once upon a time the Mežakla alp, 1350 m, flourished here. On the saddle stands a monument to fallen Partisans. The path joins a forest road and soon leads to a saddle below the main top of Jerebikovec. At this point the surrounding summits first peep through the canopy of trees. The way continues straight up through steep forest to the

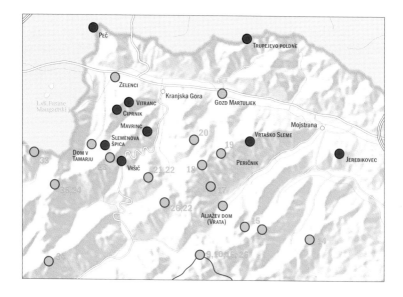

broad bald top. The view is magnificent. In the foreground are the Julian Alps above the valleys of Krma, Kot and Vrata, with Triglav appearing in the major role. The star of the northern panorama is the Karavanke summit of Kepa (whose regular outline is reminiscent of Fuji). A local lover of Jerebikovec has constructed a cheerful shelter among the branches of a great beech at the highest point. Barely 2 hours from the road; the path is waymarked and quite easy, though rather steep.

VRTAŠKO SLEME

Despite its being a two-thousander, the pleasant grassy pyramid of Sleme, 2077 m, can't be included among the real high mountains, and so is placed here in the category of trips. This gently shaped mountain is the easternmost outcrop of the mighty Martuljek ridge, which right here loses its powerful character. Sleme is an easily accessible viewpoint and doesn't lack visitors. Moreover the broad eastern flank where the forested Vrtaški vrh rises also attracts skiers. Sleme is similarly blanketed as far as the base of the crowning pyramid with continuous spruce forest.

Once more the starting point – this time for the ascent of Sleme – is Mojstrana, 650 m. You leave the road that runs through the Vrata valley at the end of the village, at the top of the first incline. Here the waymarked path turns up the slope, bending towards the initial hill of Grančiše, then winding towards the left through steep forest. The otherwise safe path offers anything but a gentle gradient, so that the extensive forest clearing of **Vrtaška planina**, 1462 m, reached after a good two hours' walk, is a veritable relief. This offers a fantastic view of the majestic mountains surrounding the Vrata valley and many visitors end their trip here. But above the alp there soon opens up a charming world above the treeline; between the scattered larches the big

Rjavina, Triglav and Cmir above Kot, Stenar and Dolkova špica above Vrata (right)

mountains dazzle the eyes, and along the ridge the view of the Julians is joined by that of the Karavanke summits. The rounded Vrtaški vrh, 1898 m, is bypassed by the path on the southern side but it's well worth the effort of climbing it. Then above the green saddle of Njivice you reach the start of the high grassy slopes. Making your way wherever you wish, you reach the narrow summit ridge not far right of the highest point of Sleme. Undoubtedly the star character in the panorama now seen is Kukova špica – a formidable rock fortress guarded with jagged arêtes. In the background are ranged the ridges that surround Vrata, finally merging into the magnificent massif of Triglav, here displaying his famous North Face. From Vrtaška planina 2 h, from Mojstrana 4 h. Descent by the same route.

VRŠIČ, 1611 m,

is the highest road pass in Slovenia. The road links the Upper Sava Valley with Trenta, where the Soča River has its source. Nowhere else in the country can you so easily approach the alpine summits. The road was built during the turbulent war years of 1914-18 to meet the strategic plans of the Austrian army. Mostly Russian prisoners of war were engaged in the work and experienced terrible suffering. Unused to the mountains, they were mowed down in masses by avalanches and other weather disasters. The Russian Chapel is devoted to their memory. Even if you view your surroundings from behind the steering wheel, you'll be drawn willy-nilly to brake on the picturesque serpentine bends, where the Vršič giants soar upwards. Unforgettable scenes slide past your windows and at times you seem to come close to touching true mountain wildness. (If you are aiming at Vršič from Kranjska Gora by bus, be sure to choose a seat on the left side!) Right now you catch sight of a petrified woman's face in the midst of the rocky crags, then a piece

The view from Vrtaško Sleme

of sky shines through a dark shaft among grey rock faces, while below boisterous waters gush over precipices and all around the peaks are unbelievably high. Vršič is an important mountaineers' starting-point, it is assaulted by crowds of cyclists and skiers, and at times the hustle and bustle is really too much in the face of all this beauty. It is nowhere stipulated that you must drive or ride up there; because the asphalt can mostly be avoided, the footpath to Vršič is appealing and considerably used – indeed in winter, when the road is often closed by snow, it is obligatory.

Immediately beyond Kranjska Gora, 810 m, the footpath bears right into the forest above the road, crosses the Mala Pišnica stream and continues along a gentle cart- track to the Erika Hotel. Three kilometres of asphalt on to the mountain hut Mihov dom can be avoided if before the bridge you take the forest road and follow it along the east bank of the Pišnica. Where this crosses the stream-bed a good half hour later, you must look for the waymarked path on the right taking you to Mihov dom. This valley section of the way features views of the lofty peaks around the Krnica valley with turreted Razor in the middle. The waymarked shortcut slices off the bends above Mihov dom but the short bend on the 8th serpentine must be taken, because there stands the picturesque, well-maintained **Ruska kapelica** (Russian Chapel) – in memory of the unfortunate road-builders who died here far from their homeland for foreigners. You are soon back on the asphalt, but only to cross it and the footpath again seeks the shade among the spruces. (Five minutes to the left stands the mountain hut Koča na Gozdu by the roadside, while to the right a path branches off to Mavrinc – see the next paragraph.) For a time a little stream keeps you company, and the road is reached again on the 17th serpentine, above the 21st you bear left to the nearby mountain hut

Looking towards Vršič: Prisank (left) and Mojstrovka (right)

Erjavčeva koča, 1525 m. Its very position invites you to take a rest and enjoy the view. Prisank is the commanding presence here, hiding a host of intriguing features. Some you caught sight of lower down: for instance, the wild gully of Hudičev žleb (Devil's Gully) and the sequence of waterfalls at its foot. The view of what is the biggest natural window in the Slovene mountains is simply breath-taking. And right in front of Erjavčeva koča you have the finest sight of another play of nature: from the heart of those grey rock faces the long petrified **Ajdovska deklica** (Pagan Giantess) watches all that happens on Vršič. It is only quarter of an hour from here to the pass, 1611 m, where new expanses open up and you sense the warm breath of the south. The mountain chain of Posočje (the Soča Basin) stretches in front of you as the road rolls down into the deeply cleft Trenta valley. Kranjska Gora – Vršič 3 hours (12 km). If you wish to conclude the trip in a mountaineering manner, up on the left the true **Vršič** awaits you. Without difficulty you reach the conical rise, 1737 m, in half an hour, going past the mountain huts of Tičarjev dom and Poštarski dom. The exhaust fumes are not smelt there, and the noise dies away too. So you can feel the true mountaineer's mood as you take in these majestic views.

MAVRINC

Those who ascend to Vršič from the north don't cast a glance to the right. How could they, when such a stupendous parade is drawn up on the other side and here only unimposing, overgrown tops crowd together? This really is unvisited mountain terrain, barely accessible because of the thick cover of dwarf pine. But somewhat above Mihov dom a small side ridge with a rounded head, featuring as an independent summit, pushes itself up above the forested slopes. Mavrinc, 1562 m, is a companionable, easily accessible mountain with a fantastic view, which has won itself a fair number of friends.

Špik and Škrlatica viewed from Sleme

Many of them take it in their stride – to add variety to the Vršič route. The way to Mavrinc leaves the Vršič road together with the marked path above the 9th serpentine (5 minutes below Koča na Gozdu, approx. 1200 m). After just a few paces you leave the waymarks and turn right onto a cart-track. You turn your back on this as well 30 metres on and climb straight up by a well-trodden, unmarked path. In a bare spot 10 minutes above the road a wooden bench takes you by surprise. Somewhat higher up the slope steepens, but a comfortable forest path winds gently towards a small saddle left of the overgrown Mavrinc ridge. When you reach this, you find yourself on a narrow little crest. Turn right and a small path brings you in a few minutes to the open summit with a visitors' book and a bench. The view takes in the grand sweep of peaks above the Krnica valley and Vršič: the summits between Špik and Mojstrovka create a sumptuous fan. From the road a bare hour. The route is not marked!

SLEMENOVA ŠPICA

One of the most renowned viewpoints in the Slovene mountains lies near the northern foot of Mala Mojstrovka above the Vršič road pass. A small grassy terrace is ringed by larch-trees and a few modest pools sparkling in the hollows have been captured on photographers' film to look like tarns. Above the plateau, a broad mountain face soars skyward, a sculptured sequence of dizzying precipices, which in the world of alpinism plays the role of a climbers' university. Beyond the deep valley stretches the long chain of the Poncas, while the aesthetic culmination of the panorama is the imposing Jalovec, 2645 m, towering above Tamar. This view of Jalovec is a veritable magnet, drawing the crowds. Well, there wouldn't be so many, were it not for the Vršič road being so near and the path so pleasantly comfortable. This area is called

Late afternoon on Sleme

Sleme and most tourists end their trip here. Slemenova špica, 1911 m, is a grassy slope 10 minutes above the famed spot but it has an alpine character, since a vertiginous abyss drops off beneath your feet, as you look down with bated breath into the green depth of Tamar. The shortest route from Vršič will be described here, but you can also reach the mountain by a waymarked path from Tamar (2.30 h).

The starting-point, then, is the Vršič road pass, 1611 m. The waymarked path begins from the top of the pass itself, ascending towards the right between dwarf pine and crossing rough scree to gain the Vratica saddle, 1799 m (30 minutes), and then drops to the basin-shaped plateau near the edge that falls into the Mala Pišnica valley. The only exposed spot on this trip will surprise you behind one edge but the terrain widens out again. The gently ascending path crosses the foot of Slemenova špica and should be left around here. Any number of well-trodden tracks lead to the noted viewpoint. A very picturesque larch, seen from a distance, marks the fringe of the grassy terrace with its tarns, but if you wish to reach the top of Slemenova špica, just carry on straight there. From Vršič 1.30 h.

This is the route description, yet its bare sentences cannot capture the ravishing beauty of this place. A many-hued garden undulates between angular crags, guarded by shaggy larches. Beyond Vratica you gazed at the giants above the Pišnica valley, and now here the Planica wreath of peaks is displayed. When Jalovec appears beyond the famous dell, you feel the perfection of the scene.

VITRANC – CIPRNIK

I consider that Ciprnik, 1746 m, holds top place among the viewpoints above the Upper Sava Valley. This wide open, aesthetically perfect view from a mountain which just rises above the tree-line simply cannot be praised too highly. All the peaks

The Škrlatica group dominates the view from Ciprnik, cloaked in dwarf pine

above Pišnica, Vršič and Planica are displayed in a magnificent arc, and of course under Triglav's supervision. Below, the eye rests on the soft green of the Planica valley, with its famous ski flying arena noticeably carved out. The view of Jalovec is wonderful for you are high enough to gaze at the giant face to face. To the north are ranged the gentle tops of the Karavanke, while the entire northern horizon is filled by the silhouette of the Tauern with Grossglockner dominating. Ciprnik blends into the bulk of Vitranc, 1576 m, the mountain immediately above Kranjska Gora, which boasts a network of ski routes and ski-lifts.

To reach Ciprnik you must first aim at Vitranc, taking Kranjska Gora as your starting-point. Naturally it's most comfortable to take the chairlift, which usually operates in summer as well. Just below the summit stands a mountain hut. For walkers there isn't actually a waymarked route to Vitranc, but a number of easy paths lead you there. The orientation is simplest if you just follow the line of the ski route, which is pretty steep in the upper part. From Kranjska Gora to Vitranc is 2 hours' walk. From Vitranc itself a comfortable waymarked route leads you along the gently rising forested ridge until the last section of the path, which is steep – to gain the top of Ciprnik. Here the trees stand back to let the splendid panorama described in the first paragraph greet you. From Vitranc to Ciprnik takes barely one hour.

PEČ – TROMEJA

Peč, 1508 m, is a gently rounded mountain north of Rateče and covered in forest to the top. Here begins the long Karavanke chain, which runs along the northern edge of Slovenia as far as the distant eastern plains. We include it in this chapter on the Julian Alps for practical reasons, since an ascent of Peč starts from the same valley area as for the tours described on the northern side of the Julian Alps. Peč is better known by its unofficial name Tromeja (Triple

The impressive north faces above the Planica valley

Border*)*, since Slovenia, Italy and Austria meet on its summit. It is truly a "cosmopolitan" mountain, where visitors greet each other in all the relevant languages. Moreover, Peč is extremely accessible, with a grandstand view that attracts numerous visitors from all sides. It is even possible to drive practically to the top by a reasonably good forest road from Rateče (approx. 10 km), which starts at the Šurc inn. Remember to take the left turn at every fork! Before the last big bend of the road to the right, a signpost invites you onto a pleasant though quite steep footpath, which climbs straight up towards the summit along a broad open swathe that indicates the state border. This walk takes a good half hour. However, if you opt to walk all the way, the outing from Rateče to Peč will last two hours. The summit is adorned with various symbolic features explaining its role together with a huge TV aerial. But above all Peč – Tromeja is blessed with an outstanding view, encompassing the peaks of the Eastern Julian Alps, that rise exactly opposite on the far side of the Sava valley, and additionally the mighty mountains of the Western Julian Alps, crowned by Jôf Fuart/Viš and Montasio/Montaž. Northwards the view drops into the broad Gailtal valley, beyond which rises the long bulk of Dobratsch.

TRUPEJEVO POLDNE

Like Peč, Trupejevo poldne, 1931 m, belongs to the softly drawn Karavanke range, separated from the Julian Alps by the Upper Sava Valley. This mountain stands opposite the wildest group in the Slovene mountains – the Martuljek ridge – and provides a wonderful balcony for admiring this indescribably beautiful alpine scene. The northern panorama contrasts totally with the wild ruggedness of this group; it embraces the soft, green world of Carinthia, studded with numerous lakes. The easily accessible mountain shakes itself free of the forest only just below its summit, and then shows

On the ridge below the summit of Trupejevo poldne

some high-altitude features. Among lovers of easy yet aesthetically top quality mountain trips Trupejevo poldne is highly esteemed and quite well visited. From the valley you cannot see the top, but this is nothing special, since its modest, grassy rise doesn't markedly stand out from the gently undulating outline of the Karavanke. The starting-point is the village of Gozd - Martuljek, 750 m, or rather the hamlet **Srednji Vrh,** 960 m, reached by a narrow asphalt road from the valley bottom (4 km, a bare hour on foot). This is a lovely little settlement lying on a sunny terrace in the middle of the Karavanke flanks, with an impressive view of the Martuljek group (see pp. 95-97). You leave the hamlet west of its "centre" and follow a comfortable cart-track which climbs gently – at first along the western bank above the stream Jermanov potok, and then crossing to the other side. Soon after you have passed a large haymeadow, the valley turns right (eastwards) and acquires the name Železnica. (The name is associated with iron, which was mined in these parts in earlier centuries.) Higher up you join for a time a forest road that ends near a hunters' hut, 1635 m. From here an unmarked path gradually ascends along the valley to a saddle which separates Trupejevo poldne from its eastern neighbour Bele peči. From here to the summit, marked by a large cross, involves just a 15-minute walk to the northwest along the open ridge. From Srednji Vrh to Trupejevo poldne 3 hours.

15

Vrbanova špica - Rjavina

The circuit around Pekel

ALTITUDE: 2408, 2299, 2532 m
STARTING ALTITUDE: 2332 m
HEIGHT DIFFERENCE: 700 m

Vrbanova špica and Rjavina are two mountains that belong to the Triglav group in the narrow sense – they support his great massif in the northeast, enchaining the alpine basin of Pekel (Hell) high above the Kot valley, which offers the most solitary entrance into Triglav's kingdom. Rjavina to the east is a bulky mountain with magnificent rock faces, while Vrbanova špica is more modest, but with a rompish, playful crest that when seen close to reminds you of a gateau with its distinctive strata. Bold, vertiginous secured routes traverse these steep rocks; they are among the most attractive in the Julian Alps. You needn't fear encountering the Triglav hordes on these ridges, but you should reckon with considerably more demanding routes than those on Triglav. The ascent of Rjavina or Vrbanova špica is often begun in the early morning down

Cmir, Begunjski vrh, Vrbanova špica and Rjavina - the panorama seen from Triglav

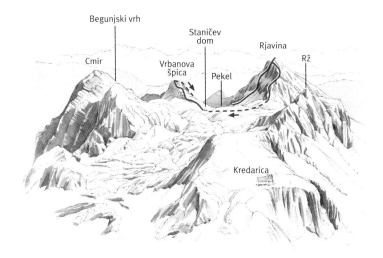

in the Kot valley, but here the round tour is described, starting from the mountain hut Staničev dom and embracing both summits. This hut has much to offer: in addition to the prestigious Triglav and our two peaks, Begunjski vrh and Cmir rise close by. So you could spend a few days up here without being short of ideas. Most visitors look on our two summits as a bonus, to be included within the framework of a visit to Triglav. The round tour is here described in clockwise fashion, although climbing the other way round is perhaps a little easier.

STARTING-POINT:
The hut Staničev dom, 2332 m, stands on level ground northeast of Triglav. Access: from the Vrata valley by the Tominšek route (Tominškova pot) or by the Prag route (4-5 h, see pp. 114-117), through the Kot valley (4 h from the end of the road), through the Krma valley (5 h from the end of the road), from Kredarica 1 h.

DESCRIPTION:
The 20-minute ascent to the gentle top of **Visoka Vrbanova špica**, 2408 m, immediately above the hut, provides a warming-up session for the demanding tour ahead. Walking is soon over as you drop over a steep grassy slope onto the right hip of the ridge, where the path follows a system of ledges. Later you keep to the ridge itself, where the finest places are waiting. The dizzying crest is particularly reminiscent of a saw. There are picturesque passages that are models of exposure. The route offers tremendous variety: at one point you step along an exiguous ledge (these are an engaging feature of the tour), and then you climb over a finely honed tower in the ridge itself. All the exposed places are well secured. To calm your nerves, the ridge eventually broadens into a fine platform called Plesišče (Dance Floor). The lower summit Spodnja Vrbanova špica, 2299 m, is then soon reached. The

111

descent into Pekel (but don't be afraid!) at first follows the continuation of the ridge, which drops sharply here. The pleasant climbing comes to an end on a steep grassy slope, where the path turns right. The grass alternates with rocky steps, while just above the scree the last tricky spot lies in wait as you pass over smooth slabs. When you gain the path running from the Kot valley up to Staničev dom, follow it uphill for about 20 minutes. As the gradient flattens, watch out for the inconspicuous path branching off for Rjavina. The more tiring part of the tour begins with a short scree section, and you soon reach the secured route. This at first follows a steep pillar and then crosses above it left into a gully, but the exit is the most difficult, involving climbing again along the exposed pillar. You finally come out of the face considerably to the right of the summit, and there are still some demanding places to be negotiated along the summit ridge. Before you reach the top of **Rjavina**, 2532 m, two picturesque windows in the ridge come as a surprise. The descent down the ridge to Staničev dom takes an hour and a half, its more difficult part you now retrace. Below the second, southwest summit (2 metres lower than the main one), the problems subside, only you still need to take care crossing the crumbly crags on to the saddle Dovška vratca. From here an easy descent is possible either into Kot or Krma; otherwise it takes half an hour back to Staničev dom up along the gentle, stony ridge.

DIFFICULTY:
The tour is very demanding. Exposed! Self-belaying is essential. The security aids are reliable. The tour can be safely carried out only in settled weather. You must not be caught in a storm on the ridge. The tour can, of course, be interrupted after descending from Vrbanova špica.

TIMES:
Staničev dom – Spodnja Vrbanova špica 2 h
Spodnja Vrbanova špica – Pekel 1 h
Pekel – Rjavina 2 h
Rjavina – Staničev dom 1.30 h
The entire circuit 7 h

16

Triglav

The northern appearance of the highest Slovene mountain

ALTITUDE: 2864 m
STARTING ALTITUDE: 1015 m
HEIGHT DIFFERENCE: 1849 m

In the Bohinj chapter (pp. 67-76), the sunny, gentle side of the highest mountain in the Julian Alps was described. Here Triglav is presented from the north, and his sober, majestic appearance above the Vrata valley. From the heart of the massive rock face 1000-metre-high pillars thrust upwards, consisting of innumerable strata of grey limestone. The sunlit edge is so immensely high up it seems to belong to some other, inaccessible world. This is the Triglav North Face. Slovene climbers are so fond of it that they affectionately shorten the name into simply the Face. How much has happened in those vertiginous walls! How many passionate, though unfortunately often tragic stories are recorded in the exploration of the Face, how much courage and daring this never completed "conquest of the useless" has demanded. And the Face still stands

The Triglav North face soars above the Vrata valley

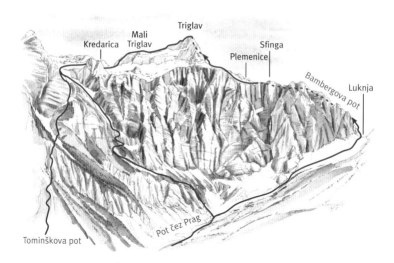

Triglav
Mali
Triglav
Kredarica
Sfinga
Plemenice
Bambergova pot
Luknja
Pot čez Prag
Tominškova pot

before us as an eternal challenge. Above it rises the beautifully formed summit section of Triglav. To the left below this, the remains of the Triglav glacier are slowly disappearing. Only steep and still steeper routes lead from the Vrata valley to Triglav, consisting of merely three "ordinary" ones and over 100 climbing routes of all grades of difficulty.

STARTING-POINT:
Aljažev dom in Vrata, 1015 m, 11 km by road from Mojstrana (2.30 h on foot).

A. TOMINŠKOVA POT (The Tominšek Route)

This is the classic Triglav route, regarded as the most beautiful and the most frequented, though not the easiest northern approach. Demanding, it will take quite some exertion. Of the trio of paths, it is the easternmost, and in the lower part runs across the face of Triglav's neighbour, Cmir. In the morning hours these sheer slopes lie in shadow. Despite its constant twists and turns, it is also regarded as the shortest route from Vrata to Triglav, and is recommendable especially for the ascent. It mostly traverses steep rocks, which are well secured. Since all around is open, it offers tremendous views. If you wish to gaze to your heart's content on the Face, then choose the Tominšek route! However, the path does cross some steep gullies, generally snow-filled until far into the summer, so an ice-axe is a compulsory piece of your equipment until mid-July.

DESCRIPTION:
From Aljažev dom go up along the valley as far as the nearby memorial (a giant karabiner in memory of fallen Partisans), where the path swings left and

climbs steeply into the forest. The trees first recede on the brink of a deep gully, and above the second gully to the right the path reaches the tree-line. Overhead are the sloping strata of the Cmir face, while your route climbs steeply rightwards to gain a green top. From here the well-secured path rises steadily towards the right across the ledges and gullies of the Cmir face; in some places it is really exposed. The most beautiful view is proffered as you reach the promontory Kozja dnina, where the terrain becomes noticeably easier. You soon reach a hollow at the foot of the yellow face of Begunjski vrh, with a pleasant jet of water issuing from the face. At this point you join the Prag route, and a little further on a path forks off left for the nearby mountain hut Staničev dom, 2332 m. Shortly above the spring the Triglav path climbs onto a gently sloping karst plateau, with characteristic features, and crosses ever more extensive snowfields. Past the edge of the former Triglav glacier, which has left behind it broad gravelly banks, you gain the saddle below the summit section of Triglav. Up on the left the big, comfortably furnished mountain hut **Triglavski dom na Kredarici,** 2516 m, is waiting to greet you. Here a marvellous view unfolds towards the south and east. From Vrata 5 h.

Now comes the grand finale. If you have successfully overcome the difficulties so far, then you have already passed the "entrance exam" for Triglav. However, a word of warning is necessary: you are now entering the upper storey, where natural forces rule more strictly than in the gentle lowlands. So set out for the summit in conditions which exclude the danger of a storm. The path from the saddle below Kredarica makes a bee-line for the steep rocks of Mali Triglav (i.e. the lower summit, "Little" Triglav). You soon encounter the first pitons and follow them left onto an edge where a sheer drop, yawning below your feet, demands respect. The well-secured route winds through

An evening view of Staničev dom with Rjavina

natural passages and in a good half hour you reach the top of **Mali Triglav**, 2725 m. The notorious ridge rising up to the main summit, along which the Triglav pioneers tremblingly hitched themselves, as if on horseback, need present no threats today, since reliable steel ropes tautly stretch up it. The walk along the ridge is indeed sheer enjoyment. Even the last climb is completely safe and a little above the memorial plaque commemorating the Slovene poet Valentin Vodnik you catch sight of the famous **Aljažev stolp** (the Aljaž turret), marking the summit of Triglav, just nearby. Then your gaze is startled by the bottomless abyss plunging down into the Trenta valley. The panorama is complete, the summit achieved. From Kredarica 1.30 h.

B. THE PRAG ROUTE

Of the northern approaches to Triglav, the Prag route is perhaps the easiest but not the most recommendable. Ascending this way, you must cross some steep screes, making the path rather unfriendly. Consequently, it is more suitable for the descent. But its attraction lies in its proximity to the North Face, as the path runs along its left edge. The spine-tingling thrill at the sight of the rocky colossus at your side creates a special atmosphere, for it seems you're only a hand's breadth away from primeval mountain wildness.

DESCRIPTION:
From Aljažev dom you go straight up the valley past the left fork for the Tominšek route and the right fork for Kriški podi and Luknja, as far as the source of the

The Bamberg route via Plemenice

River Bistrica, issuing from under a large snowfield near the foot of the North Face. Here the path swings left and climbs the first rock step. Then gently rising towards the left, it follows a long grassy ledge, until starting to ascend in numerous serpentine bends over rocky step-like terrain at the lefthand edge of the Face. You must climb several well-secured rock steps, the smoothest of which is called Medvedova skala (Bear's Rock); rumour has it that a bear once fell to its death here when fleeing from Trenta hunters. Between these rock steps are the tiring screes, but above the highest one a pleasant spring of water – in a rock hollow beneath the face of Begunjski vrh - provides a welcome surprise. Here the path joins the Tominškova pot and follows it on past Kredarica towards the summit of Triglav (see the previous section). The route over Prag takes half an hour longer than the Tominšek one.

C. VIA LUKNJA AND PLEMENICE

This, also known as the Bamberg route (Bambergova pot), is the most difficult Triglav route, but represents for the experienced mountaineer a prestigious approach. It is the longest on this side and the only one that needs to be done in one fell swoop. These details point to the demanding nature of the tour, which is one of the boldest and most dramatic in the Slovene mountains. This route leads to Triglav from the west.

DESCRIPTION:
The steep climb along the western ridge has an easy overture: the ascent to the **Luknja** saddle, 1758 m. From Aljažev dom go up the valley to the source of the Bistrica and here bear right. The walk along the foot of the gigantic face is pleasant and suggestive, but unfortunately it ends in a toilsome scree. Up on Luknja (2 h from the Vrata valley) you have the first greeting from the Trenta mountains, which will keep you company from now on. Immediately above the saddle the serious business begins. The first rock face is the most difficult but perfectly secured. Higher up, the terrain is less steep but always exposed, requiring constant concentration, and since the security aids are scarce, a less experienced mountaineer can stray into danger. The strenuous gradient does not yield for a long, long time. Only when you are really high up does the ridge level out for the first time, and a reward is waiting in the form of delightful grassy cushions. Right now you realize what a wild and splendid world you have entered. In fact it doesn't belong to the Vrata valley but to the sunlit region of the Trenta mountains, which nevertheless show not a trace of the balmy south, for they are steep and rugged. Still higher up, the north dominates in perpendicular form: from the bottomless depths of the Face the most vertical Triglav pillar soars up – the renowned **Sfinga** (the Sphinx). Soon you will step along its apex, scarcely believing that such a walk is possible just a stride away from the abyss. Above the Sfinga you enter a kingdom of stone as the path winds over the plateau-like **Plemenice**. The

terrain here is like that below Kredarica and just as treacherous if fog wraps itself around you. The path soon turns right and near the massive dilapadated stone barracks of Morbegno joins the path from the Dolič saddle. Now you tackle the rocks of the summit section. Above the sheer start the upper Triglav rocks on this side are not so steep as those above Kredarica, but they are more threatened by falling rock catapults. Above, a rough ridge forms and leads you to Slovenia's topmost point. Don't say that you aren't thoroughly tired! From Luknja 4 h.

DESCENT:

Where there is freedom of choice, one normally takes a harder route going up and an easier one going down. So the Prag route has provided the usual descent into the Vrata valley. However, many mountaineers descend from Triglav on the opposite side. The classic traverse of Triglav involves an ascent from Vrata and a descent by the Triglav Lakes Valley. This tour (in the ascending direction) is described in the Bohinj chapter (pp. 72-76).

DIFFICULTY:

The northern Triglav approaches involve long, strenuous and demanding tours. As mentioned above, the Prag and Tominšek routes are easier than the Bamberg. On this one self-belaying is essential and a climbing helmet is recommendable. The paths are in a good state. At least up to mid-July you need to take an ice-axe up to these heights. For the ascent of the summit itself there must be fine weather. Beware of any storm!

TIME AND TACTICS:

From the Vrata valley to Kredarica by the Tominšek path takes 5 h, by the Prag path 5.30 h. From Kredarica to the summit you need 1.30 h. To the summit via the Luknja saddle takes 6-7 h. Thus climbing Triglav from the north as a one-day tour is for exceptionally good walkers. Since the weather and the view from the summit are generally best of all in the morning, we recommend reaching Kredarica in the afternoon and going for the top in the early morning next day. The Bamberg route is different, of course: the only sensible tactic is to set out really early, and you can spend the night in one of the mountain huts on your descent.

17

Stenar

Face to face with the patriarch

ALTITUDE: 2501 m
STARTING ALTITUDE: 1015 m
HEIGHT DIFFERENCE: 1500 m

Stenar is the tragic hero of the Julian Alps. Its truly commanding presence attracts everyone's attention on the way into Vrata but only at the beginning. In front of Aljažev dom the genuine ruler, Triglav, presents himself in full glory and naturally all admiration is bestowed there. Thus Stenar is fated to remain overshadowed. But it is highly valued by connoisseurs, whether rock-climbers or mountaineers. The former are drawn by its very name (Stenar means 'mountain of faces'), which absolutely holds true; the latter are offered one single possibility, but that is really gentle, making Stenar one of the most easily accessible giants. The mountain with its tremendous faces closes in the head of the Vrata valley on the right; because it stands close to busy main routes for mountaineers, it is not accustomed to solitude. The leading motive for

Bivak IV nestles at the foot of Stenar

Bovški
Gamsovec

Stenar

Dovška
vrata

Sovatna

visiting Stenar is the stunning view of Triglav's majestic pillars on the far side of the valley.

STARTING-POINT:
Aljažev dom in Vrata, 1015 m; 11 km along the road from Mojstrana (2.30 h on foot).
DESCRIPTION:
From the mountain hut go up along the valley. You pleasantly warm up for 20 minutes on the level, then above the first small incline a signpost directs you up into the forest on the right. This area is called Bukovje (Beech Forest) and shade is assured for almost an hour's walk. Sometimes there is a pleasant trickle below an overhang in the conglomerate rock in the middle of the forest.

As you come into the open, you must soon contend with the rubbly bottom of the steep valley **Sovatna**, squeezed between the high faces of Bovški Gamsovec and Stenar. Two hours of unrelentingly steep gradient you must simply accept, for after all you are aiming for a high mountain. Perhaps the suffering will be lightened for a moment by seeing a frolicsome band of ibex, which often roam around here. Sovatna is steepest in the middle part, where you even come upon an iron piton or two, but above, the valley becomes easier and changes into a succession of basins. Finally you recover your breath on the pass **Dovška vrata**, 2180 m. Now the plateau of Kriški podi lies before you, with solitary mountain tarns hiding in the hollows. Below, you notice the mountain hut Pogačnikov dom, while the champion of the expansive panorama is the mighty Razor. On the left your gaze slips into the depth of the Trenta valley, in which you feel the warm breath of the south. Stenar stands to the right and appears quite tame. And indeed the ascent is easy and pleasant. The path leads through lifeless high-altitude karst in the direction of the col Stenarska vratca on the left under the mountain. You traverse the upper steep slopes by making a long curve to the right, and then step onto the ample, wonderfully panoramic summit. By just one metre you've overstepped the boundary which places Stenar in the elite 2500 club.

DESCENT:

On the return you can add on a visit to the southern neighbour Bovški Gamsovec, 2392 m (Bovški refers to Bovec, and Gamsovec means Chamois Mountain) with a descent into Vrata via the Luknja saddle; this route is described on p. 144. The nearby mountain hut Pogačnikov dom, 2050 m, just half an hour from Dovška vrata, is the starting-point for the approach to Razor, 2601 m, (see pp. 175-177). Škrlatica, 2740 m, the second highest Slovene mountain, also belongs to the repertoire of Pogačnikov dom (pp. 122-127). So – no lack of ideas.

DIFFICULTY:

This technically easy tour is quite a big undertaking, for which you need excellent condition. On such a high mountain snow can lie far into the summer, and an ice-axe is essential until the middle of July.

TIMES:

Vrata – Stenar 4.30 h

Stenar – Bovški Gamsovec - Luknja – Vrata 4-5 h

18

Škrlatica

Winner of the silver medal

ALTITUDE: 2740 m
STARTING ALTITUDE: 1015, 1113 m
HEIGHT DIFFERENCE: 1700-1800 m

Škrlatica (Scarlet Mountain) is a mighty, tower-shaped mountain, which represents the culmination of the tremendously wild and dynamically moulded mountain chain between the valleys of Vrata and Pišnica. In the time of the first ascents it was known as Suhi plaz (Dry Avalanche) on account of the insignificant scree above the Vrata valley. The present name originated later, given by some unknown person who one late afternoon admired the play of colours across the western faces; today's visitors to the Vršič pass are convinced that he took it down from their tongues. The reason for such a luxuriant symphony of colours is the reddish rock of the faces above the Krnica valley, which towards evening change into a burning torch. The scarlet colour of the rock is a synonym for brittleness in the Slovene mountains. The sunny side is

Dolkova and Rakova špica, Škrlatica (centre), the Rokavi, Oltar and Dovški križ

somewhat milder, but precipitous faces are not lacking here either. Škrlatica is reckoned a difficult mountain, although a well-secured route leads to its top. For a long time it resisted the efforts of "conquerors of the useless" and major alpinists of the classical period took part in the competition for the first ascent. How full of suspense is Kugy's description of the winning ascent in 1880, when his Trenta companions Andrej Komac and Matija Kravanja finally succeeded in finding the correct way and leading the roped team to the summit! The mighty fortress has a weak point on the southern side, and three different routes lead to the foot of the summit section: from Krnica, from the plateau of Kriški podi and from Vrata.

A. APPROACH FROM VRATA

The most direct approach to Škrlatica as a one-day tour is among the most strenuous, but half-way there a friendly tin bivouac – Bivak IV – offers a more comfortable version of the ascent.

STARTING-POINT:
Aljažev dom in Vrata, 1015 m; 11 km by road from Mojstrana (2.30 h on foot).
DESCRIPTION:
The signpost in front of Aljažev dom directs you northwards across the forest clearing, then the path begins to climb through the forest. Above a gentle gully it makes a bend to the right, and beneath a smooth face leaves the forest, ascending over open ground towards the left. In the basin-like valley on the right below Stenar the path turns right and climbs to a small plateau. Behind one edge there suddenly appears an unexpected gift of civilization. This tin little house bears the name **Bivak IV**, 1980 m (2.30 h from Vrata), and in this solitary place it gives the impression of a luxury hotel. The simple shelter (no supplies) brings precious relief; if you've taken time for a two-day tour, a night awaits you in the embrace of mountain summits. The path continues towards the right and reaches a green promontory in the middle of the rocky flanks of Dolkova špica. It is an exceptionally beautiful resting-place. As you think of the storms that often rage in these heights, you cannot admire enough the tenderness of the tiny flowers in this Arcadian garden. Behind the edge your goal reveals itself in all its power and beauty, while the path winds gently downwards around the foot of Dolkova špica. In early summer you will often encounter here a steep snowfield! The route soon ascends and that quite considerably. You notice above you the sharp Kucelj, an interesting little peak dividing the hollow gap between Dolkova špica and Škrlatica. The path skirts it on the right and brings you into the scree-filled cwm of **Zadnji Dolek**. A steep scree falls down here from the right; there's no help for it but to grind your way up it to the top. Only now do you start on the "real" Škrlatica – above you soars the southwest face, characterized by huge smooth bellies. The passage through lies to your right with a narrow ledge leading to it. A

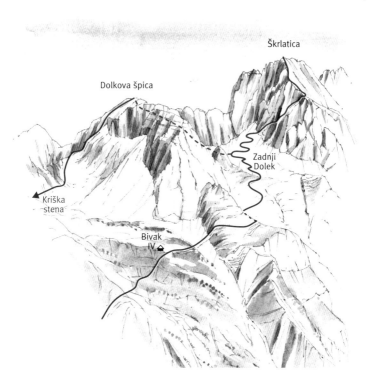

well-secured chimney takes you to a small tower, above which iron aids give plentiful help in clambering over the pot-bellied slabs that represent the crux. To the right above them the ground is easier, but friable. Soon you step onto the southern ridge and over the edge the countless towers of the Rokavi group thrust up. The steepness is now over and the panoramic ascent along the easy broad ridge is a reward for the previous strenuous efforts. From a fair distance a mighty cross greets you. Beside it one of the most magnificent views in the mountains is waiting for you.

DESCENT:

The described route is the only one leading back to the starting-point.

DIFFICULTY:

Demanding climbing along the secured route is short, as far as Zadnji Dolek the way is completely easy. However, the tour is very long and strenuous. Experience and good condition are equally valid requirements for success on Škrlatica. If you don't feel strong enough to do it all in one day, make use of Bival IV. Again be on your guard about the steep snowfields, making an ice-axe obligatory at least until mid-July.

TIMES:

Vrata – Bivak IV 2.30 h
Bivak IV – Škrlatica 3 h
Descent 4 h

B. APPROACH FROM KRNICA

This route is even longer than the one just described, and technically it is more demanding. The starting-point lies in the west and the atmosphere along the way is more serious, quite different from the sunny path from Vrata. The summit rocks will be climbed in the same manner as previously described and the approach from the Krnica valley is full of variety. The route is not even roughly a direct one, because it must skirt on the right the long, precipitous barrier above Krnica. Only above the head of the valley a useful passage presents itself, which is called Kriška stena. And then, of course, it is necessary to go far back again towards Škrlatica. A tour for the strong!

STARTING-POINT:
The mountain hut Koča v Krnici, 1113 m, 2 h on foot from Kranjska Gora, 1 h from the 3rd serpentine bend on the Vršič road.

DESCRIPTION:
From the hut go up along the valley. On the easy way to the foot of the face Kriška stena you don't need to look very much where you put your feet, which is very welcome, for there's really something to see up above. The trees soon give way to dwarf pine and grass, and the uphill going is pleasantly gradual. Impressive grandeur is typical of the head of the Pišnica valley. Beside the chaotic pile of Razor (in the centre) the wild scene is complemented by the monolithic face of Zadnji Prisank (on the right) while beyond the valley are the dark walls of Škrlatica and its neighbours, which, maybe when you return, will glow in their wonderful scarlet evening dress.

Škrlatica glows in evening splendour

The route aims for a basin on the left at the foot of Razor, and a spring offers its greeting. Up above it looks as though you've reached the end of the world. This scree-filled head of the valley, snow-covered far into the summer, is overwhelmed by a gloomy atmosphere as of a cage. Wherever you turn, you see nothing but stern rock faces, furrowed by gullies whose black tongues drip with melting snow. An hour of climbing over **Kriška stena** separates you from relaxation in the sun. From your small platform the path bears left and takes a leap into the steep rocks. Don't come here too early in the summer or you will have problems with the snow! The face is not overly steep but neither is the path overly secured. Natural passages wind along ledges and gullies. Above on the sunny ridge, 2289 m, your qualms are forgotten and the view once more embraces 360° (from Krnica 3 h).

Another path leads here from **Pogačnikov dom** on Kriški podi, 2050 m. (The approach from Vrata is described on p. 144 - see also tour no. 22.) This path begins on the saddle west below the mountain hut and leads over the slopes above the lake Zgornje Kriško jezero to the edge of Kriška stena (1.30 h). Many mountaineers enrich their collection of summits at this spot by going up to the nearby **Križ**, 2410 m, which shows itself in the southeast like a gentle back. It is half an hour to the top.

On the edge of Kriška stena you orient yourself towards Škrlatica, and follow the path twisting over the slopes above the Vrata valley. First you gently drop down over lifeless stony ground and then in a long diagonal ascend to **Rdeča škrbina** (Red Notch), where the great massif of **Dolkova špica**, 2591 m, adjoins the main ridge (you can easily reach this summit in 15 minutes; recommendable). Only here does the lofty goal reveal itself in full glory, seemingly it's quite near. The truth is rather different, though, since a deep

The rugged mountains of the Škrlatica group seen from Špik

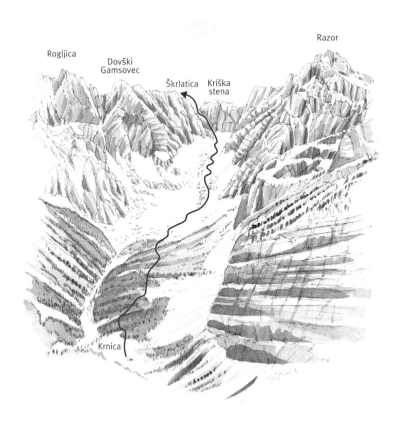

drop into the cwm of Zadnji Dolek awaits you before you gain the foot of the summit section. Here you join the path from Vrata (described under A). It is still 1.30 hours to the very top.

DESCENT:
You can return to the starting-point only by the route described, while the shortest descent is into Vrata.

DIFFICULTY:
A very demanding and strenuous tour, reserved for experienced mountaineers with excellent condition. The snow lies under Kriška stena sometimes even in August, ice-axe!

TIMES:
Krnica – edge of Kriška stena 3 h
Edge of Kriška stena – Škrlatica 3 h
Total 6-7 h, for the descent 5 h
Descent into Vrata 4 h

Dovški križ

In the heart of Martuljek's wildness

ALTITUDE: 2542 m
STARTING ALTITUDE: c. 950 m
HEIGHT DIFFERENCE: c. 1600 m

The alpine world in the heart of the Julian Alps, hemmed in by the Vrata and Pišnica valleys, which presents itself so impressively above the Upper Sava Valley, holds a special place in the Julians. Mountaineers name this region simply Martuljek, and it is linked with the Škrlatica group by a wild ridge. The region's exceptional character derives primarily from its great steepness. Nowhere else in the Slovene mountains are steep and perpendicular lines so predominant. Everything leaps upwards, the ridges are sharp and jagged. These mountains have elements of Gothic architecture built into their form, and on average they are very high. Such features make them difficult of access, so the summits are the reserve of alpinists. Only famous Špik can be reached by a waymarked path; its neighbours are pathless and possible only to rock-

The Škrnatarica-Dovški križ ridge above Amfiteater; Široka peč in the foreground

Dovški
križ

Rokavi
Visoki   Oltar
Srednji   Grlo

Šplevta

Bivak II
Mali
Matterhorn

climbers. Consequently a mountaineer without alpinist experience can venture there only in the company of a guide. But we can't resist showing a way into this enchanting wildness at least in the place where it shows its friendliest face. The approach from the Vrata valley to Dovški križ is in fact pathless, but still doesn't belong to the real climbing routes. Experienced and discerning, a responsible and well-equipped mountaineer, who is not dependent on the safe guidance of waymarks and iron security aids, will certainly be up to Dovški križ. As a one-day tour it is pretty strenuous, but the shelter Bivak II at the foot of the summit section offers a possibility for carrying out the tour more comfortably.

STARTING-POINT:
The Vrata valley. You leave the road in the forest clearing Poldov rovt, c. 950 m. This is about 8 km from Mojstrana, 2 h on foot. (Poldov rovt lies above the road, approximately 2 km on from the place where the long hill above the Peričnik waterfall levels out. The clearing is marked right at the beginning by an old log cabin. A good 2 km from Aljažev dom.)

DESCRIPTION:
On the right at the edge of the clearing a comfortable hunters' path climbs up through the forest. For half an hour it winds leftwards as far as the gully of Rdeči potok (Red Stream), where the terrain becomes steep. The tiny, barely trodden path at first ascends over rough scree left of the gully, and then winds

over rather difficult, overgrown ground, interrupted by rock steps, in the direction of the incredibly bold, pointed summit of Šplevta. To the left below this you notice a considerable barrier, with a waterfall cascading over it. The scarcely visible path now skirts this perpendicular obstacle to the right and continues along a small narrow ledge leftwards to the source of the waterfall at the foot of a steep tongue of scree. The steep ascent between larches is right of the scree, which you soon cross and come into a more friendly wood. Higher up you follow a trodden passage through the dwarf pine as far as a large hollow at the foot of the sharply pointed Mali (Little) Matterhorn. Skirting this on the right, you reach a grassy trough, which runs out above onto a sort of plateau at the foot of the faces in the main ridge. On a rise to the right stands the precious mountaineers' shelter **Bivak II**, 2118 m. (This tin bivouac is open, but without supplies; it offers 6 mattresses with blankets.) It doesn't need any special emphasis that the tour to Dovški križ will be much more comfortable if you cuddle down overnight in this friendly nest set in the heart of primeval nature. Its position is indescribably beautiful. Nearby the jagged ridges of the Rokavi, 2646 m (left), Oltar, 2621 m and Dovški križ, 2542 m pierce the sky, the last mentioned being partly hidden on the right by Šplevta, 2272 m. To the south the glorious massif of Triglav fills half the horizon, while eastwards another fair slice of Gorenjska is seen across the deep Vrata valley. Above the bivouac you advance northwards to a small saddle between Dovški križ and **Šplevta** (the climb to this nearby top you can add on as a bonus). Towards the summit of Dovški križ you first cross a steep, grassy slope by a barely visible little path but then you must keep right at the foot of broken rocks and cross two crumbly ridges. The passage across the last gully below the top is the only rather demanding spot. The Dovški vrh summit is a rich place high above Vrata and Martuljek, where you find yourself surrounded by a host of incredibly jagged ridges. Your exertions have borne noble fruit, for here you are in a world of wild, sharp-edged grandeur which not everyone is privileged to enter. You descend by the same route.

DIFFICULTY:

This pathless tour is very demanding and one of the most difficult included in this guidebook. It requires a highly experienced mountaineer, capable of easier rock-climbing and orientation in pathless terrain. Without such qualifications you must not attempt Dovški križ unless in the company of a guide.

TIMES:

Vrata – Bivak II 2.30-3 h
Bivak II – Dovški križ 1.30-2 h
Descent 4 h

19

Špik

The champion of the Martuljek mountains

ALTITUDE: 2472 m
STARTING ALTITUDE: 1113 m
HEIGHT DIFFERENCE: 1400 m

Although in the Martuljek panorama Špik occupies a modest sixth place, it indisputably and deservedly holds first place according to a different, for many people more important scale of values. The north face of Špik with its audacity, its aesthetic and architectonic perfection, is the ideal symbolization of a mountaineer's concept of what a mountain means to him. If Triglav is the national shrine of Slovenes, then Špik is the mountaineers'. Its very name (Spear-point) rings in his ears as something enterprising and vigorous. In the 1920s and 1930s the famous north face was recorded in the brilliant history of Slovene classical alpinism. Even today it is only the most experienced climbers who dare enter this magnificent but stern face. But because the mountain on its western flank does not challenge the sky so martially as on the Martuljek

The view of Špik from Vršič

Rušica Rusa peč Frdamane police Špik Lipnica

side, even the non-climber may win this noble trophy. Špik is the only Martuljek stalwart that has allowed waymarks to reach its peak. To the south the sister mountain of Lipnica leans upon Špik and the most recommendable approach lies this way. Another route climbs directly from the Pišnica valley through the steep Kačji graben (Snake Gully). The characteristics of the route and the convenient starting-point at the mountain hut Koča v Krnici leave no doubts about the best strategy for this tour: the sequence described is sensible and recommendable. As for the technical aspect, the tour is moderately demanding, but like all Martuljek expeditions decidedly steep and strenuous. Yet for aesthetics and memorable experience it is one of the finest in the Julian Alps.

STARTING-POINT:
Koča v Krnici, 1113 m; 2 h on foot from Kranjska Gora, a bare hour from the 3rd serpentine bend on the Vršič road.
DESCRIPTION:
The path sets off from the mountain hut westwards towards the foot of Škrlatica. Soon shaking itself free from the beech forest, it winds gently upwards a long way through dwarf pine to reach the foot of the giants. The head of this valley is named Gruntovnica. In a stony basin on the right you can fill your water bottle from the only spring on the route. After some climbing over huge boulders in the gully, the path retreats to the left edge and mounts through dwarf pine to a scree. Here it turns sharp left and crosses the stones in a long traverse. At the base of Gamsova špica (Chamois Peak) the path steepens among the larches. A steep trough runs out onto grassy slopes, over which the route gains the summit ridge. Here you must climb some rocks along by the fixed steel rope, before reaching the summit of **Lipnica**, 2418 m, which provides a view of your not-so-distant goal. A short descent to

the base of Špik's head runs over rocks left under the ridge, and the final gradient is steep and strenuous, for the rock is very jagged and brittle. There is no easing off all the way to the top. Before you devote yourself to admiring Špik's alpine neighbours, the view straight down into the abyss on the north side will probably make your heart quake. But – you have reached the summit of the ideal mountain!

DESCENT:

You already know the rocks forming the head of Špik, and further down the path turns right through a scree-filled valley. Then the ground drops away with the scree aiding a quick descent. A detour to the right around a rocky spur is followed by a long, leftwards diagonal scree section, which ends among the highest larches, where you can shake the stones out from your boots on a cushion of grass. From here the path drops straight down through steep stony troughs among the dwarf pine. Even below this, in the forest, the ground is still pretty steep; and there's a fair amount of energetic gymnastics involved in getting over rock steps, where protruding roots can be useful. The route then allows a short breathing space as it curves around to the right, to touch the edge of **Kačji graben**. Still the last steep gradient, and you can give your trembling legs a break on the relaxing scree. You soon reach the bank of the tumbling Pišnica, above which runs the forest road from Kranjska Gora. Nothing gives more pleasure than to dip your hot feet in the clear alpine water.

DIFFICULTY:

This tour is more strenuous than demanding, but nevertheless it does require some mountaineering experience. Rising early is recommended because of the length of the tour, while the morning's shade makes life much easier.

TIME:

Krnica – Špik 4-5 h

Descent 3 h

pp. 134-135: The awe-inspiring face of Široka peč

21

Prisank

The giant above Vršič

ALTITUDE: 2547 m
STARTING ALTITUDE: 1611 m
HEIGHT DIFFERENCE: 1000 m

Prisank (also named Prisojnik) is a mountain with a hundred faces and particularities, with a colossal "weight" and naturally a tremendous attractiveness for mountaineers and alpinists alike. It is a great all-rounder, proffering inviting goals to visitors of every orientation – only novices should rather wait a bit. Prisank belongs together with Triglav, Razor, Jalovec and Mangart to the main summits that constitute the backbone of the Julian Alps, and there is never a shortage of visitors. Especially not, when you can jump up there from the advantageous altitude of the Vršič road pass – 1611 m. This solidly ramified mountain, rising east of the pass, is riven by deep gullies among its numerous ridges and subsidiary summits; as many as ten of these have independent names! Judged by the number of its paths, Prisank is undoubtedly the champion of Slovene mountains, nor do these paths represent any repetition,

Prisank viewed from Mojstrovka

136

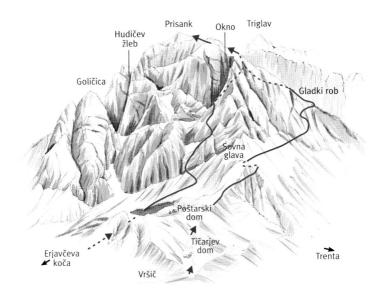

for each one has its own characteristics. So if you wish to count as one of the connoisseurs of Prisank, you have plenty of work ahead. To gaze from close at hand into the rocky countenance of Ajdovska deklica (Pagan Giantess), who silently observes the bustle on Vršič from her central position in the north face, to climb through both celebrated natural windows, to peep into the terrifying darkness of Hudičev žleb (Devil's Gully), from the vertiginous ledges of the Jubilee path (Jubilejna pot) to notice deep below the solitary cwm V Škednju .... these are stations on the demanding routes across the shadowed side of Prisank. Of course the mountain also has its friendlier face: the otherwise equally mighty Trenta side is more gradual, and extravaganzas of flowering gardens reach high up its flanks. Here only a selection from Prisank's rich repertoire will be offered.

A. FROM VRŠIČ PAST THE FRONT WINDOW (PREDNJE OKNO)

This approach is one of the less demanding, though not the easiest. It leads to Prisank from the west, partly over the southern slopes. On the way you can peep through the majestic natural window, but the finest part of the tour is the panoramic summit ridge. In its level of difficulty the tour is reminiscent of Triglav.

STARTING-POINT:
The road pass of Vršič, 1611 m; 12 km from Kranjska Gora, the same distance from Na Logu in the Trenta valley (34 km from Bovec).

DESCRIPTION:

From Vršič you take the small steep road past the mountain hut Tičarjev dom as far as the serpentine bend where the road bears left to another hut, Poštarski dom (10 minutes). The waymarked path sets off to the right, almost horizontally skirting the top Sovna glava on your right, and gains the saddle at the foot of Prisank. There follows a long, gradual traverse across extensive scree, and then the route climbs onto the ridge **Gladki rob** (Smooth Edge). At the first fork you keep going steeply leftwards along the ridge but later across the grassy slope on your right. All of a sudden there yawns beneath your feet a huge natural window (**Prednje okno**, Front Window, c. 80 m high and c. 40 m wide), through which your gaze drops down through the depth of the north face. To the right of the window the path ascends over steep rocks (the first secured section) and soon reaches the summit ridge. From now on it mostly keeps to the ridge, which at first is narrow and exposed (steel ropes), but then increasingly easier. You'll continue walking a good hour before achieving the summit, but the time slips quickly by as you delight in the abundant views.

DESCENT:

It isn't essential to return the same way. From the first notch in the ridge west of the summit a path, considered the easiest on Prisank, drops down to the Trenta side. This primarily aims towards the southwest, leading over steep and often unpleasantly brittle scree. There are a few rocky places, and occasionally you find some iron aid. Lower down the gradient eases off as you enter the world of alpine gardens. A pleasant walk towards the right brings you again to the ridge Gladki rob, near the place where your ascent route heads towards the window. Finish the tour by the already described route.

DIFFICULTY:

A moderately demanding secured route.

TIMES:

Vršič – Prisank 3.30 h
Descent 3 h

B. KOPIŠČARJEVA POT

To climb Prisank via the north face is naturally a challenge for every good mountaineer. Kopiščarjeva pot (the Kopiščar Path) is one of the most beautiful but also one of the most demanding secured climbing routes in the Slovene mountains. It runs in the western part of the majestic face in the fall-line of the great window (Prednje okno) and through this comes out onto the previously described path. Thus climbing the sombre north face is followed by the sunny walk along the summit ridge. The demanding nature of the route dictates the necessity of self-belaying and wearing a climbing helmet. In this shadowed face you can be surprised far into the summer by some steep snowfield, so you must take an ice-axe with you up to August. The security aids are generally in perfect condition.

STARTING-POINT:

Vršič, 1611 m, or the mountain hut Erjavčeva koča, 1525 m.

DESCRIPTION:

The path enters the north face of Prisank approximately in the fall-line of the great window. This point can be reached almost horizontally from Erjavčeva koča. If you start the tour on the top of the pass, follow the previously described path to the saddle at the foot of Prisank, from where another path takes you down left over rough scree to the entry-point for the face. An arched ledge just above the scree-filled gully leads you leftwards to the first rocks. This first part of the face is very steep, but higher up the going is easier. The route follows a steep system of ledges where the friable terrain demands constant carefulness. A good hour above the entry-point you climb to the base of a great perpendicular barrier of black rock. Towards the left, this is sliced open by a noticeable cleft, which offers the only possibility of a passage through. A comfortable ledge takes you from the right to the beginning of the cleft, which at first is formed like a somewhat overhanging chimney that narrows higher up and turns to the left. The narrow shaft wants to prevent your rucksack from also reaching the summit - you outwit it by pushing the rucksack up in front of you. The reliable security aids enable you to make a safe climb over this very demanding (even athletic) and exposed place. Again the terrain becomes easier. The route leads leftwards over a brittle slope, while up above the enormous recess in the mountainside reveals itself; at any moment now the Trenta sky will be seen through it. Before entering into the majestic window (**Prednje okno**), you must still climb a steep face towards the left. The threshold below the window is often covered in snow and requires sufficient caution. You clamber across greasy, red rubble towards the inviting light, but immediately below the exit the last steep slab, studded with pitons, awaits you. Up there the Trenta sun greets you and the gloomy atmosphere of the north face is forgotten. Here you join the path described in section A and follow it for an hour and a half to the summit. The descent is also given above.

DIFFICULTY:

A very demanding secured climbing route! Because of the narrow chimney the slimmest possible rucksack is advised.

TIME:

Vršič - Prisank 4 h

(the same from Erjavčeva koča)

p. 139: The face of Ajdovska deklica can be clearly seen from Vršič

22

Prisank - Razor - Triglav

Along the ridges from Vršič eastwards

The backbone of the Julian Alps is at the same time the watershed between the sources of the Sava and the Soča. The former belongs to the river basin of the distant Black Sea, while the latter, incomparably nearer, empties itself into the Adriatic Sea. The major links in this majestic chain are Triglav, Razor, Prisank, Jalovec and Mangart. Of course, a connected tour traversing all these champions would be a glorious challenge for a mountaineer, but for the majority would represent too big an undertaking. The most distinctive cleft in this chain is the pass of Vršič. The western part of the ridge, dominated by Jalovec and Mangart, is complicated and demanding, and thus will not be described here. But in the east the summits are arranged in such a handy, sensible sequence, and linked with good paths, that even they themselves invite one to undertake this bold ridge tour. The following description will run from west to east. From Vršič over Prisank, Razor and Bovški Gamsovec to Triglav, plus the descent into the valley of course, takes at least three days; in the Julian Alps you could scarcely succeed in experiencing anything more magnificent. Such a tour naturally demands a very experienced mountaineer with excellent condition and equipment, not to mention good fortune with the weather. But then it goes without saying that various alternative routes are possible and – why not? – also extensions.

STARTING-POINT:
The Vršič road pass, 1611 m; 12 km from Kranjska Gora, the same distance from Na Logu in the Trenta valley (34 km from Bovec).

DESCRIPTION:
Our grand ridge tour begins with the approach to **Prisank**, 2547 m, described in the previous section. From Prisank you descend eastwards along the extremely picturesque **Jubilejna pot** (Jubilee Path), built in 1953 on the 60th anniversary of the Slovensko planinsko društvo (Slovene Alpine Society). The first part of the route runs southwards over scree-covered rock into a notch, beyond which two bold towers rise up, called **Zvoniki** (Bell Towers). Here you step onto a ledge that will lead you far across the northern face of the eastern Prisank chain. At the foot of the Zvoniki the ledge is easy and broad, but as you pass into the massif of **Zadnji Prisojnik,** it narrows into a scarcely negotiable line. As you pass around the most exposed edge, it virtually disappears, so that only with the help of the steel rope can you climb around the corner.

141

Deep below, you look into the solitary cwm V Škednju, filled by a real little glacier. Behind the edge the ledge broadens again and soon leads to the biggest natural sight along the Jubilee path – **Zadnje okno** (Back Window). This is smaller than its western counterpart, but strikingly picturesque, formed in true Gothic style. Unfortunately the last earthquake in these parts caused considerable damage, partly demolishing this natural curiosity. The passage through the window is now quite difficult, as collapsed rocks lie in all directions. A warning is also necessary about the steep snowfields which remain in the region far into the summer.

So from the north you have crossed onto the sunny side of Prisank. Here as well you'll notice the aftermath of earthquakes, for the descent is made harder by demolished rocks. But in between there are increasingly more green stretches. Further down the path turns left and for a moment you can peep over the notch in the ridge into the deep valley of the Pišnica. From here you drop down through a narrow gully to the grassy steep slopes near **Škrbina** (Notch), 1989 m, a deep gash between the massifs of Razor and Prisank. Here you join the path coming from Vršič over the southern flanks of Prisank. (This path would, of course, immensely shorten and facilitate your tour, but it would greatly impoverish the glory of traversing Prisank as well. It follows the first described approach from Vršič to Prisank as far as the Gladki rob ridge, and then drops 200 metres down to **Kranjska planina**. Maintaining this contour line, it crosses numerous gullies and edges to reach the fall-line of Škrbina, and then begins to climb towards Razor. A little above the excellent spring where the Mlinarica stream issues forth, it joins the Jubilee path.)

Now comes the next big mountain on the tour. **Razor**, 2601 m, has not been suitably presented as yet, so some words should be devoted to this excellent

Prisank, Razor and Triglav from Vršič (right); the Škrlatica group is on the left

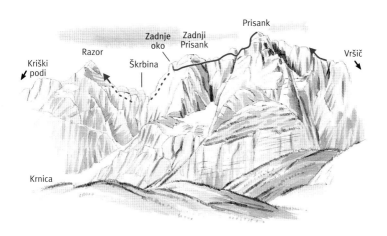

member of the Julian Alps. This mighty, impressively delineated tower-shaped mountain with its furrowed faces dominates the head of the Pišnica valley, while stretching southwest from it one of the wildest and most inaccessible ridges in the Julian Alps stabs deep into the heart of Trenta. Here are the important Goličica summits, the crazily jagged Kanceljni and Razor's neighbour, Planja, 2447 m. Only to the east does Razor show a more friendly face; there at the base of its summit bulk the extensive karst plateau of Kriški podi bathes in the sun – the goal of the first stage of our tour. In the western face of Razor, now before you, a cut-out system of ledges and gullies in the shape of the letter S can be discerned. All the time the path follows this formation and is not even too demanding. Only gaining the first ledge can be complicated by a hard, steep snowfield. The bend to the left is more difficult than the two oriented to the right, but above them you step onto the saddle (2349 m) between Planja and Razor with its sudden, breath-taking view. From here to the summit of Razor takes only a good half hour. (If hard pressed you can, of course, omit the summit itself and descend straight on to Kriški podi.) The path first climbs to a saddle south under the peak, then turns left into the west face and ascends over broken rock to the highest point.

The first stage is now approaching the end. You will need an hour and a half to gain the safe shelter of the mountain hut **Pogačnikov dom** on Kriški podi, which you see clearly below you, a helpful detail when reckoning how much time you can enjoy on the wonderfully panoramic lofty peak. When finally you must descend, return to the saddle between Razor and Planja, then drop to the left down onto Kriški podi. At first you cross quite an extensive scree and then on the last steep rocks to be encountered on this strenuous day there is the final secured stretch. Right at the end you must go upwards still once more, but fortunately not too high, before you cross the threshold of Pogačnikov dom, 2050 m.

This complete route from Vršič to the mountain hut is an enormous portion for one day. If you wish to manage both giants – Prisank and Razor – you'll barely manage it in less than 10 hours. Pogačnikov dom stands at the intersection of many paths and is an important starting-point for many summits. If you have time and the will, you can enrich the tour described here even further and take another day or two for some enticing "side path". Škrlatica, Stenar, Križ and Pihavec are the surrounding mountains, as well as Bovški Gamsovec, of course, across which the route leads on towards Triglav. But if you are forced to interrupt the tour, you can descend from here into the Trenta, Pišnica or Vrata valley.

The second stage takes you over Bovški Gamsovec, descends to the Luknja saddle and then climbs to Triglav by the western ridge. If the previous day's marathon hasn't left you with terribly aching legs, you'll manage this in a shorter time than the first one. From Pogačnikov dom you first head upwards and eastwards for a bare hour to reach the saddle Dovška vrata, 2178 m, situated between Stenar and Bovški Gamsovec. The path gently gains altitude as it crosses the eroded karst plateau; in the hollows on both sides you catch sight of two small lakes. Once on the saddle you bear right and climb to the summit ridge along the ledges of the low west face. Soon afterwards you reach the summit of **Gamsovec** (Chamois Mountain), 2392 m. Here in all their magnificence the pillars of Triglav's north face display themselves, crowned by the goal of our tour and the leading light of all the Slovene mountains. From Gamsovec you return to the nearby fork, where the path begins to drop towards the Luknja saddle below Triglav. At first you descend along a small, dizzyingly exposed ledge (safe steel rope) and then the path winds along a grassy ridge that is reminiscent of an alpine botanical garden. Below you step into a broad basin and the further descent is completely easy. On **Luknja** (Gap), 1758 m, you finally cross to the foot of Triglav. From Pogačnikov dom to Luknja is 3 hours' walk. Here as well it's possible to interrupt the tour, taking an easy, comfortable path, whether you descend into Vrata or Trenta.

From Luknja you climb towards Triglav by the steep ridge with its demanding secured route, as described on pp. 117-118. For the descent you have a considerable choice of routes available, as can be seen in the sections on Triglav.

DIFFICULTY:

It is self-evident that only a trained mountaineer can undertake such a long and demanding route. For such a person the technical difficulties along the way should not represent severe obstacles. We should just mention that Prisank and Triglav are harder than Razor and Bovški Gamsovec. Don't fail to put in your rucksack equipment for self-belaying on the secured sections, a climbing helmet is recommended and until the end of July an ice-axe as well. And understandably you need an abundance of healthy enthusiasm and stamina.

TIMES:

Vršič – Prisank 3.30-4 h
Prisank – Škrbina – Razor 4-5 h
Razor – Pogačnikov dom 1.30 h
Pogačnikov dom – Bovški Gamsovec – Luknja 3 h
Luknja – Triglav 4 h
Triglav – Kredarica 1.15 h

23

Mala Mojstrovka

Off to a two-thousander after lunch

ALTITUDE: 2332 m
STARTING ALTITUDE: 1611 m
HEIGHT DIFFERENCE: 721 m

Above Vršič there begins a long, uniformly shaped ridge, which far to the west culminates in Jalovec, the handsome prince of the Slovene mountains. The first three heads in the ridge are called Mojstrovka – Mala, Velika and Zadnja (these adjectives mean Small, Great and Last). The lowest and nearest one is Mala Mojstrovka. This mountain has solitude only at night and in truly hopeless weather. Not surprisingly either, when it rises right above one of the most frequented spots in the Slovene mountains – the road pass of Vršič. The reason why these abundant visitors didn't pounce upon the even nearer summits of Šitna glava and Robičje probably lies in Mojstrovka's considerable height, fine figure and especially the attractive approach. It is a universal mountain: accessible to practically everyone by its normal route, in winter it teems with

The view towards Mala Mojstrovka from Vršič

145

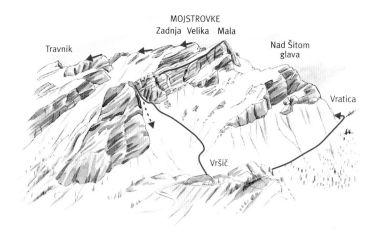

MOJSTROVKE
Zadnja Velika Mala

Travnik

Nad Šitom
glava

Vratica

Vršič

skiers, several tempting climbing routes lie in the north face, among which the popular secured route Hanzova pot may be included. Otherwise, compared with its sisters and other stalwarts in the vicinity, it is really "small". Thanks to its high starting-point, Mojstrovka is a comfortable mountain and cut out for mountaineering lazy-bones, as you can guess from the subtitle. If it seems too small a mouthful for the hungrier mountaineer, you can make a detour to the famous viewpoint Sleme, and some additional hints are offered at the end of this description.

STARTING-POINT:
The Vršič road pass, 1611 m; 12 km from Kranjska Gora, the same distance from Na Logu in the Trenta valley (34 km from Bovec).

A. THE USUAL ROUTE

Near the highest point of Vršič a signpost directs you to the path ascending leftwards in the direction of a deep gash in the southern ridge of Mala Mojstrovka. The going is easy, only that just below this gash your comfort is disturbed by a steep slope made slippery by so many visitors. Now the path heads towards the summit, proving at first pleasant and very panoramic. Nor is the upper part of the ridge demanding either, but the scree-covered rocky slabs are somewhat unfriendly. From Vršič to Mala Mojstrovka 2 h. The route is easy.

B. BY THE HANZOVA POT ACROSS THE NORTH FACE

This is something different! The Hanzova pot leads across the steep north face that rises above the plateau where Sleme, the famous viewpoint, is situated. It is demanding and exposed, but an excellently secured route, one of the most popular and most frequented of such routes in the Slovene mountains. It was built during the inter-war period, when an absurd state border ran across Vršič, rendering the southern approach to Mojstrovka impossible for Slovene mountaineers.

DESCRIPTION:
The north face cannot be seen from Vršič; the way to it lies over the pass **Vratica**, 1799 m, east of the mountain. A comfortable path sets off between the dwarf pine and alpine rhododendron from the road pass. Half an hour after you've left the asphalt behind, the broad panorama you've enjoyed so far is joined by a veritable sea of mountains to the north as you reach Vratica. Here the path turns sharp left towards the face (the righthand path leads to Sleme and down into Tamar). Even from this point you can observe a clear passage along a steep gully under the mighty, yellow overhangs. From the saddle to the face takes 15 minutes. You enter the face from the steep gully and immediately encounter the secured section – indeed there's an almost unbroken sequence of pitons and steel ropes that from now on guides you safely towards the summit. Any detailed description is redundant, since you can't go astray. The steepest places lie in wait at the end of the entrance gully,

The prominent ledge on the Hanzova pot

147

where the path makes an exposed bend to the right, while higher up it runs along a long ledge, excellently secured. You step out of the face via steep gullies, peep for a moment over the edge down to Vršič, and then ascend to an expansive terrace just below the peak. Only the odd piton or two remains in these last rocks and then on an exposed promontory you stare in amazement at the part of the panorama that has been absent so far – all the majesty of the faces above the Planica valley is revealed. A moment later you get your breath back on the capacious summit. From Vršič 2.30 h.

DESCENT:

The tempting tit-bit of the descent by the usual route southwards towards Vršič is the lengthy tongue of scree above the pass, which offers the possibility of helter-skeltering down, if you are good at this form of "transport" and if you are not too fussy about your boots.

DIFFICULTY:

The Hanzova pot is a demanding secured route and requires obligatory self-belaying and wearing a climbing helmet. Snow lies under the face far into the summer and complicates the entry-point into the face.

C. ALONG THE RIDGE TOWARDS TRAVNIK

In the introductory paragraph we promised something for the "hungry". So, if Mala Mojstrovka has not sufficiently quenched your passion, or you haven't shed enough sweat, then you're invited to engage on a wonderful ridge walk across her bigger sisters. Be warned that it's a pathless tour, but with quite straightforward orientation, and in general it's not too demanding – only just in front of Travnik a certain passage is a little trickier. The first ascent over shattered boulders to **Velika Mojstrovka**, 2366 m, is unpleasant though easy, but from then on you have a broad, undulating ridge where you really can enjoy the finest that mountains can offer. The destination is quite unimportant – you can continue to **Zadnja Mojstrovka**, 2354 m, or, if you're specially light-footed, all the way to **Travnik**, 2379 m. From this high bridge your gaze can slide down the staggering perpendicular line of the Tamar rock faces or into the sunbathed gentleness of Trenta and the Primorska horizons while all the time the ideal crystal formation of Jalovec glitters in front of you. Although the southern flanks are quite passable, we recommend returning to Mala Mojstrovka by the same way. The extension as far as Travnik lengthens the tour by three hours.

24

Jalovec

The alpine crystal of the Julian Alps

ALTITUDE: 2645 m
STARTING ALTITUDE: 1108 m
HEIGHT DIFFERENCE: 1537 m

If we should want to represent the Julian Alps in three selected pictures, one of them would assuredly depict Jalovec. Only Triglav receives so much glory and exalted eulogies. One of the most beautifully shaped Slovene mountains, formed like a mighty crystal, it glows above the head of the Planica valley, and dominates the Trenta and Koritnica valleys, too, with the same might and majesty. Jalovec is indeed a peak with a sterling character; on every side it presents an image with an inbuilt fundamental trait in common that gives it the seal of "personality". This common trait is difficult to define, but we come near the truth if we say Jalovec's character has something audacious and challenging about it. Special emphasis is given to it by the uplifting Gothic lines of its ridges and arêtes and the sharply pointed summit that literally pierces the sky. Jalovec is a lofty and difficult mountain, and this has particular significance for the northern approach; from Tamar the tour must be accomplished in one fell swoop. It is a mountain of many parts, for it offers excellent climbing routes while slopes beloved by ski tourers reach far up its flanks. The approach described here leads along the northwestern ridge and represents the most difficult route to Jalovec. But at the same time this long and strenuous tour is one of the finest alpine ascents in the Slovene mountains.

STARTING-POINT:
The mountain hut Dom v Tamarju, 1108 m; 6 km by road from Rateče (1.30 h on foot). The road is open for public use from 18.00 to 8.00.

DESCRIPTION:
In the expectation of enjoyment on the lofty ridge, the approach to the saddle Kotovo sedlo will seem a somewhat lengthy overture. For quite a long time you walk almost on the level, and when the valley eventually begins to rise, you wade into rough scree. If the monotony of this section has left you daydreaming, you must be careful not to miss the beginning of a steep bank to the right at an altitude of roughly 1500 m. The path takes to it and in a trice the going is more pleasant. The path winds over green patches and quickly gains height. This section ends on a ridge covered in dwarf pine, the path

turns left and beyond an exposed, secured ledge runs out onto a spacious flat area. The route now continues through a medley of huge, scattered boulders, and then climbs to the saddle **Kotovo sedlo**, 2138 m. Here a deep abyss breaks off below your feet and your gaze takes in the wonderful alpine surroundings of the Koritnica valley with Mangart, 2678 m, at the head. But this is just the start of the real tour. Above the first rocks the path turns right into the Koritnica face and you won't touch the ridge any more. You are already so high that the view overleaps the nearby ridges and extends to the distant peaks of the Dolomites. Mali Jalovec is skirted by a gently rising traverse. The path is demanding only in those places where you must exchange one ledge for another. The security aids are scanty but reliable. A difficult descent into a gully serves as introduction to steep climbing across the summit face. Winding through gullies, the path doesn't head directly for the top and you gain the summit ridge south of the peak. When you surveyed the mountain down below in Tamar, you were probably concerned whether you'd have anywhere to sit down on the summit. Pleasantly surprised, you now discover your fears were ungrounded. At this point the Trenta valley also lies before you and the panorama is completed.

DESCENT:

You can make a fine round tour by descending over the notch Jalovška škrbina. You drop down over the summit crags by the path coming from the south, which counts as the usual approach. It begins with a pleasant ridge walk, then the well-secured route turns left, descending by a system of ledges and gullies to the small plateau Na jezercih. Before that you cross the mouth of the gully Loški žleb, which falls steeply into Koritnica. At times a steep and exposed snowfield lies here far into the summer. The path into the Trenta valley continues over the steep slopes of Ozebnik, but our route veers left immediately beneath the rocks of Jalovec and climbs to the nearby saddle. Down to the left yawns a dark chasm, and your gaze slides into immeasurable depths before coming to rest on the green calm of Tamar. It's true that the renowned Jalovec couloir offers the most direct route for the descent, but we cannot recommend it. This murky narrow slit is constantly bombarded by falling stones, and most of the year it is covered by a steep snowfield. A clear-headed mountaineer will therefore rather choose the route over Jalovška škrbina. This drops into a scree-filled funnel to the right of the pointed top of Goličica. Further down the ground falls away and the descent over this steep, smooth face is probably the most demanding part of the tour. The secured route at first drops steeply and then by an exposed passage crosses over to the left. Below the face is an extensive scree, but in early summer a snowfield, which can prove a real hindrance. Now you embark on a short ascent to **Jalovška škrbina**, 2138 m, and behind it the final stretch of climbing. A covered ledge cuts across the steep face. You finally turn your back on the rocks at the couloir exit, which is not always simple because of the bergschrund. Now only a long scree separates you from the blessed greenness of Tamar.

DIFFICULTY:

A very demanding, long and strenuous tour! Jalovec is a significant degree more difficult than Triglav. Take into consideration the warnings about steep snowfields and go suitably equipped. An ice-axe is compulsory.

TIMES:

Tamar – Kotovo sedlo 2.30-3 h
Kotovo sedlo – Jalovec 2-2.30 h
Descent via Jalovška škrbina 4-6 h
Total 10-11 h

pp. 152-153: One of the finest views of Jalovec opens up from Sleme

The mountains above the Soča

The great classical alpinist and writer Julius Kugy called the Soča the most beautiful river in Europe. Another artist, the Slovene poet Simon Gregorčič, who rarely departed from the Soča during his lifetime, called it "the clear daughter of the mountains". We must confirm both of them. Truly the Soča is a mirror reflecting the intoxicating beauty of the sunny side of the Julian Alps. The fact that the mountains above the Soča are sunny is their most noticeable characteristic. Thus they are bright, friendly, inviting, a character such as you can observe in the wonderful turquoise colour of the river's deep pools. The Soča source area includes all the southwestern part of the Eastern Julian Alps and a tiny portion of the Western Julian Alps in the Kanin group. This extensive area branches out into numerous valleys, divided by mountain ridges. Here the upper Soča valley (upper Posočje) will be described, i.e. that part of the basin that belongs to the high mountains of the Julian Alps.

The Soča arises in the heart of the Julian Alps – from the slopes of Travnik west of the Vršič pass. With youthful energy it foams through narrow gorges and over rapids in the Trenta valley, calms down in the broad Bovec basin and then, fortified by strong tributaries, again foams through deep gorges. At Kobarid it finally quietens and slowly but powerfully flows towards the Adriatic Sea. The Soča valley in its alpine region is more inhabited than the valleys of the Sava Bohinjka and the Sava Dolinka, which can well be attributed to the more favourable climate, in which the beneficent breath of the nearby Adriatic is felt. Only in the valleys of the upper region, in Trenta, Bavšica, and Lepena, where life is hard and nature, for all its beauty, is unfriendly and begrudging, often even cruel, are there just a few well-tried and persistent inhabitants. Among the numerous settlements, which often nestle high up on the mountain slopes, are the centres of upper Posočje - the small towns of Tolmin, Kobarid and Bovec. The last mentioned lies highest, right in the heart of the mountains, and is an immediate starting-point for mountaineers. The sources of the Soča and its upper tributaries burst forth at the foot of the mountain groups of Kanin, Mangart, Jalovec, Bavški Grintavec, Prisank, Razor, Triglav and Krn.

Contemporary tourism is entering the Soča valley and its mountains with a slower step than the Sava valley, so it is attractive especially for lovers of peace and unspoilt nature. The mountains above the Soča are mostly difficult to reach despite their previously mentioned friendly features. Since the foot of these mountains is at a modest altitude, the differences in height are very great and in general steepness and wildness predominate. It's true that the crowds have conquered Kanin and Mangart, but elsewhere you will rarely meet a kindred spirit on your mountain path. Some regions, such as the mountains above the Bala and Možnica valleys, make you feel as if you walk through a world where life has died out. So the peaks above the Soča are a promised land for romantically minded mountaineers. The significance of the upper Soča valley as a starting-point will be explained in more detail in the descriptions of individual valleys.

No presentation of this region is complete, of course, without mention of the tragic happenings that have incised painful lines through the friendly image of this very beautiful realm. The first one is the still living memory of the years of the terrible world conflict in 1914-1918, when right here, in the midst of these proud summits of the Julian Alps, along the wonderful Soča River, one of the most decisive and bloody actions of this war took place. The mountain giants of Rombon and Krn are still marked with the horrifying remains of this world slaughter, and in many another place you may stumble upon some scrap of rusted weaponry. The excellent Kobarid Museum is devoted to this dark period, and every visitor will leave it deeply shocked and moved. But even in times of peace, the inhabitants of this apparently idyllic region must often face hard calamities caused by the forces of nature. Earthquakes, for instance, are quite frequent in these parts, the latest one in 1998 demolished many homes in the small villages under Krn and around Bovec. The abundant rain- and snowfall, due to the clash of mountain and maritime climates, and the incredibly high, steep slopes give rise to threatening avalanches and landslides. But this is the only shadow lying across the picture of Posočje, which in the aesthetic sense can hardly be compared with anywhere else.

The crystal pools of the Soča

Valleys

TRENTA

is the heart of Posočje, for in it the loveliest Slovene alpine river is born. This marvellous valley with its southlike charm has captivated and inspired numerous visitors, including great alpinists and artistic revealers of the beauties of the mountain world. The Soča valley in its upper part is called Trenta, and it begins some 3 kilometres above the village of Soča. Even the valley here seems to belong to the high mountain world, so steep are its sides, which from their lofty ridges press down into the narrow ravine through which the Soča flows. In its upper course this is youthfully vivacious, foaming in wild gorges and only occasionally calming down to slide over its white pebbly bed. Its pleasant tumult reaches into every nook of Trenta, adding to the valley a characteristic accompaniment. Because the river must constantly leap over rocky thresholds, it froths and sparkles with bubbles. Thus "the most beautiful river in Europe", as Kugy called it, has an incomparably lovely and unique turquoise colour. In the character of Trenta it appears as something fragile and mysterious, allowing only a rare visitor to penetrate to its soul.

Trenta is an inhabited valley. With incredible tenacity its people have grappled through the centuries with this cruel alpine realm that offered them modest possibilities of survival only if they knew it really well, managed it and – loved it. The humble plots in the valley produced too few *čompe* (a Trenta type of potato) to feed the admittedly scanty population. And so the inhabitants (in Slovene called Trentarji) were always intimately linked with their mountains

The Trenta valley

in the role of foresters, hunters and shepherds. In their daily hard labour they turned into practised masters of the mountains and in the classical period of alpinism became outstanding Slovene mountain guides. Their eminent client, co-traveller and friend was the great herald of the beauties of the Julian Alps, the alpinist and mountain writer Julius Kugy, who wrote the finest pages of his opus precisely about the Trenta valley.

Trenta is winding and narrow, quite often more like a gorge than a proper valley. From the bottom you frequently can't see the summits at all, so steep and high are the slopes. The Soča's true source area is the valley Zadnja Trenta (Back Trenta), above which rise the giants Bavški Grintavec, the Pelci, Jalovec, Prisank and Razor. At the village of Na Logu the valley turns sharply towards the southwest and acquires the name Spodnja Trenta (Lower Trenta). Here the Zadnjica valley, carved into the foot of Triglav, branches off eastwards from the main valley. Lower down the Vrsnik and Lepena valleys decant into Trenta from the east, and finally the Soča emerges from behind Svinjak into the flat Bovec basin.

The central settlement is the village **Na Logu** (or simply Trenta), 620 m. Today's tourist development is only slowly advancing into this remote hamlet, as descendants of the famous guides strive to protect as far as possible the elementary nature of one of the furthermost corners in the Alps. In this the **Dom Trenta**, managed by the Triglav National Park, plays an important role. This information and tourist centre offers accommodation and the services of guides, and also houses the finely arranged Trenta Museum. Here you can become acquainted with Trenta's glorious mountaineering history as well as the difficulties the local people have long struggled with in their none-too-easy existence. The very winding Bovec – Vršič road runs along the valley,

A view of Jalovec from Zadnja Trenta

with turnings reaching into the side valleys. From Bovec to Na Logu is 22 km, and from here to Vršič 12 km.

Trenta is a first-class starting-point for mountaineers and alpinists, but compared with the Upper Sava Valley and Bohinj it is unsuitably far less frequented. The reason is its distance from central Slovenia (in both the geographical and traffic route senses), the modest degree of tourist development, and particularly the demanding nature of its mountaineering goals that results from primeval nature, the considerable height differences, and the lack of mountain huts and easy paths. But precisely in this lies its great appeal for lovers of untouched wildness, which in our contemporary world becomes an ever more precious, rare and eagerly sought-after good thing.

On your way into Trenta (if coming from Bovec), you shouldn't hurry unaffected past the wild gorges of the Soča, which can be viewed immediately below the road. In quite a few places hanging bridges are strung across them. The most picturesque "troughs" (korita) are a little below and a little above the village of Soča, where the road branches off to the village Vas na Skali. Somewhat more detail will be given in the following description of the easy, pleasant but quite lengthy trip (shorter versions are possible, of course, as you wish) that shows some of Trenta's main beauties and points of interest – those which are scattered along the valley and easily reached. The starting-point is **Na Logu** (Trenta), 620 m. In fact Trenta's main interesting sights are found along the road, but generally it is not so busy with traffic as to make walking along it unpleasant. Setting out in the upward direction, you find the valley levels out after the first incline. Passing by individual homesteads and a campsite you soon reach a graveyard where you can pay your respects to the men of Trenta's mountaineering history, including members of the famous mountain

The village of Trenta - an idyllic image of the valley

guide families Tožbar, Komac, Kravanja, etc. By the roadside you notice several mysterious, old-fashioned wayside shrines with simple sketches and inscriptions. These are typical folk memorials to those Trentarji who met their death in accidents at work in the forest or while out poaching. These simple shrines are a touching testimonial to the difficult life lived in these parts. A few hundred metres further on stands the church of St Mary (cerkev sv. Marije) to the right of the road; it preserves beautiful frescoes by the Slovene painter Tone Kralj. This hamlet is named **Pri Cerkvi** (By the Church) and in former times it was the centre of Trenta. Traces of long-past iron working have already disappeared. Immediately behind the church is the finely arranged botanical garden **Alpinum Juliana,** which extends far up into the forest. In a suitable season (early summer is best) everything glows with the colours of alpine flowers. A little further on you notice on a large rock a memorial plaque in honour of Trenta mountain guides, and then the road crosses to the Soča's opposite bank. Soon a signpost invites you to cross a hanging bridge (these are a typical feature of Trenta, though unfortunately only a few are still preserved in their original form) into the **Mlinarica** gorge. This is one of Trenta's real pearls. Just a few minutes from the road the path disappears into a dark, deeply riven cleft, from which the Mlinarica stream emerges roaring and rushing; its source lies high above under Razor. The path leads to the beginning of this impassable canyon, which is so wild, deep and twisted that it gives the impression of being a tunnel. A very suggestive place! As you return towards the road, it is best to stay on the Soča's northern bank (before the hanging bridge) for a waymarked tourist path leads straight on northwards to the **Kugy monument**. The sculptor Savinšek has modelled this great lover of Trenta and the Julian Alps sitting in a reverie, gazing at one of his favourite mountains,

The Mlinarica gorge twists and turns only one kilometre below the Kugy monument

Jalovec. The monument stands at an altitude of approximately 800 m near one of the first serpentine bends of the road to Vršič; here the high-mountain world around Trenta begins to reveal itself. Kugy's beloved peak with its distinctive crystal form plays the major role in this dramatic scene. From the starting-point to here is a good hour's walk (not including stops).

From the monument return to the road and descend along it to the nearby turning for the **Koča pri izviru Soče** (Hut by the Source of the Soča), 886 m, a good kilometre away. It is only 10 minutes' walk from the hut to the source, **izvir Soče**, though the path is not quite easy; at the end you must climb some steep rocks with the reliable help of a steel rope. When the water level is high, the Soča gushes thundering out from a deep cave, but usually it springs forth somewhat lower down and then flows in lovely cascades into the valley. At those times you can look down into the cave and see the surface of a subterranean lake in the mountain's interior.

If you finish your outing here, we recommend returning by the waymarked tourist path, which mostly avoids the road. Shortly below the hut a signpost invites you down rightwards to the river. By the bridge somewhat lower you come onto the road and follow it to the second bridge (below the Mlinarica gorge), but leave the asphalt before that and keep all the time to the right bank of the Soča. This pleasant path winds through the forest and over solitary haymeadows, ascends somewhat opposite the village Na Logu and then drops again to the picturesque Končar farmhouse standing by itself. Here you can cross the river by a hanging bridge or continue as far as the road bridge about one kilometre below Na Logu. The route given (Na Logu – the Kugy monument – Izvir Soče and back) lasts 3-4 hours. But if you wish to really experience all the "stations" described, the trip can well occupy you all day.

The source of the Soča

It is by the source of the Soča that the real, wildly romantic Trenta begins, closely associated with the jagged ridges of the surrounding mountains and creating together with them an indivisible whole. The rather rough road continues on for about a kilometre, but no valley noise or bustle reaches into **Zadnja Trenta** (the local people prefer the ancient name **Zapoden**). Actully only a few inhabitants still persevere in this remote corner, and the solitary farmsteads are scattered far apart. The flat valley bottom is covered with extensive pebble beds that bear witness to the force of the waters, whenever fierce storms rage high above. Both sides are scoured by wild gullies, down which springtime avalanches roar right into the valley. It's not unusual for their soiled remains to lie near the highest farmhouses far into the summer. The Trentarji must carry on a ceaseless, direct battle with these forces of the high mountains.

The road previously mentioned comes to an end by the well-preserved homestead Florijeva domačija, 963 m. Here a path to Jalovec starts, while the route towards Bavški Grintavec mounts straight on up the valley. Before this point a signpost invites you to bear left to the old-time Kverh house, now adapted as an inn, **Kekčeva domačija**, in traditional Trenta style. You can wander along Zadnja Trenta without any particular goal in mind. If you have a taste for adventure and it's a hot day, we recommend a trip right into the heart of the valley, where a stream pleasantly burbles along. Beside this stream, or even wading along it, if necessary, you can pass through a narrow gorge to reach a beautiful waterfall. But here you bump up against the inexorable wall of the high mountains. From the source of the Soča to the waterfall takes 1.30 h.

By the village Na Logu there branches off to the east a deep valley carved between the towering faces of Razor, Pihavec, Triglav, Kanjavec and Ozebnik – this is **Zadnjica**. A forest road runs along it but public traffic is allowed only as far as the barrier, 2 km beyond the village, where a route to Kriški podi turns off to the left. The Krajcarica stream has its picturesque source just here, with the water cascading down over moss-covered stones. People also live in Zadnjica, though most of the old homesteads are nowadays converted into holiday cottages. The lively Beli potok (White Stream) bursts out from under Kriški podi, leaping over a rock threshold just above the valley. Below is a deep pool where the water is pleasantly warmed in summer and engagingly invites you to take a dip. The only problem is finding it! If you follow the road as far as it goes, you will find yourself in one of the wildest valley ends. Majestic rock faces press down into the valley on all sides, including the highest face in the Slovene mountains, the 1500-m-high north face of Kanjavec. From the road barrier to here is an hour's walk. Here at the head of the Zadnjica valley routes begin that aim for Triglav and the Prehodavci saddle at the beginning of the Triglav Lakes Valley.

LEPENA

Lepena is a shortish, transverse valley that runs out into the Soča valley somewhat above the village of Soča. It bites into the heart of the Krn mountain group. Along it flows the small river Lepenjica, which issues forth in a lovely waterfall from the flanks of the mighty mountain Lemež. Just as in Bavšica and Zadnja Trenta, there is no compact settlement here and farmsteads are scattered all around. Yet compared with these two other valleys, Lepena has a more lowland character, making it more lively and populated, while tourist facilities are also developed to a much higher degree. The road into Lepena turns off 2 km below the village of Soča, runs along the northern bank of the river and leads to the large mountain hut, **Dom dr. Klementa Juga**, 680 m, standing at the head of the valley. Above there are steep slopes rising towards the high mountains of the Krn group, but some hundreds of metres higher the terrain again levels out into a broad basin, adorned by the large **Krnsko jezero (Lake Krn)**, 1394 m. A little below it stands another mountain hut. From here the much frequented path continues on towards the summit of Krn, while to the east a path branches off for the Komna plateau, which belongs to the Bohinj mountains.

Lepena is a pleasant, recommendable destination for a trip with plenty of additional possibilities, e.g. continuing to Lake Krn. Even down in the valley you don't need to tramp all the way along the asphalt. Three kilometres after turning off the Trenta road you will notice a hanging bridge, and an attractive footpath then runs along the opposite river bank all the way to the mountain hut. An enterprising, inquiring visitor should make the effort to find a hidden, little-known ravine in the middle of the valley, and certainly won't regret it. From the mountain hut a waymarked path leads to the previously mentioned waterfall (30 minutes, care needed if the way is slippery). It is a good two hours' walk to Krnsko jezero along a comfortable, gentle path. For the sake of nature conservation bathing in the lake is not allowed.

KORITNICA

A little above Bovec the river Koritnica, which flows from the right into the Soča, has given its name to one of the wonderful valleys of Posočje. This deep glacial valley is broader and sunnier than Trenta, and green with forests. Its level bottom is covered with lovely fields and meadows such as the Trentarji can only dream of. In the lower part, the side valley of **Možnica** turns westwards, cutting into the heart of the Kanin group. Koritnica is dominated by the tremendous mountain **Mangart**, 2678 m. Somewhat to one side stands Jalovec, here showing its least characteristic, although most impressive image. The western flank of the valley is hemmed in by the finely shaped Jerebica, and between this peak and Mangart the ridge drops sufficiently to be crossed by the road reaching the **Predel** (Predil) saddle, 1156 m. The state border runs along these ridges. From the east one of the most magnificent rock faces soars above the valley. **Loška stena** with its monolithic nature and uninterrupted steepness appears as a single mass, although the summit ridge comprises no less than ten peaks, which are all barely accessible loners. The head of Koritnica, squeezed in between Mangart and Jalovec, is one of the most beautiful in the Julian Alps. Koritnica in general is characterized by exceptional grandeur, and the surrounding mountains are for the most part extremely diffiult to attain on account of their tremendous height differences and relentless gradients. The river's exit from Koritnica is pressed into a narrow gorge with 60-m-high walls. You can enjoy the view into this chasm, where the water whirls and foams far below, from the road bridge by the former fortress of **Kluže**.

The village of **Log pod Mangartom**, 651 m, is situated where the road starts to climb up towards the Predel pass. On a sunny terrace somewhat higher up lies the hamlet of **Strmec**, with which only Srednji Vrh above Martuljek can vie for the beauty of the view and the position itself. Between Strmec and Predel a road branches off towards Mangart, the only road in Slovenia to surpass 2000 m.

This description could lead the reader to create an image of Koritnica as a pure idyll, but unfortunately this is not the case. The wild, elementary world of the surrounding mountain ridges presses so directly into the valley that this too must often feel the impact of the natural forces that rule at high altitudes. Like the Trentarji, the inhabitants of Koritnica frequently have to face the devastation of raging waters and avalanches. The worst disaster befell the region in the autumn of 2000, when heavy rains dislodged a colossal landslide under Mangart, which crashed into the valley, demolishing part of the village Log pod Mangartom. The results of this catastrophe, which also exacted a human toll, will be visible for a long time to come. At that time life came to a standstill in Koritnica but now it is returning and the valley invites visitors again with its eternal beauty.

There is a fine trip from Log to the head of **Loška Koritnica**, as the upper part of the valley is named. The forest road is closed to public traffic and ends in the middle of sunny haymeadows approximately 5 km above Log. Higher up, on the flanks of Mangart, lies the abandoned pasture Koritniška planina, about 1000 m. From here long and demanding routes diverge towards Mangart and Jalovec.

Mangart and Jalovec above the Koritnica valley

Branching off by the bridge a good 2 km below Log, a rough road leads into the side valley of **Možnica**, but it's more recommendable to take the footpath that crosses the Koritnica by a hanging bridge about one kilometre lower, leads past the solitary Koc farmstead, and then winds close by the stream. This hides itself in a very picturesque gorge with numerous waterfalls, deep pools and tiny basins, which the enterprising visitor can view if inventive enough. In the middle of the valley stands a holiday home (at times offering refreshments), 793 m, which has been adapted from a former border barracks. An hour's walk from the road.

BAVŠICA

with its side valley of **Bala** cuts into the solitary alpine world south of Jalovec, in between Trenta and Koritnica. This trough-like valley, open to the west, is the loneliest and most untouched of all these Posočje nooks. The lovely haymeadows that cover the valley bottom are here and there invaded by scurries of scree from the surrounding rock faces, while enormous boulders are scattered everywhere, whether glacial deposits or runaways from the almost perpendicular slopes. Although Bavšica is blessed with the warm Primorska sun, life there is hard. The local inhabitants retreat to the more favourable lowland regions, many homesteads, scattered far around, are deserted, and there is no single settlement anywhere. As you walk through Bavšica, you can't shake off the feeling that this is a dying countryside. In many ways, this valley is reminiscent of the neighbouring Zadnja Trenta. It is hemmed in by the ridges of Bavški Grintavec and Loška stena, between them the exceptionally sharp, wedge-shaped ridge, Pihavec, cuts in like a dragon's flaming tongue. Lower down, Bavšica runs out into Koritnica, and here there is a permanent stream, otherwise the valley is dry. The road into it branches off by the great

Rombon rises above the Možnica valley, viewed here from Log pod Mangartom

164

fortress of Kluže, precisely by the bridge over the deepest gorge in Slovenia, and penetrates to the last farmhouses at the head of the valley. Nearby stands the **Mladinski vzgojni center PZS** (TheYouth Training Centre of the Alpine Association of Slovenia), 715 m, which offers tented accommodation for the night (8 km from Bovec, 1 h from Kluže on foot). From here it is possible to climb Bavški Grintavec by very demanding routes.

High-mountain features also characterize the side valley of **Bala**, which advances in steps towards the north, squeezed between the high slopes of the Loška stena chain and the ridge of the Pelci summits. It ends at the Brežice pass, 1980 m, where Bala abruptly plunges into Koritnica. Above the first "step" in the lower part of Bala you find the deserted farmhouses of the hamlet Logje, which the inhabitants have abandoned totally. Along this valley runs a rarely used path towards Jalovec, while the approach to the highest summit of Loška stena, Briceljk, 2346 m, is still more demanding.

Bavšica and Bala with their solitary, barely accessible mountains are inviting in quite a different way from the better known and more frequented alpine valleys. You need to be something of a romantic or a recluse if you decide on visiting this remote little world, which offers no help to the spoilt tourist. You must take everything with you, even water. But what you take away from Bavšica depends on you and your personal relationship with untouched nature.

Waterfalls

Waterfalls always captivate us with their foaming whiteness and the wealth of ever-changing sparkling light. The sound of falling water is also pleasantly natural, so different from the wearisome racket of town life. If anywhere at all, then certainly in the upper Soča valley you can gaze to your heart's content at every kind of waterfall and cascade. The configuration of this alpine world and its climatic conditions produce an optimal combination for waterfalls to form. In the mountains above Trenta, Lepena and Koritnica there isn't a single stream that doesn't hollow out trough-like gorges through the rock and leap over precipices in its way into the valley. It sounds almost unbelievable, but above the Koritnica valley alone about 120 waterfalls are known so far! Alas, the most beautiful of them are so hidden and inaccessible that we cannot present them here. Some waterfalls have already been mentioned in preceding paragraphs, while the mightiest ones in Posočje resound further down, in the surroundings of Bovec and Kobarid.

SLAP BRINTA, GREGORČIČEV SLAP (the Brinta waterfall, Gregorčič's waterfall) On the southern flank of Krn, which towers over 2000 metres above the Soča, a sunny terrace has formed a few hundred metres above the valley, and here lies the lovely little village of Vrsno, where the Slovene poet Simon Gregorčič was born and spent his young years. The beauties of this mountain region powerfully influenced his poetry, which Slovenes are particularly fond of, and he dedicated his most famous poem to the river Soča. Below the village the ground abruptly falls away and two mighty waterfalls plunge over the edge. The one well seen from the village is called Gregorčičev slap, somewhat lower but with a lesser volume of water is the slap Brinta near the village of Selce. If you want to see them both, you must first find this small village. Leave the main road between Tolmin and Kobarid by the signpost Kamno - Vrsno. A bare kilometre above Kamno you turn right into Selce. On the meadows above the village you first glimpse the mighty 88-m-high Gregorčičev slap, and from here a path leads over the edge into the gully of the Malenščak stream, where the more hidden, 104-m-high Brinta plunges across overhangs. If you want to get closer to Gregorčič's waterfall, you must cross another edge to reach the gully of the Volarja stream. This takes half an hour from the village, but the path is not marked and is somewhat dangerous.

SLAP KOZJAK (the Kozjak waterfall) is near Kobarid. The stream of the same name has traced its way from the western flanks of Krn through a wild gorge and just above the valley overleaps two big precipices. The upper waterfall, Veliki Kozjak, is one of the most beautiful, and due to the short and easy access, one of the most often visited as well. In Kobarid look for the turning towards Drežnica, and Napoleon's bridge will present itself crossing the Soča. On the other side, by a campsite, a waymarked path forks off left towards the waterfall. Passing the remains of some old fortifications, you soon reach the Kozjak stream, cross it above the lower waterfall and continue through the

The Kozjak waterfall

narrowing gorge until you come to a wooden platform just above a big pool in the middle of this dark basin, into which the extremely full and booming Veliki Kozjak waterfall plunges. Half an hour's walk from the road by an easy, waymarked path.

SLAP BOKA (the Boka waterfall)

The Kanin group with its vast, high-altitude plateaus forms an enormous collection area for water. The karst nature of these mountains explains why the water immediately percolates into the unchartered subterranean world. Only deep below does it encounter impermeable strata and then bursts out to the surface. This happens in the most spectacular fashion west of Bovec, opposite the village of Log Čezsoški where, about 400 metres above the valley, the Boka waterfall pounds from a cleft in the flank of Kanin. It is 106 metres high and especially in spring, when the snows on Kanin are melting, it is incredibly majestic. You have a fine view of it from the main road about one kilometre above the village of Žaga (parking place and café). You can approach the waterfall as near as you wish by a waymarked path along the overgrown edge left above the stream bed. However, to reach the source of the waterfall you should take a waymarked and (modestly) secured path along the northern bank of the gully – 1.30 h, demanding and exposed.

p. 167: The Boka waterfall

Lower viewpoints

MATAJUR

Matajur, 1641 m, is the highest summit in the small group in the extreme southwest of the Slovene alpine "foothills". It rises above the Soča valley opposite Krn, to the southwest above Kobarid. The state border runs along its ridge. This is a friendly, easily accessible mountain though with quite steep, overgrown slopes above the Soča, while its Italian side is somewhat denuded with varied relief. At the extended foot of Matajur lies a small region with a predominantly Slovene population living in numerous little villages; it is thus known as Slovenska Benečija (Slovene Venetia). Matajur is regarded as one of the finest viewpoints of the Slovene foothills. To the north shines the long succession of high Julian peaks, with nearby Krn especially commanding respect, while to the south the view reaches across the soft flanks of Slovene Venetia as far as Venice. In fine weather you can even see the Adriatic Sea sparkling. In the west stand the distant massed summits of the Dolomites. There's no lack of paths leading to this spreading mountain, as you might expect; we recommend the eastern approach, starting from the village of Livek.

Down in the valley the road to Livek forks off from the main road in the village of Idrsko 2 km south of Kobarid. From here a narrow road climbs westwards a further good kilometre to the village of **Avsa**, 860 m, where the marked path to Matajur begins. The route runs along the right side of the gently rising broad ridge, alternately winding through forest and across meadows. When you reach the dairy herdsmen's huts on Idrska planina, you join a forest road for a short

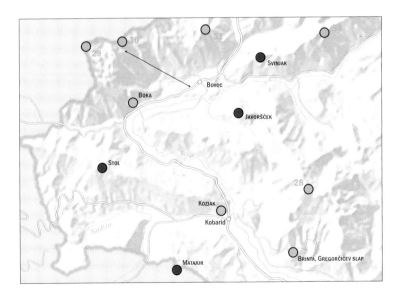

time, and soon afterwards the path forks. The righthand path is the more recommendable, leading across the northern slope. In one spot it is interrupted by a rock step, which offers a little piece of pleasant gymnastics. The summit of Matajur is broad and open, so your gaze can float at will around the extensive horizon. On the highest point stands an attractive chapel. From the village of Avsa 3 h. You can descend by the same route, and higher up you can choose a path which leads along the summit ridge and occasionally winds over Italian territory.

And a hint for diehard walkers – you can begin your ascent of Matajur right in Kobarid. You walk to the neighbouring village of Svino (1 km towards the southwest), where the waymarked path starts. It climbs steeply through the forest, higher up crosses more gentle open stretches and half an hour below the summit joins the usual path. From Kobarid 4 h.

STOL

There are two summits in the Slovene mountains with the name Stol (literally Chair): the mighty champion of the Karavanke range and this more modest one above the Soča river. Kobariški Stol, 1673 m, is the name of an immensely long upland back, which stretches eastwards towards Kobarid for as much as 34 kilometres and represents the southern boundary marker of the Julian Alps. A good half of this uniformly shaped ridge lies in Italy, where the highest point is found – Karman/Chiampon, 1709 m. On the Slovene side, the Stol ridge separates the Soča valley and the Breginjski kot valley. It's interesting that this ridge is formed in exactly the opposite way to the majority of ridges in the Julian Alps, where the northern side is usually steep and precipitous. That side of Stol is gentle and covered in vegetation. The southern side is one long, uninterrupted steep grassy slope, with rough precipices here and there.

The two long ridges of Stol and Kanin seen from Matajur

From a distance the Stol ridge gives the impression of a mighty wall, visible from Venice and even further away. Naturally such a subalpine ridge is exceptionally panoramic and competes with Matajur in this respect. Access is also perfectly easy.

Approaching by car can simplify a trip to Stol into a mere walk, accomplished in a good hour. If you decide on this version, then in the village of Žaga on the main Kobarid – Bovec road turn westwards along the valley of the River Učja. Somewhat before the border crossing of the same name a forest road branches up to the left and winds over the forested slope of Stol (turn left at the only fork), after 6 km this reaches the alp **Spodnja Božca**, 1240 m, with a hunters' hut. It's best to leave your car here and continue along the road to the upper alp, which lies just below the pass Na Verilih, 1377 m. Now you step onto the summit ridge, with its open views on every side, and the path westwards towards the top of Stol is a really pleasant walk. The summit is indicated by a TV station. A good hour from planina Božca.

As with Matajur, we'll add instructions for passionate walkers. Your waymarked path begins in Kobarid, 234 m, on the northern edge of the town. A steep climb through low forest ends after an hour and a half at the beginning of the open ridge, where you commence the long, gradual hike towards the summit. On the way you can take a rest at the modest shelter of Bivak Hlek (no supplies), 1225 m, and on the saddle Na Verilih you'll join the previously described path. From Kobarid to the top of Stol takes certainly 5 h.

JAVORŠČEK

This subalpine, forested mountain cone rises to the southeast above the Bovec basin. Lacking a specially attractive shape, it stands in the shade of Svinjak, but nevertheless is a recommendable and fairly frequented, undemanding

Rombon from the Golobar alp

mountaineers' goal. Javoršček, 1557 m, belongs to the Krn group and it is just here that the exceptionally long and mighty northwest chain of Krn begins. The mountain was indelibly marked by a great rockfall, which happened in 1950. To the east below the summit lies the fine alp Golobar, with two waymarked paths leading to it. The marks don't actually reach right to the summit, but it is prefectly easy to get there. Here we recommend a round tour, in the direction described. The starting-point is the village of **Kal-Koritnica**, 460 m, at the foot of Svinjak, 3 km east of Bovec. From the monument in Kal the waymarked path drops to the Soča, crosses it by a small footbridge above the picturesque pool Brjek, and then begins to climb through the forest towards the southeast. You soon notice a solitary farmhouse on your left, otherwise you continue for 2 hours from the Soča river before the trees give way and reveal the extensive abandoned pasture **Golobar,** where the disintegrating sheds stand as reminder of the once flourishing dairy activity here. The open expanse reaches up to the pass Čez Utro, 1305 m, where the cone of Javoršček, seen on your right, is attached to the Krn ridge. In the spring of 1943 a bloodstained wartime tragedy occurred here, marked now by a Partisan memorial. A broad forested ridge slopes gently up towards the summit with a well-trodden though unmarked path, by which you can reach the top in scarcely one hour. Javoršček's open summit offers an excellent view of the impressive mountains enclosing the Bovec basin. From the village of Kal 3.30 h.

You can avoid descending the same way by taking the path over the southern slope towards the village of Čezsoča. First return to the Čez Utro pass and then drop down in a long bend southwards to the still preserved sheds on the alp Slatniki. The path continues gently downwards high above a gorge of the Slatenik stream and leads in half an hour to a great rockfall (though this is not the biggest

Svinjak mounts up directly above the Bovec basin

one, which marks out the mountain from a distance). The passage across it is not too pleasant, but on the far side the path drops more steeply to a forest road, along which you reach the valley. By the Soča river turn left into the village Čezsoča, 3 km south of Bovec. This round tour takes at least 6 h.

SVINJAK

Zermatt has the Matterhorn, and Bovec has Svinjak, 1653 m. Such is the role this dark watchman of the Bovec basin boasts of. But it is nonetheless true that this mountain of medium height is the most noticeable one in the panorama surrounding the capital of the upper Posočje. Its image as a bold pointed peak, however, is seen only towards Bovec; from other places it is clearly seen as an unimportant rise at the end of Bavški Grintavec's long ridge. But never mind, the mountain is challenging and definitely worth visiting. Its position at the heart of the mountain chains encircling the Bovec basin assures it a favourable slot in the class of viewpoints that includes Pršivec in Bohinj, for instance, or Ciprnik above the Upper Sava Valley. In contrast to Matajur, Stol and Javoršček, Svinjak indisputably belongs to the rugged world of steep, high mountains, and such is the character of the approach. There aren't actually any technical difficulties yet Svinjak is by no means just a walk. You must shed some sweat to get there (the height difference is 1200 m), and in the full heat of summer the tour cannot be recommended due to the presence of snakes.

The path to Svinjak begins in **Koritnica**, a village 3 km east of Bovec. The first waymark is painted on the water trough at the upper edge of the village, then you climb in the direction of the steep edge straight up towards the summit. The path mostly winds to the right of the edge and is decidedly steep. Lower down small trees predominate, but above the tree line the real alpine world begins, with only a few sparse larches scattered among the dwarf pine. But the increasingly extensive view is a reward for the strenuous ascent. As you step onto the summit of Svinjak, you have the feeling of having gained a "real" mountain. From Koritnica 3 h. The same path must be used for the descent as no other options exist.

p. 174: The mountain world in autumn glory

25

Razor

The sunny side of a furrowed mountain

ALTITUDE: 2601 m
STARTING ALTITUDE: 740 m (in the valley), 2050 m (Pogačnikov dom)
HEIGHT DIFFERENCE: 1900 m (from Pogačnikov dom 600 m)

"The furrowed mountain", mentioned in the subtitle, indicates the meaning of the name of this peak, one of the highest and most beautiful in the Julian Alps. It shows its most furrowed face towards the north, where Razor dominates the Kranjska Gora panorama, but the south side, too, with its complicated structure, full of wild, lonely gullies, truly justifies the name. Razor stands right at the heart of the main ridge of the Julian Alps and is an important link in the grand ridge tour from Vršič to Triglav, described on pp. 141-144. The direct approach from the Trenta valley is attractive as well since you can become acquainted with the secrets of the high-mountain plateau Kriški podi, lying to the south under Razor, and adorned with lovely tarns. The ascent of Razor from Trenta is too big an undertaking for most people if done as a one-day tour, so we

Jalovec appears across the Pihavec-Gamsovec ridge

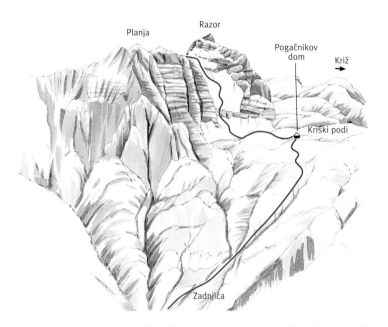

Planja
Razor
Pogačnikov
dom
Križ →
Kriški podi
Zadnjica

recommend staying overnight at the mountain hut Pogačnikov dom on Kriški podi, 2050 m. While you are there, some other idea may also come to birth.

STARTING-POINT:
The village Na Logu in Trenta; from here 2 km east along the road into the Zadnjica valley as far as the barrier, 740 m.

DESCRIPTION:
From the parking area turn left along the forest road to the load cableway. On the right below the road in the gully of Beli potok (White Stream) you'll notice a fine waterfall plunging into a deep pool, which is very enticing for a marvellous bathe on a hot summer's day. Here the road changes into a comfortable path, which climbs in gradual serpentine bends on the left beside the gully. You walk for two hours mostly in the shade of the beech forest, in between crossing two deep gullies, and then the path winds over open ground rightwards to the foot of steep Pihavec, 2419 m. The surroundings are very wild, full of deep gullies and precipitous faces. The ridge on the left is particularly picturesque, resembling a saw. Its most sharply whetted teeth are called the Kanceljni, 2133 m. The summit of Razor is hidden by mighty Planja, 2447 m, with its smooth faces. High above, you see the edge of the Kriški podi plateau, with a big building observable – this is **Pogačnikov dom**, 2050 m. Half an hour before you cross the threshold of this hospitable mountain hut, you see on your right the lower lake Spodnje Kriško jezero, and on the way a welcome spring greets you. It's a 4-hour walk to the mountain hut.

The path to Razor drops down a bit from the hut, but then you must cope with a steep climb towards the northwest. (On the saddle below the hut, the path for Škrlatica turns off to the right.) The southern slope of Razor is shaped like a bowl, covered by a big scree. You climb up to this over rocks worn smooth, but the path being secured makes things easier. The tiring ascent over rough

176

scree ends on the saddle, 2349 m, south under Razor, where the western panorama opens up, with majestic Prisank, 2547 m, claiming half the horizon. Here there is an important intersection. To the left the path turns off for the nearby summit of **Planja**, 2447 m (half an hour's walk, recommendable; on the way you can see an interesting play of nature – **Utrujeni stolp** (Weary Tower), on the other side the route drops towards Prisank and Vršič, while the path to Razor winds off to the right. It mostly follows the western flank of the main ridge, in between you pass a big hollow, where sometimes a precious rivulet of water is found. Razor's summit exchanges looks with the champions of the Julian Alps as "primus inter pares", the nearest ones are Prisank, Stenar and Pihavec – while Triglav mounts up in the background. In the northeast you admire a great host of sharp peaks belonging to the Škrlatica group.

DESCENT:

On the saddle below the top of Razor you can, instead of descending the same way, choose to continue your tour towards Vršič (described in the opposite direction on pp. 141-144) and if you're in good form, you can take in Prisank as well. Pogačnikov dom is the starting-point for the ascent of Škrlatica (pp. 122-127), Stenar (pp. 119-121), or for a grand traverse across Bovški Gamsovec and the Luknja pass towards Triglav (pp. 117-118).

DIFFICULTY:

The tour is moderately demanding. If you carry it out in one go, it is tremendously strenuous.

TIMES:

Trenta – Pogačnikov dom 4 h
Pogačnikov dom – Razor 2 h
Razor – Trenta 4 h

The Zadnjica valley

26

Triglav

Triglav is not a mountain. Triglav is a kingdom (Julius Kugy)

ALTITUDE: 2864 m
STARTING ALTITUDE: 740 m
HEIGHT DIFFERENCE: 2122 m!

It is rare to find a mountain range with such a dominant highest peak as in the Julian Alps. Triglav can be seen from a great distance as an image of majesty and it is no wonder that the predecessors of today's inhabitants saw in it the throne of the gods. This myth has been preserved in some fashion in the soul of every Slovene and so they compare Triglav with Mt Olympus or Kailash. Triglav now occurs for the third time in this guide, in this chapter as the ruler and highest mountain of Posočje. The west side of Triglav is no less magnificent than the others, but this is certainly the least well-known and least frequented face of the great mountain. At this western foot lies the valley of Zadnjica, which denotes something remote, forgotten. Indeed this valley is a sort of "blind gut" of Trenta, surrounded with a dark wreath of the highest faces of the Slovene mountains.

Triglav and Pihavec seen from Goličica

The almost two-kilometre-high western face of Triglav is interrupted at an altitude of approximately 2500 metres by the lifeless, stony plateau of Zaplanja. Above it rises the finely shaped summit structure. Far fewer mountaineers climb Triglav from the west than from Bohinj or the Vrata valley. This is not to be attributed to the difficulty or lack of paths and mountain huts, but to the remoteness of Trenta. But this fact also carries an advantage: anyone who hates crowds in the mountains and all the accompanying phenomena should choose any of the western approaches for the ascent of the mountain.

The usual approach to Triglav from the west is actually very unusual. Through all the wild and solitary steep slopes, often over real faces, all the way up to 2500 m, a comfortable "mulatiera" was built – an old military transport route, which even today could be managed with some skill and courage by a good motorbike rider. It should be explained that the Soča Basin, in the period between the two world wars, belonged to Italy and the current strategic interests demanded a strengthening of the border. Thus on the plateau just below the summit of Triglav a huge barracks was erected, with the mulatiera leading to it. We hope that the world today is different, and that these comfortable military routes - not only to Triglav - have become important mountaineers' highways. To reach Triglav from Trenta means a two-day tour, of course, and the mountain hut Tržaška koča on Dolič offers overnight accommodation.

STARTING-POINT:
The village of Na Logu in Trenta; from here 2 km east along the road into the Zadnjica valley as far as the barrier, 740 m.

DESCRIPTION:
From the parking area in front of the barrier follow the righthand road past the last homesteads up to the head of the Zadnjica valley. It would be difficult to find another place where a person can feel so hemmed in. Majestic faces press down from everywhere, the deep silence is broken only by the roar of waterfalls and the sound of falling stones. The summits appear incredibly lofty. After rising about 100 metres, the road changes into the mulatiera and here your ascent of Triglav really begins. You can't miss the way and a technical description isn't required. A good hour above the valley it is necessary, in fact, at a fork to choose the righthand path (the left one leads to the Luknja pass), but still orientation is the last thing to worry about on the way to Dolič. During your comfortable walk with its gradual gradient, which is actually, if the truth be told, a bit monotonous, you can indulge in pleasant thoughts or be absorbed by the grandeur of the alpine world, which expands with every step. Down below you walked through pleasantly shady forest, in the region of dwarf pine it's harder to find any shady nook for a break, still higher up, where grass predominates, you'll be delighted by the variegated gardens of alpine flowers. During the final hour's walk beneath the Dolič saddle, you're completely surrounded by grey rock.

Tržaška koča na Doliču, 2151 m, is very roomy and generally less crowded than the Kredarica or Planika huts. As its name shows, it stands on the Dolič saddle, which separates two massive mountains, Triglav and Kanjavec. This is an important intersection of mountain paths, since the alpine worlds of Bohinj and Soča meet right here. The mulatiera hasn't ended yet – for a good hour you can still enjoy its comfortable style as you ascend above Dolič in the direction of Triglav's summit. In this high region you'll hardly encounter any living thing, your world has changed into a stony wilderness. The mountaineering part of the tour begins on the plateau of rough scree at the base of the summit section. On the left you notice the remains of the huge military barracks of Morbegno, then you climb over steep scree to the rocks. The route is laid along natural passages towards the right; its sequence of ledges and crumbling gullies runs out at the deeply cut notch Triglavska škrbina, 2569 m. The summit is now on your left and you must still climb a fairly high, steep rock section and finally the beautiful, panoramic ridge. All the exposed places are well-secured by a steel rope. Quite some distance before the summit you catch sight of the well-known turret Aljažev stolp, which marks the highest point of Slovenia. There is no loftier mountain for miles and miles around.

DESCENT:
Only the approach route described leads back to your starting-point, but otherwise you can easily choose some other variant for the descent. Many are outlined in this guide.

DIFFICULTY:
As far as the base of the summit section it's a path "for motorbike riders", above that the route is moderately demanding, well-secured and in places quite exposed. There is also the danger of exposure to falling stones.

TIMES:
The Zadnjica valley – Tržaška koča na Doliču 4 h
Tržaška koča – Triglav 2.30 h
Triglav – Trenta 5 h

Tržaška koča on Dolič

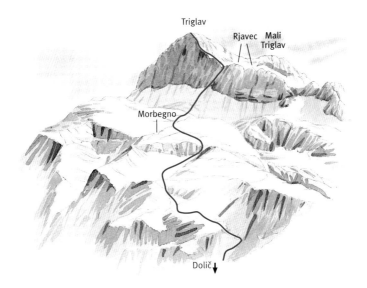

NOTE:

Only exceptionally well trained and experienced enthusiasts, can be recommended to attempt the ascent of Triglav from Trenta via the Luknja pass and along the west ridge (Bambergova pot – the Bamberg route). The enormous height difference of 2122 m must be overcome in one fell swoop, plus climbing one of the most difficult secured routes in the Slovene mountains. If you can cope with such a challenge, you deserve full honours; you will be incomparably rewarded by the tour. A similarly comfortable "mulatiera" takes you to the Luknja pass, 1785 m, as to Dolič, then the real hard work begins. The description of the Bamberg route is found on pp. 117-118. You need 3 h to Luknja, and another 4 h to the summit.

Another option is the route from Zadnjica via Prehodavci and Hribarice (4 h).

27

Lepa špica

The mountain between Trenta and Bohinj

ALTITUDE: 2398 m
STARTING ALTITUDE: 2071 m
HEIGHT DIFFERENCE: 450 m

Lepa špica (Beautiful Peak), which you will generally find on the map under the artificially created name Veliko špičje (Great Peak) and also Lepo špičje, has already been presented as a Bohinj mountain. But actually this border mountain only half belongs to the Bohinjci, showing them its mild and sunny southern slopes, rich with flowers. The mightier, northern aspect belongs to the Trentarji. Lepa špica is the highest summit in an exceptionally long and uniform ridge between Spodnja (Lower) Trenta and Dolina Triglavskih jezer (the Triglav Lakes Valley), which its impressive face supports. It is characterized by numerous parallel pillars and many an admirer has noticed the similarity to a huge organ. These faces shine beautifully and invitingly in the late sunshine; if at such a time you are rambling along the valley, where dusk is

Lepo špičje glimpsed from Zavetišče pod Špičkom

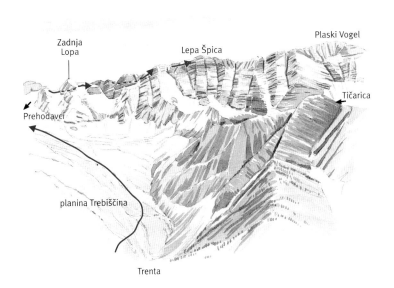

Zadnja Lopa   Lepa Špica   Plaski Vogel

Tičarica

Prehodavci

planina Trebiščina

Trenta

beginning to fall, you can be seized by a deep desire to be that moment up there. The desire can be fulfilled the next morning, and this description will come in handy. The approach from Trenta leads to Lepa špica along the east ridge from the saddle **Prehodavci**, 2071 m, where the mountain hut Zasavska koča stands. This offers the possibility of a two-day tour, which is to be recommended, for it is so beautiful on Lepa špica, as its name indicates, that it would really be a pity to hurry.

STARTING-POINT:
The mountain hut Zasavska koča na Prehodavcih, 2071 m, stands on the saddle northeast under the beginning of the long ridge of Lepa špica and its neighbours. The path from Trenta leads here into the Triglav Lakes Valley and the tour to Lepa špica can be an introduction to longer circumambulations in the mountains. Two easy though not short paths run from the valley up here, and join together an hour's walk below the hut.
- The route from the Zadnjica valley is steep and picturesque, winding through very suggestive surroundings at the foot of the highest rock faces in the Julian Alps. You begin the tour in the village Na Logu, or rather by the road barrier in Zadnjica 2 km above the village, 740 m. Continue along the road to the head of the valley, closed in by the faces of Triglav, Kanjavec, Vršac and Ozebnik. At the end of the road turn right and follow an easy path up through the steep valley of Zadnjiški dol, carved between the massifs of Vršac and Ozebnik. A good spring in the middle of these steep slopes is a joyful find. The valley ends on the pass **Čez Dol**, 1632 m, where a comfortable path for transport comes up from the other side. This climbs towards Prehodavci in almost exaggeratedly gentle serpentine bends over increasingly stony and lifeless ground. From the road barrier to Prehodavci takes 3.30 h.

- The route through the **Trebiščina** valley runs more to the west and is more gradual, but then, naturally, longer. It turns off the main road in Trenta barely one kilometre below the village Na Logu, follows the forest road for a time, and then changes into a comfortable mulatiera (transport route), winding through the gradually ascending Trebiščina valley at the southern foot of the bulky mountain Ozebnik. On the pass Čez Dol, 1632 m, (where it joins the route from Zadnjica), it turns right towards Prehodavci. From Trenta to Zasavska koča takes a good 4 h.

DESCRIPTION:

The way from Prehodavci to Lepa špica is one of the most beautiful high-altitude walks in the Slovene mountains. A detailed description is scarcely necessary, as you can't go astray anywhere. Before you ascend the first top in the ridge (Zadnja Lopa, 2115 m), you cross a series of shining white slabs, which are reminiscent of a glacier, with their sharply eroded water channels. The first and second pointed peaks (Malo špičje, 2312 m) are avoided by the path on the left, but then it grips the ridge. In places the way is exposed, and occasionally you encounter some iron security aid, but there are no serious difficulties. So you can give yourself totally to enjoyment and delight in the view. The ridge is gently undulating as far as the main summit. If you are attentive, you can observe that this rocky wilderness does have life. In crevices amidst the grey rocks a little cushion of tiny flowers suddenly glows with bright colours; don't be alarmed if all of a sudden a small herd of ibex comes running from behind the edge; precisely on Lepa špica they are often co-travellers with mountaineers.

DESCENT:

You'll return to your starting-point most easily and quickly by the same way, but numerous possibilities offer themselves for continuing your tour. For instance, you can descend into the Triglav Lakes Valley (by the path described on pp. 57-58), and choose a further route as you wish.

DIFFICULTY:

The path from Prehodavci to Lepa špica can be "dangerous" despite its modest level of difficulty because it offers so many beauties to look at that someone can forget how they walk. Real danger sometimes lurks elsewhere: you should undertake this ridge tour only in reliable weather, for a storm must not catch you out up there.

TIMES:

Trenta – Zasavska koča na Prehodavcih 3.30-4.30 h
Prehodavci – Lepa špica 2.30 h
Lepa špica – Prehodavci 2.30 h
A one-day tour: Trenta – Prehodavci –Lepa špica and back 12 h

28

Krn

It saw the raging of nature and man

Krn, 2244 m, belongs to the great champions of the Julian Alps despite its modest altitude. Solitary, proud, seen from far around and easily recognizable because of its unique outline, it stands on the southwest edge of this mountain range. It is linked most closely with the Soča, since the waters of this river basin wash against it on every side, while the river itself is forced to make a big curve around it. In a way, Krn is related to Jalovec, since it displays on all sides the regular, sculptured form of a mighty nose. If we dubbed Jalovec a challenging mountain, then we could attribute defiance to Krn.

Krn belongs to the "highest" summits of the Slovene mountains, even though its altitude doesn't merit it a place even among the top hundred. The southern slope above the Soča measures over 2000 metres! This is a sheer open slope, interrupted below by a long terrace, on which a series of lovely hamlets bask in the sun. In the west the grassy steepness erupts into Krn's mightiest face; this aspect of the mountain is the wildest and most powerful. The northern side is alpine, the mild influence of the south does not penetrate here. Below the low

The summit of Krn rewards the mountaineer with marvellous views

185

face of the summit section extend enormous stony slopes, which lower down sink into forests. In the valley to the north of Krn a large lake, Krnsko jezero, lies sparkling, a special adorment of this individualist mountain group. Nearby a mountain hut hides among the spruces. Paths of all levels of difficulty lead to Krn, the usual approach being easy. Just below the summit, on the southern side, stands a mountain shelter. Krn is reckoned to be a "personality" among its peers, and so is the desired goal of every mountaineer. It scarcely needs to be said what a marvellous panorama this high viewpoint on the periphery presents. Of course we must explain the subtitle. During the First World War Krn and its neighbours were the scene of tempestuous and bloody battles, with the mountain being changed into a veritable fortress. Numerous remains are a reminder of those sad times. Even nowadays you can find rusted fragments of weapons and military equipment among the rocks. In stony hollows the walls of old barracks are still disintegrating, or you notice an entrance in the grey rock to the dark underground. The entire mountain group is crisscrossed with a network of military transport routes, now used to advantage by mountaineers. Krn again confirmed its dark reputation of an "unhappy mountain" in 1998, when it shuddered in the whirlpool effect of a destructive earthquake. This caused much suffering in the delightful hamlets below. Thus an ineradicably carved bitter line lies across Krn's image.

Krn rises above Krnsko jezero

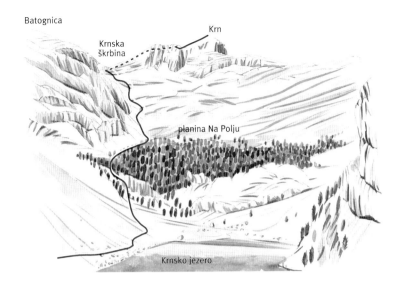

Batognica

Krn

Krnska škrbina

planina Na Polju

Krnsko jezero

A. THE NORTHERN APPROACH

ALTITUDE: 2244 m
STARTING ALTITUDE: 680 m (1385 m)
HEIGHT DIFFERENCE: 1570 m (860 m)

In hot summer weather it's best to go to Krn from the north. Below, you walk in the pleasant shade of the spruce forest, then you can refresh yourself by the lake, and even on the stony expanses of the northern slopes the sun doesn't burn so mercilessly as on the southern grassy steeps. This way is relatively gentle, and thus longer as well. The northern approach as a one-day tour is quite a strenuous undertaking, but two mountain huts, the lower one by the lake and the upper one just under the summit, make a more comfortable execution possible.

STARTING-POINT:
The Lepena valley. The road from the village of Soča ends by the mountain hut Dom dr. Klementa Juga, 680 m (18 km from Bovec, 1.30 h on foot from Soča).

DESCRIPTION:
The first part of the tour is comfortable, as the gentle path winds through the spruce forest towards the southeast. When the steep slope eases, you walk gradually up along a valley to the hut **Planinski dom pri Krnskih jezerih** (Alpine Hut by the Krn Lakes), 1385 m (2 h from Lepena). From here it's a 15 minutes' level walk across the Duplje alp to the main lake. **Krnsko jezero** is the biggest high-altitude lake in Slovenia. It lies in a cwm left by a former glacier north of the foot of Krn and east below the steep mountain of Lemež. You can observe numerous fish in the water. The lake does warm up in summer, but bathing is not allowed for reasons of nature conservation. The path runs above the eastern shore, and then

climbs steeply up to the alp Na Polju. Thereafter the gradient really increases and the surroundings begin to change into a stony desert. Below the summit section of Krn you step onto the last flat terrace, where you can slake your thirst if you find a tiny spring, hidden among the boulders. The last steep slope above this runs out onto Krnska škrbina (Krn Notch), 2058 m, east of the summit. Here an extensive view opens up to the south. Turn right and the path soon forks, with the easier path leading straight to the small hut **Gomiščkovo zavetišče**, which stands just 10 minutes' walk beneath the summit. The righthand path follows the ridge itself, ascending straight to the top.

DESCENT:

If you wish to return to your starting-point, you must descend by the same route. You can greatly enrich your tour by making a detour over Krn's eastern neighbour **Batognica**, 2164 m. This easily accessible mountain is a real textbook for the history of waging war in the mountains. On its summit plateau numerous fortifications are preserved that testify to the times when neighbours stood opposite each other with weapons in their hands. The path to Batognica begins on Krnska škrbina. Actually there are two: one marches along the broad ridge, the other winds over the northern slope. The paths rejoin on the saddle Batogniško sedlo in the east behind the mountain, making a recommendable round tour. The detour over Batognica will detain you for an hour and a half.

DIFFICULTY:

The northern approach to Krn provides an easy and pleasant tour.

TIMES:

Lepena – Koča pri Krnskih jezerih 2 h
Koča pri Krnskih jezerih – Krn 3 h
A one-day tour: Lepena – Krn – Lepena 8-10 h

B. THE SOUTHERN APPROACH

ALTITUDE: 2244 m
STARTING ALTITUDE: 991 m
HEIGHT DIFFERENCE: 1250 m

The southern side of Krn above the Soča valley measures a good 2000 metres. Below it is cloaked in low, deciduous forest, but above 900 metres there stretch the open grassy steep slopes that give the mountain, when seen from a distance, an exceptionally monolithic appearance. Life extends high up the mountainside, pleasant little villages lie on sunny terraces, and further up a whole series of alps. It's a rare mountaineer who tackles Krn right from its foot, the majority make use of the road that covers almost half the height difference and makes it possible to carry out a fine one-day tour.

STARTING-POINT:

Planina Kuhinja (*Kitchen*), approximately 1000 m. Access by road from the Soča valley; turn off at the village of Kamno, 205 m, halfway between Kobarid and Tolmin, then through the hamlets of Vrsno and Krn to the alp (12 km). A waymarked footpath partly avoids the road (2 h). On the lower edge of the alp stands a mountain hut, which is manned only at weekends.

DESCRIPTION:

From planina Kuhinja the path sets out precisely towards the summit of Krn, crosses a serpentine bend of the road, which is here closed to public use, and gradually mounts up to reach the highest Krn alp, **Zaslap**, 1360 m. Here the steep grassy summit slope begins, which is so uniform it produces a wicked optical deception, making the top seem quite near. The path climbs upwards near the left edge of this slope, but swings right to avoid the intervening Kožljak. Now follows an endless series of serpentines, where in the summer heat the mountaineer looks in vain for some shadow. The monotonous ascent is given variety here and there by a view of the precipitous west face. Ten minutes below the summit of Krn you reach Gomiščkovo zavetišče. In the middle of the steepness a path branches off to the right leading in the same style to Krnska škrbina to the east below Krn, offering an alternative approach (and a recommendable one, so that you also include Batognica, 2164 m, known for its remains from the tempests of war).

DESCENT:

The descent to the starting-point can only be by the way described. In the upper section you can make the circular tour mentioned above.

DIFFICULTY:

The tour is easy, but in summer can be terribly hot because of the sunny, open position.

TIMES:

Planina Kuhinja – Krn 3-3.30 h
Descent 2.30 h

View of the Krn massif and the Western Julian Alps

C. THE WESTERN APPROACH

ALTITUDE: 2244 m
STARTING ALTITUDE: 554 m
HEIGHT DIFFERENCE: 1700 m

Towards the west Krn shows its wildest and mightiest image. This high rock face, furrowed with gullies, is in complete contrast to its gentle foot, where the green Drežnica plateau spreads around with its pleasant little villages. Two demanding secured routes lead across the face, which are intended for experienced and well-equipped mountaineers.

STARTING-POINT:
The village of Drežnica, 554 m; access by road from Kobarid, 6 km.
DESCRIPTION:
The waymarked path begins on the eastern edge of the village. The path first crosses easy haymeadows and then continues through the forest eastwards, for a short time joining a forest road bearing right. Beyond the Ročica stream the path forks. The righthand route is the easiest western approach to Krn, which will be described for the descent, so turn left for the **Zahodna Drežniška smer** (Western Drežnica Route). The path climbs through forest as far as the face, on the way you notice on the right a modest shelter (no supplies), where you can stay the night, and also quench your thirst at a little spring of pure water (1.30 h from Drežnica). You soon enter a basin at the foot of the west face, surrounded on all sides by precipices, while above, you notice a big

A resting-spot on the Silvo Koren Route

190

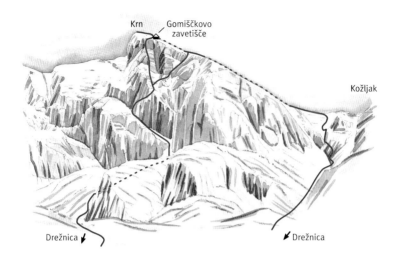

gully oriented to the left, squeezed between two steep faces. The path climbs for quite a long time along this until a passage appears towards the right onto a promontory in the middle of a big pillar. At this spot, called Lev (Lion) by the locals, the path forks again. The original Western Route winds to the right on a long, exposed traverse to reach Krn's southwest ridge, where (half an hour below the hut) it joins the usual southern path. Otherwise the very demanding **Pot Silva Korena** (Silvo Koren Route) pushes straight ahead. This follows the pillar all the time, involving a steep climb, and finishes at the shelter Gomiščkovo zavetišče, 10 minutes below the summit.

DESCENT:
Right of the west face lies a steep valley, which offers the only easy route from this side. A waymarked path runs along it, which is recommended for the descent. You drop down from the summit along the southern path over the big, steep grassy slope to the little saddle by Kožljak, 1591 m, and bear right down through the steep valley until you reach the easier, forested terrain beneath the west face. By the Ročica stream you join the path you know from the early morning.

DIFFICULTY:
The Western Drežnica Route is a moderately demanding, and the Silvo Koren Route a very demanding secured route. Both have been newly equipped, since they were badly damaged by the earthquake in 1998. Self-belaying and wearing a helmet are recommended. The rock climb runs through really majestic and wild surroundings.

TIMES:
Drežnica – Krn by the Western Drežnica Route 6 h
– by the Silvo Koren Route 4.30 h
Descent by the path described 3.30-4 h

29

Visoki Kanin

The ruler of a rock kingdom

AALTITUDE: 2587 m
STARTING ALTITUDE: 2202 m
HEIGHT DIFFERENCE: 385 m

Kanin is a lofty, expansive, uniquely shaped mountain range to the northwest of the Bovec basin. It belongs to the Western Julian Alps, separated from the Eastern half by the Predel pass. The Slovene - Italian border runs along the entire length of its water-shed ridge. (Most of the Western Julians – the Jôf Fuart/ Viš and Montasio/Montaž groups – lie on Italian territory, and Slovenia has only "half" of Kanin as well.) The uniqueness of Kanin is best expressed in its amazingly vast karst-fields, which extend on both sides of the massif. It is formed in a very unified way; the summits between Črnelska špica in the east and Visoki Kanin are unusually alike, appearing as regular pyramids with an emphatic layered or step-like construction. The karst-fields (*podi*) are the really picturesque feature of Kanin, completely bare due to their high altitude, and

Kaninski podi below Visoki Kanin

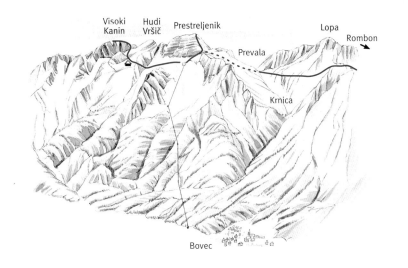

often the light-coloured limestone glitters as if the plateau were covered in snow. If you observe this kingdom of rock at close quarters you'll be dumbfounded at the incredible dynamics of minute details that the millenial activity of water has wrought in Kanin's stony face. Sharp little grooves in picturesque curves plough through the shining slabs and yet one stride away you must take care not to drop into the dark underworld, which has innumerable entrances on these plateaus. Because of the great height difference the water has bored immensely deep abysses in the limestone, some of them being the deepest of all, so that Kanin has won an international reputation as a goal of speleological research. Formerly this was a remote, unfrequented alpine region, but nowadays the cableways that reach high up on both sides have made it easily accessible. The cable cars and chairlifts primarily serve skiers but they also operate in the summer tourist season. Nevertheless, the Kanin range has slopes of true alpine steepness as well. The eastern "border stone" groups of Rombon and Jerebica can boast of such gradients and especially Kanin's western façade above the Resia valley is formed with gigantic sweeps. In this sequestered mountain nook, surrounded by "skyscraper" summits, its centuries-long loneliness and isolation have preserved many things that died out long ago in more lively places. Resia is a veritable ethnological treasure-chest.

Kanin is a mighty barrier on the edge of the high-mountain region and all the climatic blows from the southwest first strike against it. Consequently it has the highest rainfall in the Julian Alps and of course in winter the deepest blanket of snow. This and its favourable configuration make it particularly attractive to skiers, who can quite often continue their enjoyment until the late spring. Yet because natural forces have so powerful an influence here, one must also reckon with the increased danger of sudden storms and lightning. In fine weather Kanin offers exceptional views on account of its solitary position and great height.

Visoki (High) Kanin is the highest summit in the group and stands on the western edge of the central chain. The former paths, which started right down in the valley, are immensely long and tiring; today practically no-one attempts them. The majority of mountaineers make use of the cableway, which has changed Visoki Kanin into one of the most comfortably accessible high summits in the Slovene mountains.

STARTING-POINT:

The bottom station of the Kanin cableway is on the western edge of Bovec, 436 m, and the top station at an altitude of 2202 m at the foot of Prestreljenik. The journey lasts 40 minutes, and you need to enquire in Bovec about the summer timetable.

DESCRIPTION:

From the upper cable car station you climb westwards to the nearby pass, from where the path drops somewhat towards the deep, trough-like valley of Veliki graben, where snow lies far into the summer. Up above you notice the great Prestreljenik window. Soon afterwards a path branches off left to the mountain hut **Dom Petra Skalarja**, 2268 m, which is open only occasionally, and invites you to make this detour, which adds scarcely one hour to the walking time. The path heading for the summit climbs over some steepish rocks (secured) to gain a small saddle at the foot of the next pyramid-shaped mountain (Hudi Vršič, 2478 m). Now this vast rock kingdom, Kaninski podi, stretches out in front of you. The path leads over screes at the base of the summit chain, and at a suitable spot you climb over easy rock onto the wonderfully open ridge, where the giants of the Western Julian Alps, assembled in the Jôf Fuart/Viš and Montasio/Montaž groups, present themselves in full glory. Below, you notice a large snow-covered surface (Kaninski led), which almost deserves the designation of glacier. The Italian route comes from there up to the ridge. The further way on to the summit is exposed in places, but the ridge is well secured so that the level of difficulty is relatively modest. When your view slides unhindered into the depths of the Resia valley, this signals that you've stepped onto the highest point of Kanin. The same route is recommended for the descent.

DIFFICULTY:

A moderately demanding secured route. A comfortable tour with the use of the cable car.

TIMES:

The top cable car station – Visoki Kanin 2 h
Descent 1.30 h
The top cable car station – Dom Petra Skalarja – summit 3 h

Prestreljenik

A shot-through mountain. Monte Forato in Italian

ALTITUDE: 2499 m
STARTING ALTITUDE: 2202 m
HEIGHT DIFFERENCE: 300 m

There is an unwritten rule in the Slovene Alps that a mountain is "very high" if it exceeds 2500 metres. Approximately 25 summits belong to this elite club; Prestreljenik is an unfortunate soul barred from admittance among the chosen few by just one metre. (But what about in the winter?) This mountain, built like a pyramid, stands in the central part of the Kanin group and is even better known than Visoki Kanin itself due to its original appearance. The great curiosity of Prestreljenik is its enormous natural window, which pierces the main ridge to the west below its summit and gives the mountain its name (elucidated in the subtitle). Nobody actually shot through the mountain, but it is said that the devil himself made this gaping hole when he was once in such a hurry he couldn't avoid it in his forceful leap. The peak is exceptional for yet another

The renowned window in the Prestreljenik ridge

reason, but this is a rather humbling particularity – it is the nearest of all the stalwarts. Of course, if you start legging it down below in Bovec, it'll be quite a different matter, and you'll sweat your way 7 hours to the summit. It is the cable car that has brought Prestreljenik down to the level of a short hike; this disgorges you an hour's walk below the summit. It doesn't need stressing that on fine summer days visitors flock up here in crowds and there is really something to see, for the Prestreljenik view is a real "Kanin" one (the term denotes first-class). The approach to the window is also a popular trip.

STARTING-POINT:
From Bovec you come by cable car to an altitude of 2202 m.

DESCRIPTION:
Follow the ski route northwards up to the saddle, 2292 m, and then bear left over the stony slope to the summit of Prestreljenik. Return the same way to the upper cable car station.

The trip to the window is shorter (45 minutes). At first you follow the path for Visoki Kanin, beyond the first saddle a path branches off that climbs over steep screes to the window (with some easy rocky steps higher up). The passage from here to the summit itself is feasible only with pretty demanding rock climbing. Use the way up for the descent.

DIFFICULTY:
The path is easy but quite steep. The ground is crumbling and slippery in places.

TIMES:
The upper cable car station – Prestreljenik 1 h
The upper cable car station – window 45 minutes

31

Rombon

Along the traces of a world slaughter

ALTITUDE: 2208 m
STARTING ALTITUDE: 2202 m, 460 m
HEIGHT DIFFERENCE: 6 m (in fact approx. 400 m), 1750 m

Rombon is the only big mountain of the Kanin group that stands entirely on Slovene territory. From Bovec you see it on the right looking like an incredibly mighty, lonely border stone of the chain, but the view from elsewhere, especially from the Možnica valley, shows that Rombon has completely deserted its relatives. The reason is that a real "Julian" north face, so typical of the central stalwarts of these mountains, falls right here. The approach to Rombon is relatively easy, but long and tiring, and terribly hot in summer. Nevertheless, it doesn't lack visitors, but entices them with its fine, imposing figure and tremendously extensive views. But these unfortunately are not the predominating features of this splendid mountain.

In fact Rombon is burdened with the dark reputation of being the most

Rombon from Svinjak

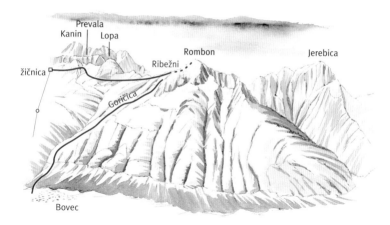

Prevala
Kanin Lopa
Rombon   Jerebica
Ribežni
žičnica
Goričica
Bovec

bloodstained Slovene mountain. In the tempestuous years of 1914-1918 fateful
battles that almost changed the outcome of the war were waged around here.
The front line ran right over Rombon, which at that time was a real mountain
– a fortress. Thousands of innocent soldiers lie below in half-forgotten war
cemeteries, while on the mountain itself the traces of their appalling suffering
will remain for a long time to come. Rombon is marked out by numerous scars,
which today's visitor can in no way overlook. This mountain will forever remain
as a grave warning.

STARTING-POINTS:
The upper cable car station, 2202 m; Bovec, 460 m.
DESCRIPTION:
The way to Rombon that starts with the cable car is absurd for a mountaineer,
as you will mostly walk downhill. The summit is a ridiculous 6 metres higher
than the starting-point, and even the sum of all the ups and downs hardly sounds
like a real mountain tour. We could say that this tour is particularly characteristic
of the Kanin group, which by some strange geological coincidence lacks the vertical
line that is essential for the alpine world. On Kanin it is the horizontal line that
dominates, emphasized by its extensive plateaus and ledge-type structure. All
the same, you'll have a thoroughly good walk, because it's a considerable
distance, even if "on the level". Not to mention the really deep descent.
The ascent to the saddle below Prestreljenik, accomplished in some minutes in
the northerly direction, is a pleasant warming-up exercise for the morning, and
then the promised "path downhill to the mountain" begins. The goal of the first
half-hour descent is the saddle **Prevala**, 2067 m, which divides the central Kanin
chain into two. From here on both the Slovene and Italian sides two deeply cut
valleys such as ski tourers dream of drop away. Here the path orients itself
towards the east and winds over the foot of a finely shaped, steep and barely
accessible mountain, Lopa, 2406 m. For a long time you keep on the level, and
very comfortably so, since the former military transport route is excellently
preserved. Precisely this section explains why you were invited to make the

198

tour from the cableway instead of ascending Rombon in mountaineering fashion, from the valley. All around, the Kanin "kingdom of stone" is spread out, a sobering karst world, reminiscent of a petrified glacier. If you're not in a hurry, do allow yourself a short hike of discovery in this wonderful world of rock dynamics frozen in time. Only take care not to break your leg on the knife-sharp limestone sculptures, and not to fall into some abyss, for there is no shortage of them here. Some are over 1000 metres deep! But never mind, the path itself is completely safe; when you pass over the foot of the most regularly shaped mountain pyramid in the Kanin group (Črnelska špica, 2332 m), this horizontal walk suddenly ends with a view down into the bowels of the Možnica valley. From this point the ridge **Ribežni** stretches eastwards towards Rombon, with the path winding mostly to the right of it. You approach the distinctive summit structure of Rombon as you gently descend, here and there peeping over some notch into the vertiginous depths of Možnica, but you must, of course, after all climb upwards to reach the summit itself. Up above a reward is waiting for you in the form of one of the most beautiful views in the Julian Alps.

DESCENT:

Down to Bovec you have 1750 metres' height difference! The path descends towards the south; to reach an intermediate summit, named **Čukla**, 1767 m, you can choose between the more demanding direct route or the easier detour to the right. On Čukla stands a well-preserved monument to the unfortunate soldiers who died on the mountain for goals which were not their own. As you continue the descent, the numerous remains of this world slaughter will command your thoughtful consideration. Lower down you finally come in front of remains of buildings which did not serve the ends of destruction. In earlier times the sheep pasture of **Goričica**, 1336 m, flourished here. The further descent is quite a hard nut for your knees. The steep path twists partly through the forest, but more often over open ground exposed to the heat. Even when you reach the first farmstead, Bovec is still half an hour's distance away.

The route just outlined is, of course, a uphill challenge to be tackled by the "real mountaineers", for whom the cable car is "infra dig". If you do decide on this very strenuous route, you need to look in the northern "suburb" of Bovec, Kaninska vas, for the turning with the waymarked path which winds northwestwards to the last farmhouses, where you can fill your water bottle by a drinking trough. The way is long and hot. You need a good 2 h to planina Goričica, walking more in the sun than in the shade of the forest. The main route then runs left of the foot of Čukla, but the ascent to this historical point is essential. An hour's walk above Čukla brings you to the summit of Rombon.

DIFFICULTY:

This tour is more strenuous and hot than demanding. The waymarks are reliable but do keep a good eye on them so as not to go astray on any of the numerous side paths.

TIMES:

The cableway – Rombon 5 h
Rombon – Bovec 3 h
Bovec – Rombon 5-6 h

32

Jerebica

The easternmost mountain of the Western Julian Alps

ALTITUDE: 2126 m
STARTING ALTITUDE: 793 m
HEIGHT DIFFERENCE: 1400 m

Jerebica is an exceptionally fine and independent mountain in the eastern chain of the Kanin group. It stands near the Predel road pass, where the Eastern and Western Julian Alps meet, with Jerebica having precisely the position mentioned in the above subtitle. The state border runs along these ridges, so Jerebica naturally has an Italian name too: Cima del Lago, referring to the lake that lies at its foot. The Slovene name has a completely different meaning as the mountain is called after the alpine hen partridge, goodness knows why. The best view of Jerebica is from the Koritnica valley, where it displays the noble appearance of some grand mansion with numerous supporting pillars. To the west below the mountain the Možnica valley rests in solitude. Surrounded by mighty faces from the south, east and north, it gives the impression of inaccessibility. It's certainly true that only

The view from the Ribežni towards Jerebica (left), Mangart and Jalovec

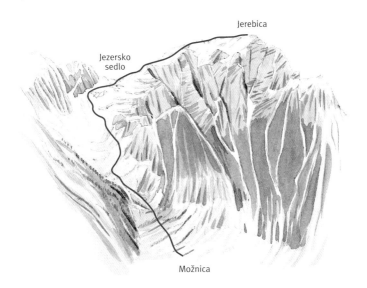

Jerebica

Jezersko
sedlo

Možnica

experienced rock-climbers can reach it directly from Možnica, Koritnica or from Predel. But like the majority of mountains, Jerebica also has its weak point, which is the west ridge, linking it with the central Kanin group. An easy, marvellously panoramic waymarked path runs along it, yet even the approach to the ridge from Možnica or from the Italian side is relatively simple, so that Jerebica is open to a very wide circle of mountaineers. The view is one of the most beautiful. It's difficult to decide where to turn one's attention first, to the Eastern Julians, undulating beyond the nearest ridge scenery of Loška stena, to the majestic pair Mangart and Jalovec above the head of Koritnica, or to the towering Jôf Fuart/Viš and Montasio/Montaž groups to the west. Below, your gaze rests on the green carpets drawn up at the foot of the peaks and on the rippling blue surface of a lake. Despite Jerebica's decidedly enticing trump card, only a few mountaineers make their way up there. Jerebica stands somewhat to the side within the Slovene alpine world, and the tour itself, notwithstanding its technically undemanding nature, is also quite long and strenuous. So the visitor to its summit has the pleasant feeling of belonging to a select band. Nature in this solitary corner is generous with surprises as well. Perhaps you will jump aside, startled, when some shy wild partridge (a reminder of the mountain's name) flutters away from behind a rock.

STARTING-POINT:

The Možnica valley. A rather rough forest road leads into it, branching off from the main road above the bridge over the River Koritnica approximately 2 km below Log pod Mangartom. After three kilometres you reach a guest house, **Dom v Možnici**, 793 m, an unusual building adapted from a former border guardhouse (it is open in summer, and later at the weekends, overnight accommodation is possible, parking area).

DESCRIPTION:

The road above the guest house is no longer practicable, but you notice waymarks on trees along the remnants of it. For half an hour the path runs along the valley bottom, then beyond a broad scree in the beech forest turns sharply right and begins to ascend towards Jerebica. Shortly afterwards it climbs over a band of rock, where the mountain's only security aids provide help. Higher up the forest begins to yield to grassy stretches, and here you must carefully follow the waymarks which indicate the scarcely visible path. The route makes a considerable bend to the left, rising at the foot of the pillared face of Snežni vrh. A long diagonal towards the right across rough scree then runs out onto the saddle **Jezersko sedlo** (Lake Saddle), 1720 m, in the main ridge. All of a sudden the mighty peaks of the Western Julian Alps appear before you as you reach the spot where the Italian path from the other side intersects. A good 3 h to here.

The ridge walk towards the summit of Jerebica (on your right of course) is the finest part of the tour. In fact the path keeps to the ridge only here and there, mostly it drops just below it on the Italian side, thus avoiding two outcrops. This easy, gentle walk providing wonderful views is indeed pure enjoyment. The final ascent over grassy slopes to the crown of Jerebica is on the Slovene side, and the summit is like a broad plateau, open all around. From Jezersko sedlo 1.30 h. Use the same route for the descent.

DIFFICULTY:

Technically a relatively easy tour but long and strenuous. The renewed waymarks are reliable, only you must watch out for them in deep grass, where the path can hardly be seen.

TIMES:

Možnica – Jerebica 5 h

Jerebica – Možnica 3-4 h

The Možnica valley

33

Mangart

The humbled giant above Koritnica

ALTITUDE: 2679 m
STARTING ALTITUDE: 2055 m
HEIGHT DIFFERENCE: 620 m

Why such a subtitle? This will be explained a little later, first the mountain should be presented. Mangart is the alpine champion of the ridges above Koritnica, along which the state border partly runs. This third highest Slovene mountain is one of the mightiest. Its finely shaped summit cupola rises far above the Koritnica valley on the Slovene side, where the extensive faces are sliced by wild gullies. The Italian side is even steeper; here extends one of the most majestic north faces in the entire Julian Alps. Especially its monolithically carved eastern part belongs to the most demanding and highly desired goals of rock-climbers. These mighty faces are seen reflected in the mirror of the twin lakes Laghi di Fusine (Slovene Belopeška jezera), the superb ornament of the Mangart valley. With its long, barely passable eastern ridge Mangart is

Looking from the Predel pass towards Mangartsko sedlo and Mangart

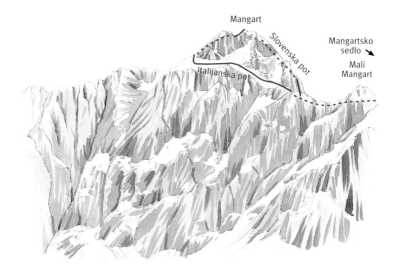

Mangart

Slovenska pot

Italijanska pot

Mangartsko sedlo

Mali Mangart

linked with the Jalovec and Ponca groups. Only on the western side is the mountain shaped somewhat more kindly. Below the summit cupola lies a small plateau, but unfortunately it smells rather of petrol because the highest Slovene road reaches right up to a saddle in the border ridge, at 2055 m. Slightly below this saddle stands the mountain hut **Mangartska koča**, 1906 m, so it scarcely needs explaining why Mangart is one of the most frequented Slovene summits. This reputation, however, was temporarily interrupted by the catastrophic landslide in the year 2000, which destroyed part of the road; in the summer of 2002 the improved road was reopened. Paths at all levels of difficulty lead up to Mangart, the combination of the Slovene and Italian routes chosen here constitutes a fine though quite demanding round tour. If you are not sufficiently trained for the steep Slovene route, then climb to the summit by the much easier Italian route, described for the descent.

STARTING-POINT:
Mangartsko sedlo (Mangart Saddle), 2055 m, to the west at the foot of the summit structure of Mangart. Access is by road from Koritnica (17 km from Log pod Mangartom, 27 km from Bovec). Road toll! Half an hour below the saddle stands Mangartska koča, 1906 m. The road is extremely picturesque and in places very boldly constructed; a number of tunnels add variety. Generally it is well maintained. Passionate walkers can mostly avoid the road, for a marked footpath winds left of the road down below (and crosses the alp Mangartska planina, where you can buy good sheep's cheese), while higher up it keeps mostly to the right. On foot to the saddle takes 3 h.

DESCRIPTION:
From the parking area set your direction towards Mangart and at first it's a leisurely walk over grass and gently sloping rocks on the Slovene side of the ridge. Thus you traverse the foot of Mali Mangart, on the small saddle behind

it you step onto the main ridge, which is very precipitous here. From the north the very demanding Italian secured route, a "via ferrata", leads to this point. Soon afterwards you reach the fork where the Slovene route turns right. You climb over rough scree to the foot of Mangart's west face. Decisively cut into it, from left to right, is a steep gully, which the route follows. Immediately on entry you take hold of the steel rope, which guides you safely over the face. We recommend self-belaying and wearing a helmet. The gully runs out onto a promontory giving a fine view, and then the path bears left and climbs over the last steep places. Just below the summit a jet of water springing out takes you by surprise. The summit of Mangart is really ample, and the view that greets you is tremendously embracing. Naturally, since you reached a very high mountain.

If you've chosen the Italian route for the approach, turn left at the above-mentioned fork and in a long traverse across the easy rock of the northern flank of this summit section you climb to a saddle to the east below the summit. There you swing sharply right and along the panoramic ridge reach the nearby summit.

DESCENT:

From the summit the Italian route descends eastwards along a broad ridge, and after 15 minutes turns left onto the mountain's northern flank. A long traverse to the left across easy rock leads you to the fork where the round tour is completed. Snow can lie on the north side of Mangart far into the summer. At that time the Italian route is safely negotiable only by experienced mountaineers, accomplished in the use of ice-axe and crampons.

DIFFICULTY:

The Slovene route is steep and exposed, but well secured. If self-belaying is used and a helmet worn, it is safe and very recommendable. The Italian route is much easier, but often lies under snow until late summer. Under such conditions we warn against using it. The round tour described is comfortable and extremely beautiful. Elsewhere you certainly won't easily come to such a proud mountain with so little effort!

TIMES:

Mangartsko sedlo – Mangart 2 h (the Italian route is somewhat longer)
Descent 1.15 h

34

Bavški Grintavec

In the heart of Posočje

ALTITUDE: 2347 m
STARTING ALTITUDE: 962 m
HEIGHT DIFFERENCE: 1400 m

Unlike Kanin, Mangart, Jalovec, Prisank, Triglav and Lepa špica, which only half belong to the wonderful Posočje realm, Bavški Grintavec is a true "Trentar". This imposing, finely shaped mountain with its cupola summit section dominates the heads of two valleys: Zadnja Trenta and Bavšica. From here Grintavec displays its extensive northern face, which rises above its massive, forested foot. The southern aspect above the Soča valley is one single, almost two-thousand-metre-high sheer slope, marked out by unusually shaped, vertically projecting rock strata. From this side there was an old path to Grintavec, which nowadays is used only very rarely. 2000 metres of burning steepness without any real relief is a challenge only for mountaineering "masochists". A new route from the north is used now, but

Bavški Grintavec seen from Kriški podi

this also isn't easy and Bavški Grintavec comes to be seen sooner or later as a demanding mountain. Compared with other champions of the Julian Alps, it is an oasis of wild and solitary nature.

STARTING-POINT:
The Zadnja Trenta valley. Parking area by the homestead Florijeva domačija at the end of the road, 962 m (2 km from the mountain hut Koča pri izviru Soče).

DESCRIPTION:
The waymarks cross over the extensive shingle and then up to the head of the valley the path winds along the southern bank of this dry river-bed. Before a real ascent begins you turn onto the right side and walk for a good hour in the pleasant shade of the beech forest. The path is quite steep but easy. Later the gradient eases off and a broad basin opens up in front of you that already has a high-mountain character. Bavški Grintavec now appears in full splendour as you notice the old wooden hut of the abandoned alp **Zapotok,** 1385 m (1.30 h to here). This truly delightful spot breathes an air of the bygone times when dairy farming flourished here, and beckons you to enjoy a pleasant rest by the lively stream. The old shepherd's hut still offers unspoilt romantic souls its simple shelter for the night.

From here the path climbs steeeply towards the left into a lovely larch forest. Easier walking follows over the increasingly stony slopes to a fork beneath the entry into an oval basin at the foot of the summit structure of Grintavec. If you wish to gain the summit by an easier route, turn left. You enter the basin just mentioned through a rocky gap, and then climb from it over well-secured rock in a rightward direction onto the northern ridge, shaped just here like a level shoulder (connection with the more difficult route). The further rock-climbing

Autumn on the Zapotok alp

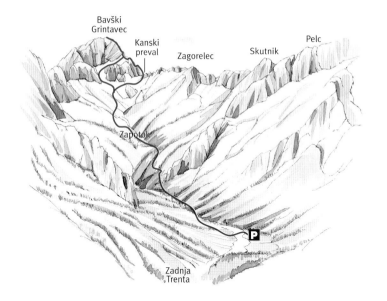

towards the summit is steep and exposed. The reliable steel rope is strung across rather brittle rocks, shaped in one place into a picturesque chimney. The steep gradient ceases only just below the summit. Bavški Grintavec stands at the heart of a really majestic mountain arc, so the view is one of the most spectacular.

For the very experienced, "sporty" type of mountaineer, the righthand route can be recommended. This gradually ascends from the fork over rough scree and then climbs over broken rocks to gain the saddle **Kanski preval**, 2030 m, at the foot of the Grintavec north ridge. Practically at once the ridge soars up, almost vertically. A few steps above the saddle you take hold of the steel rope and don't let it go for a good half hour, until you reach the level shoulder where you join the previously described route. In this demanding section the path winds along natural passages and is extremely exposed, in places even "athletic". Self-belaying is obligatory.

DESCENT:
Naturally you'll return by the easier route.

DIFFICULTY:
The path is easy as far as the foot of the summit structure of Grintavec, but above that the terrain is very demanding. The harder variant is one of the most demanding climbing routes in Slovenia. The security aids are reliable. Self-belaying and wearing a helmet are recommended. The orientation is easy.

TIMES:
Zadnja Trenta – Zapotok 1.30-2 h
Zapotok – Bavški Grintavec 3 h
Descent to the valley 3 h

35

Jalovec

The sunny side of the mountain-crystal

ALTITUDE: 2645 m
STARTING ALTITUDE: 2064 m
HEIGHT DIFFERENCE: 600 m (+ 500–1600 m from the valley to the starting-point)

The architecture of Jalovec has a built-in feature which you notice from wherever you look at it. The straight lines of the ridges and the abrupt "fractures" emphasize its stylistic unity. The mountain reminds you of a huge crystal. The northern side above the Planica valley (see pp. 149-151) with its steep lines shows elements of a strictly Gothic structure, but Jalovec presents two faces on its sunny side. The southeast face above Zadnja Trenta rises above its extensive base, while the magnificent west face, hidden and solitary, falls right into the Koritnica valley. On the whole, the sunny side is more gentle than the northern one, so that the easiest route to Jalovec is that from the south. But then everything is relative, and this "easiest" route is actually quite demanding, noticeably more difficult than the approaches to Triglav and

A view of Jalovec from Zadnja Trenta

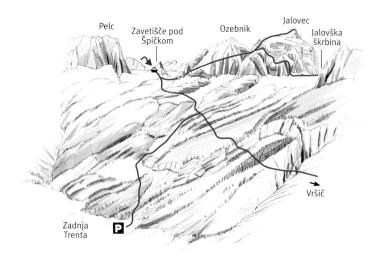

Prisank, for instance. Because these valleys are so tremendously deep, making the ascent at one fell swoop is more strenuous than managing it from Tamar, but fortunately the tour can be greatly alleviated by using the small mountain hut **Zavetišče pod Špičkom**, 2064 m, in the south at the foot of the summit structure of Jalovec. Thus the ascent from the Soča side will be recommended as a two-day tour.

STARTING-POINT:

Zavetišče pod Špičkom, 2064 m. As many as four paths lead to it, and still some other little variant, and it may be difficult to decide on one. It will be best to describe all four.

- The path from **Zadnja Trenta** is the most direct, and the natural approach to Jalovec from the south. It begins by the picturesque homestead Florijeva domačija near the parking area, 962 m, at the end of the road into this valley (2 km from the hut Koča pri izviru Soče, see the description on pp. 160-161). At first the path winds in steep serpentine bends in pleasant shade; the gradient is easier above the tree-line. You must carefully follow the signposts at the fairly numerous forks, but in fact you can spot the hut from quite a distance, pressed into the slope of a steep little peak left of Jalovec (called Špiček). The way seems to drag somewhat in the last section. From Zadnja Trenta to the hut 3 h.

- The path from the road pass **Vršič**, 1611 m (34 km from Bovec, 12 km from Na Logu in Trenta) is more frequently used than the previous route. It's difficult to explain why, as it is longer and quite monotonous, and in the height of summer exceedingly hot. But one has to admit that this comfortable, gradual ascent offers exceptional views. From Vršič the path first drops a little to avoid the rocky outlying spurs of Mojstrovka, then gently winds uphill towards the west. The forest increasingly gives way to open slopes. These flanks are very extensive and Jalovec seems reluctant to appear any nearer. After two hours' walking, a path branches off right by a hunters' hut which leads directly towards Jalovec, but the path to Špiček continues in the same direction, slowly becoming steeper. Only above the intersection with the path from Zadnja Trenta does the slope really slant uphill, so that the last hour approaching the hut visible from a distance does feel "mountain-like". From Vršič to the hut takes 4 h.

- From the **Koritnica** valley the path is very steep and demanding, recommendable only to experienced lovers of solitude and alpine wildness. It begins at the head of this valley, reached by a forest road (closed for public use) from the village of Log pod Mangartom, 4 km (see the description on pp. 162-163). About 15 minutes' walk above the road and the last shepherd's hut a not very noticeable path branches off right, which crosses a stream and then, gently ascending towards the right, traverses an extensive scree to the foot of a steep face. You enter the face below a deep black cleft. A sort of ledge climbs steeply leftwards from here, which involves exposed climbing but is facilitated by a reliable steel rope. The gradient is sustained as far as the tree-line. Higher up, between the massifs of Jalovec and Loška stena, a step-like valley is formed, which finally runs out onto the saddle **Čez Brežice**, 1980 m, where the long ridge of Loška stena adjoins the Jalovec group. From the end of the road 2.30 h. From here bear left (eastwards) over a steep section onto the grassy ridge. Using a small, exposed ledge to avoid the small peak of Mali Ozebnik on the right, you climb along a gully to the notch **Škrbina za Gradom**, 2277 m, which divides the central Jalovec group from the Pelci ridge. Now the path descends to a plateau of rough scree and heads towards the hut, which stands on the right below the steep peak Špiček. From the end of the road at the head of Koritnica 4.30 h. A very demanding route.

- The path from the **Bavšica** valley through **Bala** is a variant of the approach

Below the summit of Jalovec

just described, and joins it on the saddle Čez Brežice. The walk there is perfectly easy though long, and exceptionally romantic and picturesque due to the utter remoteness of this region. (For Bavšica see the description on pp. 164-165.) You leave the road by the water trough at the head of the valley, 700 m, and set off along a comfortable path towards the northeast. Above the first steep stretch you come to the houses of the abandoned hamlet of Logje, where you enter the Bala valley, squeezed between the great heights of Loška stena (on the left) and the two ridges of Pihavec and the Pelci. The valley ascends in steps. In the first basin you notice the remains of the alp Bala, 1181 m, soon afterwards passing a solitary hunters' hut. From behind the saddle Preval, 1560 m, the expansive cwm of Lanževica opens up, above which a high steep slope awaits you beneath the **Čez Brežice** saddle, 1980 m. 3.30 h to here. The path is insufficiently waymarked, but the orientation isn't difficult. Now the more demanding section of the route begins, as outlined in the preceding paragraph. You begin, of course, towards the right, climb to Škrbina za Gradom, then descend to Zavetišče pod Špičkom. From Bavšica 5-6 h (the height difference is 1600 m!).

DESCRIPTION:

If you have come to Zavetišče pod Špičkom from Vršič or from Trenta, the demanding part of the route will only begin now, whereas the route from Koritnica or Bavšica is more demanding than the actual climb to the summit. From the hut the path drops towards the northeast to the foot of the south face of Jalovec's neighbour, Ozebnik. You then bypass this mountain on the right by a steep, exposed climb. The dangerous places are well-secured. At the base of the summit structure of Jalovec you can recover your breath on a small plateau and then make for the final steep stretch. As your gaze sweeps through the steep gully of Loški žleb down into Koritnica (a dangerous snowfield lies here far into the summer), the path ascends leftwards over step-like rocks towards the summit ridge. You reach this about half an hour below the top. The last part of the climb you are occupied with the wonderful vistas, but you're also aware you will soon mount upon this very high and imposing peak. To climb Jalovec is a prestigious tour, in no way lagging behind the ascent of Triglav.

DESCENT:

If you're returning to the south, you must descend to Zavetišče pod Špičkom the same way, and then make your own choice of route to the valley.

DIFFICULTY:

Jalovec is a demanding mountain. The southern approaches are somewhat easier than the northern one, but nevertheless require the mountaineer to be excellently prepared in terms of experience and condition. Of the combinations described, the easiest two routes are from Trenta and Vršič, while the most difficult is from Koritnica.

TIMES:

These are given in the individual sections. The shortest route is from Trenta, the longest from Bavšica.

Zavetišče pod Špičkom – Jalovec 2.30-3 h

p. 213: Jalovec from Zadnja Trenta

The Karavanke

The Karavanke are the longest Slovene mountain range. This succession of summits extends for 120 km from the extreme northwest corner of the country to the town of Slovenj Gradec, which marks the beginning of Štajerska (Styria). The mountains represent Slovenia's fringe on the north, for the Slovene-Austrian border runs along this ridge. In contrast to the Julian or Kamnik-Savinja Alps, which are built in groups and branch out in different directions, the Karavanke have a simple form, basically a uniform ridge, which stretches in an unusually straight line from west to east. The simple structure is especially evident in the western part, where the summits line up like a cohort of soldiers. In the east the ridge is somewhat more varied and branches out in places. In the middle section the Karavanke touch and almost intertwine with the Kamnik-Savinja Alps, so that sometimes it's quite difficult to determine where a summit belongs. In altitude the Karavanke lag behind the highest summits of the Slovene Alps and only rarely exceed 2000 metres. On average the western part is higher, and here rises the highest peak of all, Stol, 2236 m. The contrast between the northern and southern sides is very noticeable, which is a general characteristic of Slovene mountain ridges. Thus the Karavanke show the Austrians real alpine north faces, while the Slovenes see mostly grassy slopes, sinking into extensive forests.

The Karavanke represent a gentle, friendly mountain range, inviting the visitor with relatively unspoilt nature, an abundance of alpine flowers, easy access and wonderful views. No mountaineers' "highway" reaches these ridges and here you can enjoy blessed mountain solitude. So let lovers of steep, demanding approaches and alpine grandeur simply stay in the Julian and Kamnik-Savinja Alps. The state border, running along the entire Karavanke ridge, doesn't signify any hindrance for the mountaineer.

There follows a description of a modest selection of the most recommendable goals in the Karavanke. These are arranged unequally and do not have any starting-points in common. Thus they can't be placed in a self-contained subsection, as in the description of other mountains. Two lovely, easy summits from the western Karavanke chain (Peč and Trupejevo poldne) have already been described; because of their common starting-point they were simply appended to the chapter Northern Approaches, which otherwise comprises tours in the Julian Alps (see pp. 107-109).

pp. 214-215: Lake Bled with the Karavanke as backdrop

36

Golica

Botanical garden of the Karavanke

ALTITUDE: 1835 m
STARTING ALTITUDE: 933 m
HEIGHT DIFFERENCE: 902 m

Golica is a beautiful, broadly extended mountain in the western chain of the Karavanke above the Upper Sava Valley. It rises west of Stol, the chief summit, and together with it dominates the surroundings of the iron-mining town Jesenice. The southern side is characteristic, the forest ceases at about 1500 m, as if it were cut off, and above it rise steep grassy slopes right up to the summit, without a single rock or bush to disturb them. So the name makes excellent sense, Golica denoting "Gola gora", i.e. Bare Mountain. At about mid height the slopes are shaped into a broad basin, with the scattered homesteads of the village Planina pod Golico. Thanks to its comfortable access and exceptional view of the Julian Alps, revealed in all their glory across the valley, Golica is the most frequently visited mountain in the Karavanke. It owes

A narcissi meadow with a herdsmen's hut below Golica

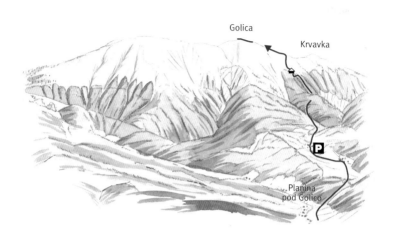

Golica

Krvavka

Planina pod Golico

its reputation to a large extent to the exceptional wealth of its flora. The slopes of Golica form a real alpine garden, which you can never tire of looking at. The biggest holiday takes place in May when narcissi bloom there in stupendous abundance, making the mountain look from far around as if white with snow. This wonderful natural phenomenon generally occurs in the second half of May.

STARTING-POINT:

The starting-point is the village **Planina pod Golico**, 933 m. This is reached by road from Jesenice (the turning is in the western part of the town); 4 km, with a regular bus service. From the village centre with its church and inn, the road reaches a bare kilometre further towards the northeast, to the guest house Pri Fencu.

DESCRIPTION:

Here the waymarked path begins, winding quite steeply through the forest. At the bottom end of the load cableway, it swings somewhat to the right and climbs through ever sparser forest to the mountain hut **Koča na Golici**, 1582 m, which stands on the already open slope. Heading for the summit, the path continues through a little grassy valley left above the hut and leads to the border ridge 15 minutes' walk east of the summit. Your last steps bring great enjoyment, which naturally reaches its climax on the top. The extremely extensive view embraces the entire northern side of the Julian Alps to the south, while far to the north in undulating line stride the giants of the Hohe Tauern. Below you sparkle the lakes of Austrian Carinthia. The descent is easiest by the same route.

TIMES:

Planina pod Golico - Koča na Golici 2 h

Koča na Golici - Golica 1 h

Descent 2.30 h

37

Stol

The highest summit

ALTITUDE: 2236 m
STARTING ALTITUDE: 1171 m (557 m)
HEIGHT DIFFERENCE: 1065 m (1679 m)

Stol is one of the most distinctive and renowned Slovene mountains. Its dominant position above the Gorenjska plain and its broad-shouldered figure explain why Stol is eye-catching from near and far. Lake Bled, with which it comprises one of the loveliest and most renowned views of the Slovene landscape, would be sadly impoverished without this majestic alpine backcloth. Since its slopes fall steeply from the ridges with hardly any interruption right to the bottom of the valley, Stol is an incredibly mighty mountain and a great challenge for the mountaineer. Yet despite its steep appearance, it is easily accessible, and numerous paths lead up to it. The view from the summit is simply incomparable. The usual approach will be described from the mountain hut Valvasorjev dom.

Towards the summit of Stol

If you tackle Stol right from its foot, it will prove fine condition training, but the tour is considerably facilitated by using the road as far as Valvasorjev dom. The footpath begins in the village of **Žirovnica,** 557 m (approximately 8 km east of Jesenice, and about the same from Bled), from where you go by the old road northwards to the beginning of the Završnica valley. Immediately behind the bridge turn right (signpost Završnica) and ascend to the road past some old mills. You will soon notice a comfortable path branching off left (signpost Valvasorjev dom), which gently ascends across a meadow to the beginning of the Rečica valley. When you touch the forest road, the path bears left, and then soon begins to climb straight up through the forest. Higher up you cross the road and before long reach a small plateau where **Valvasorjev dom** stands at 1171 m. 2 h from Žirovnica, 1.30 h from Završnica. The road to the mountain hut branches off on the western edge of Žirovnica (Moste), and runs through the Završnica valley. Near the artificial lake, a pretty rutted road turns off left from the asphalt (signpost Valvasorjev dom). Two intersections are marked with a signpost. 6 km to Valvasorjev dom.

DESCRIPTION:

From here the path runs eastwards. A 10-minute walk on the level ends on Žirovniška planina. In front of a former shepherd's hut the path swings uphill and climbs alternately through the forest and over open slopes. Although the gradient is fairly steep, the walking is comfortable, as the path is arranged in gentle bends. The surroundings are becoming more and more like the high mountains, since the trees remind you of tousled dwarfs. Other vegetation becomes more modest too, high grass changes into soft little cushions, with

Prešernova koča just below the summit of Stol

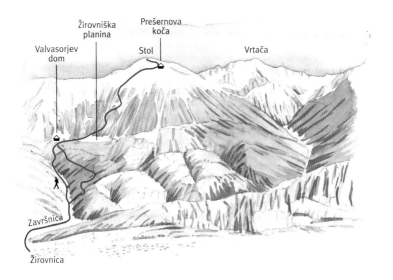

Valvasorjev dom — Žirovniška planina — Prešernova koča — Stol — Vrtača — Završnica — Žirovnica

tiny high-altitude flowers shining among them. The dwarf pine also increases. All of this testifies to the harsh conditions in the high mountains, where nevertheless life persists. The rocky towers and steep gullies also belong to this wild scene, which is steadily becoming barer and more sombre. Above the highest trees and bushes the path ascends along a grassy ridge right of a steep gully, until suddenly the mountain hut **Prešernova koča**, 2174 m, appears, perched on a hummock. It is named after the great Slovene poet France Prešeren, who was born in the village of Vrba at the foot of Stol. Now you see the summit really close. A little above the hut you drop to a saddle just below the head of the mountain, looking forward to reaching the nearby goal. When the snow has melted away, the path is easy and without any danger, but it is not an advisable ascent on hot days. The most favourable descent is by the same route.

Some words must be added about the truly fantastic panorama which this champion of the Karavanke offers. You look from the playful sharp peaks of the Julian Alps to the distant icy giants of the Hohe Tauern in the northwest. To the east it is similarly full of variety, with the ridges of the Kamnik-Savinja Alps and the Karavanke stretching to the horizon. To the north, green Carinthia lies at your feet with the lake Wörther See, and behind that innumerable side-wings, the last outcrops of the Alps, are blended together. You look down on the broad Gorenjska plain as if from an aeroplane, with the bright eye of Lake Bled twinkling happily. On this side, towards the southeast, you can see the furthest: right to the hazy horizon rise gently formed mountain backs, belonging to the Dinaric range.

TIMES:

Valvasorjev dom - Stol 2.30 h

Žirovnica - Stol 4-5 h

38

Košuta

A mighty ridge

ALTITUDE: 2094 m
STARTING ALTITUDE: 1488 m
HEIGHT DIFFERENCE: 606 m

In this mountain group, which lies in the central part of the range between the two passes Ljubelj and Jezersko sedlo, all the features of the Karavanke described in the introduction are gathered together. So Košuta is really a sort of "concentrated mass". The ridge, over 10 kilometres long, has an extremely uniform shape, giving the group a mighty appearance. To the north Košuta shows an extensive face, but the south side is one almost uninterrupted steep grassy slope. Along its foot stretches a long terrace dotted with numerous alps. There isn't any particularly distinctive cut in the line of the ridge, and such a mountain group is inviting in itself for a ridge tour. To traverse the whole of Košuta is an alpinist activity, but here the easy ridge tour in the western part of Košuta, one of the most beautiful in the Karavanke, will be described. Unfortunately Košuta can't be seen as a whole anywhere from the valley on the Slovene side, but it does display itself in majestic form from Storžič, for example. Six independent summits rise above 2000 metres (half the two-thousanders in the entire range!). To enumerate them from west to east: the mighty Veliki vrh (Great Summit), well seen from the Ljubelj road, is the most often visited, Kladivo (Hammer) stands out because of its distinctly rocky form, Tegoška gora and Macesje (Larches) are less noticeable grassy excrescences, but Košutnikov turn, 2133 m (the highest summit in the group, and the most difficult of access), with its rocky, steeply pointed peak boldly jumps up from the row. The ridge is concluded by Tolsta (Corpulent) Košuta. Between Kladivo and Tegoška gora, Škrbina (Notch) is carved out of the ridge, the only noticeable saddle in Košuta. The ridge tour between Veliki vrh and Škrbina will be described.

STARTING-POINT:

The starting point is the mountain hut **Dom na Kofcah**, 1488 m, which stands on the western edge of the above-mentioned terrace at the middle height of the southern slopes of Košuta. The hut is a popular destination for trips because of its fine panoramic position on the broad alp Kofce and comfortable access. The starting-point in the valley is the village of **Podljubelj**, 680 m, on the road from Tržič to the Ljubelj border crossing. The road (signpost Dom na Kofcah) branches off in the northern part of the village. The steep asphalt climbs towards the northeast, and higher up changes to a macadam surface. The road leads to the farm **Matizovec,** approximately 950 m, 4 km, a good 2 h on foot. From here a good waymarked path runs through the forest to the hut, which you reach in a good hour.

DESCRIPTION:

From Kofce you can see Veliki vrh on the left and Kladivo on the right, in between the ridge climbs to a less noticeable rise, Kofce gora. Of course you can climb each mountain individually, but a connecting ridge tour is much finer. The path pushes straight up over the gentle meadow, which at the foot of the steep slope levels out into a lovely terrace. Here the path turns left and diagonally ascends the extensive grassy slope to the summit ridge (and border) between Kofce gora and Veliki vrh. You climb to Veliki vrh, 2088 m, mostly across the lefthand slopes; up there a typical Karavanke view is waiting for you, which cannot be overpraised, since it embraces tremendous expanses to the north and similarly to the south. From Kofce 1.30 h. The path is easy and gradual.

From Veliki vrh you return along the ridge eastwards and continue over **Kofce gora,** 1967 m, towards Kladivo. The walk along the undulating ridge is easy and extremely pleasant. The path mostly winds along the ridge, which is abruptly sliced off on the north side, but on the south side one great field of flowers slips down. **Kladivo,** 2094 m, is a finely shaped, distinctively rocky mountain, with a path leading to it over the southern slope. From Veliki vrh a good hour. You continue the ridge traverse eastwards with a descent to **Škrbina,** 1869 m, the most noticeable saddle in the Košuta ridge. You reach it in half an hour over steep terrain, which demands more attentiveness. From here you descend to the south across the grassy slope to the Pungrat alp, which lies on the same lengthwise terrace as Kofce. You turn right onto the road and follow it on level

Dom na Kofcah with Kofce gora and Kladivo in the background

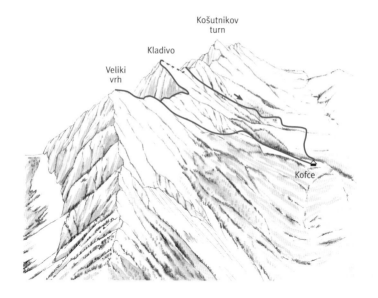

towards the west, past the herdmen's huts on planina Šija to Dom na Kofcah, where the round tour, lasting 5 to 6 hours, is completed. The walking is mostly easy, only the descent from Kladivo to Škrbina is more demanding. A very recommendable tour with exceptional views.

TIMES:

Dom na Kofcah - Veliki vrh 1.30 h
Veliki vrh - Kladivo 1 h
Kladivo - Škrbina 30 min
A circular tour 5-6 h

The view of Veliki vrh from Dom na Kofcah

39

Olševa

In the tracks of prehistoric man

ALTITUDE: 1929 m
STARTING ALTITUDE: 1232 m (642 m)
HEIGHT DIFFERENCE: 697 m (1287 m)

Olševa will be the only mountain included from the eastern Karavanke, thus rounding off this collection of mountaineering goals above the Upper Savinja Valley. Olševa is a typical Karavanke mountain. If Košuta was dubbed a sort of "concentrated mass" of the range, then this comparison can be extended: Olševa is "Košuta in miniature". And indeed these two mountain backs are similar in several respects. The summit ridge with its scarcely noticeable ups and downs, the steep grassy slopes above its expansive forested base, the friendly sunny terrace across the entire southern slope at middle height, and still some other common point could be found. Only that on Olševa, everything is in reduced form, including the altitude, which doesn't exceed 2000 metres, even on the highest summit Govca. Olševa is famous for its wealth of alpine flora, its solitude and wonderful views, especially of the magnificent fan of the Kamnik-Savinja Alps to the north. But the greatest point of interest is the karst cave of Potočka zijalka, carved into the mountain's eastern flank at a height of 1700 m. Finds were excavated here from the Stone Age, including remains of people, bone and stone tools and numerous bones of the cave bear. Olševa is a distinctive mountain, visible even from the summits of the distant Julian Alps. Unlike other Karavanke mountains, Olševa stands entirely on Slovene territory except for its extreme western corner. The forested northern side falls into the Koprivna valley. To the south its appears like a great trapezium. The western part of the mountain has some high-altitude features, but otherwise the walking is easy and pleasant. A round tour will be described, making acquaintance with the main characteristics of this beautiful, friendly mountain.

STARTING-POINT:

The starting-point in the valley is the village of **Solčava**, 642 m, in the Upper Savinja Valley. The ascent begins at the mountain hut **Koča pod Olševo**, 1232 m, near the church of the Holy Spirit (cerkev sv. Duha), which represents the centre of the village Podolševa. (On this extensive, very panoramic terrace, which runs across the whole southern side of Olševa, the homesteads comprising the village are scattered about.) From Solčava by road 8 km.

DESCRIPTION:

The most favourable footpath begins by the Firšt inn beside the River Savinja 2 km above Solčava. It leads west above the gully of the Lašek stream, 2 h to the hut. The drive along the panoramic road from the valley Logarska dolina is also recommendable. It branches off by the guest-house Sestre Logar and climbs to the above-mentioned lengthwise terrace. Offering marvellous views, it winds eastwards, passing by a source of mineral water, and continues towards Raduha. 13 km to the above-mentioned church.

From the church a gentle forest track climbs northwards and in half an hour leads to the western foot of the summit structure of Olševa. The going gets steeper, the path climbs left beside a rocky face, then for the last time through forest, which now begins to give way to grassy slopes. It is joined from the left by the path from Austria. 15 minutes higher you stand in front of the impressive entrance to **Potočka zijalka**. If you want to see the interior of this 115-metre-long cave, you'll need a torch. Above the cave the slope is steeper, and in places the way is exposed. Here and there you'll encounter some iron security aid. You're now coming into high-mountain terrain, as seen by the rocky towers which thrust up above the steep grassy slopes. In early summer there is a brightly coloured mountain garden here. The path winds across the southern slope somewhat below the ridge, but mounts it 10 minutes before you reach the highest summit of Olševa – **Govca**, 1929 m.

DESCENT:

Instead of descending the same way we recommend the ridge path eastwards. This is an enjoyable high promenade, which begins with a descent by a rather narrow, partly rocky ridge, and then you walk along a broad, gently undulating back, a soft carpet, while you take in the extremely expansive view on all sides.

Flowers in abundance at the foot of Olševa

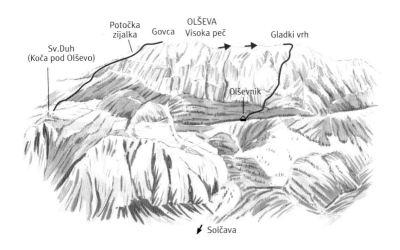

Sv.Duh
(Koča pod Olševo)

Potočka
zijalka

Govca

OLŠEVA
Visoka peč

Gladki vrh

Olševnik

Solčava

The eastern summit of Olševa is called **Gladki vrh**, 1810 m, a bare hour on from Govca. Now you head straight downhill to the south over a steep, grassy slope, which lower down is covered with forest. You gain the road by the Olševnik farm. The circular tour is completed by hiking along the road (3 km) back to the church. (From the Olševnik farmstead you can drop straight down into Solčava by a waymarked path which partly joins the road, 1.30 h.)

TIMES:
(Solčava - Koča pod Olševo 2 h)
Koča pod Olševo - Govca 2 h
Govca - Gladki vrh 1 h
Gladki vrh - Koča pod Olševo 1 h
The entire circle 5 h

The Kamnik-Savinja Alps

The Slovene capital Ljubljana prides itself on having a beautiful and dynamic panorama. It lies in a basin surrounded on three sides by medium hills which are so near the people of Ljubljana can escape the city's hustle and bustle amid pleasant greenery and even rocks, if they have just a couple of hours to spare. The northern horizon is composed of a glorious array of high mountains, with distinctive, finely shaped outlines. These are the Kamnik-Savinja Alps. Why the two names? At the foot of the southern side of the chain lies the small town of Kamnik, while the northern side is marked out by the River Savinja, which has its source in the heart of the mountains. The inhabitants of these two regions, both of them in love with their own corner, have agreed on a compromise name – the Kamnik-Savinja Alps. It's a pity that the old, neutral name of **the Grintovci** is dying out. In their extent, appearance and character these mountains are a sort of Julian Alps on a small scale. The major summits greatly exceed 2000 metres. The backbone of the range is precisely oriented from east to west. The outstanding summits here are Ojstrica, Planjava, Brana, Turska gora, Skuta, Grintovec (this is the highest – 2558 m) and Kočna. Where the ridge continues, beyond the deep Kokra valley, stands the solitary stalwart Storžič. Along the side ridges some other summits rise high, such as Raduha and Mrzla gora in the north and Kalški greben in the south. The visitor to the Kamnik-Savinja Alps has three main starting-points. The southern approaches begin in the Kamniška Bistrica valley, the northwestern ones in Jezersko, the name for the upper part of the Kokra valley, and the northeastern ones in the valley Logarska dolina, where the Savinja river has its source. The density of paths and mountain huts is similar to that in the Julian Alps.

pp. 228-229: A view of the Kamnik Alps from Stari grad above Kamnik

Kamniška Bistrica

The valley of the River Kamniška Bistrica bites into the heart of the mountains from the south. Like the majority of Slovene alpine valleys, this was shaped in its upper part by a former glacier into a broad trough, from which the river pushes its way through wild gorges. Above the head of the valley the "cream" of the range is gathered together. Apart from Kočna, all the champions of the major chain appear in this magnificent necklace. This region is characterized by exceptionally big height differences, for the steep slopes rise directly to the summits above the head of the valley, which lies at an altitude of approximately 600 metres. Consequently one-day tours to the peaks above Kamniška Bistrica are quite strenuous and the majority of mountaineers accomplish them by staying overnight high up – there is no lack of mountain huts. Eastwards above the valley stretches the plateau of Velika planina, 1666 m, which can be reached by a cableway. In the west Kamniška Bistrica is fringed by the small group of Kalški greben, 2224 m, with its popular ski centre Krvavec. There is no compact settlement in this valley, only a solitary farmhouse here and there. A good asphalt road leads to Kamniška Bistrica (13 km from Kamnik, 36 km from Ljubljana, regular bus services), which ends at the mountain hut **Dom v Kamniški Bistrici**, 601 m, situated near by the river which gave the valley its name.

Skuta seen from Kamniška Bistrica

40

Grintovec

The highest peak in the range

ALTITUDE: 2558 m
STARTING ALTITUDE: 601 m
HEIGHT DIFFERENCE: 1957 m

The view from the south presents the leading mountain in the form of a beautiful pyramid. It rises northwest above the Kamniška Bistrica valley as the concluding peak. Compared with Triglav, it is less dominant in its own company, since the neighbouring Kočna and Skuta come only a little behind in altitude, and still less in terms of beauty and mighty character. But all the same, Grintovec is the highest summit in the range and never lacks visitors. This is also partly due to its easy access. The path from Bistrica is considered the normal route, but the height difference of almost 2000 metres makes one seriously consider spending the night in the mountain hut Cojzova koča on the saddle Kokrsko sedlo.

Grintovec from Kokrsko sedlo

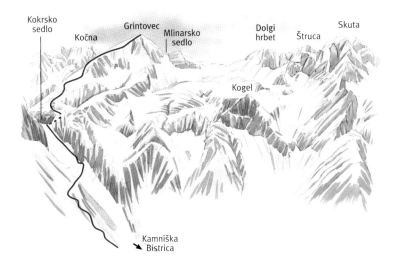

Kokrsko sedlo   Grintovec   Mlinarsko sedlo   Dolgi hrbet   Štruca   Skuta

Kočna

Kogel

Kamniška Bistrica

STARTING-POINT:

From Kamniška Bistrica, 601 m, a forest road leads right up to the head of the valley, which a footpath avoids for some time by a waymarked shortcut. The road ends at the bottom station of a load cableway; a good half hour to here.

DESCRIPTION:

The path now swings left into the forest and begins to climb in fairly steep serpentine bends. After a good hour's walk you emerge from the forest and ascend over grassy slopes to the foot of overhanging faces on the right side of the valley. Now a steep, tiring scree, which fills the narrowing valley, awaits you. This ends on the saddle **Kokrsko sedlo,** 1793 m, where to the south Kalški greben leans upon the Grintovec massif. On the saddle stands **Cojzova koča**. (There is also a path from the other side, from the Kokra valley, leading here. In the village of Zgornja Kokra a forest road branches off, leading to the Suhadolnik farm at an altitude of about 900 m. The easy, waymarked path from there takes a good 2 h to Kokrsko sedlo.)

Above the saddle the path at first ascends steeply, at the first fork you bear left over plateauish terrain to the foot of the summit structure of Grintovec. From here you climb leftwards along a steep bank, then straight up over grass and along a gully of rough scree to the beginning of the summit "roof". This is a steep, stony slope, which narrows like a cone to its highest point. Above the saddle the route runs over open slopes, so the views outweigh the rather monotonous walking. From the summit there is really something to see. The easiest descent is naturally by the same way.

TIMES:

Kamniška Bistrica - Kokrsko sedlo 3.30 h
(from the end of the road half an hour less)
Kokrsko sedlo - Grintovec 2 h
(from the valley 6 h)

41

Skuta

In the middle of the central chain

ALTITUDE: 2532 m
STARTING ALTITUDE: 601 m
HEIGHT DIFFERENCE: 1931 m

In the central chain of the range Skuta occupies a position more or less in the middle. So from the south it appears to the right of Grintovec. With its beautiful image it rather overshadows the highest summit in the range. This slender peak displays to the south a steep, smooth face, which is highly rated by rock-climbers. From Kamniška Bistrica to Skuta is even further than to Grintovec, because you must make a big detour over Kokrsko sedlo. So staying the night in the mountain hut Cojzova koča is recommended. The tour is not among the very demanding ones, but it has at least one exposed place, requiring experience from the mountaineer. Skuta will also appear in the next section, where the ridge tour from the saddle Kamniško sedlo will be described.

Štruca and Skuta above Veliki podi

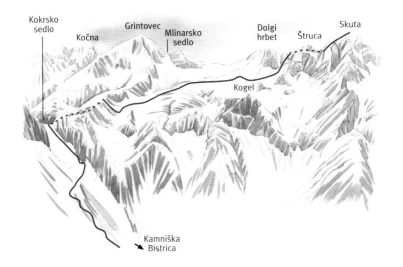

Kokrsko sedlo · Kočna · Grintovec · Mlinarsko sedlo · Kogel · Dolgi hrbet · Štruca · Skuta · Kamniška Bistrica

STARTING-POINT:

The starting-point is Cojzova koča on Kokrsko sedlo, 1793 m.

DESCRIPTION:

The access is described for the ascent of Grintovec (see pp. 232-233). At the top of the first steep stretch above the hut the way forks, with the left path leading to Grintovec and the right to Skuta. You soon step into the sharp cleft Mala vratca (Small Gate) in the southeast ridge of Grintovec, from where the path drops over steep, quite exposed rocks (secured section), and then ascends to the high-altitude plateau of Veliki podi. The path takes you past a tin-built shelter to reach a second fork. The lefthand, north-pointing path leads to Skuta. It runs through markedly karst terrain among rock hollows and over polished slabs. Here you must carefully follow the waymarks, since the terrain is difficult to survey as everything looks the same – especially in mist. Thus you come to a deep scree-filled hollow at the foot of Dolgi hrbet (Long Back), and notice on the right the picturesquely shaped **Štruca** (Round Loaf), 2437 m. Its unusual swollen belly really reminds you of a long round loaf of bread. There are quite a few paths in this area; at each fork you must always watch out for the direction Skuta. The path climbs over steep, rough scree and easy rock to the saddle between Dolgi hrbet and Skuta, avoiding the round top of Štruca on the north (though you can reach the summit in 5 minutes), then without any difficulty pushes over the stony summit slope to gain Skuta. It is easiest to descend by the same route.

TIMES:

Kamniška Bistrica - Kokrsko sedlo 3.30 h
Kokrsko sedlo - Skuta 3 h
Skuta - Kokrsko sedlo 2 h
Kokrsko sedlo - Kamniška Bistrica 2 h

42

Brana-Turska gora-Skuta

A grand traverse for more demanding mountaineers

ALTITUDE: 1835 m
STARTING ALTITUDE: 933 m
HEIGHT DIFFERENCE: 902 m

The central chain of the Kamnik-Savinja Alps is cut in half by the deeply cut saddle, Kamniško sedlo, 1885 m. The easiest passage from Kamniška Bistrica into the valley Logarska dolina leads over it. This is an exceptionally popular and much frequented point, due also to its large mountain hut. To the west above the saddle rises a distinctive mountain with high faces and a cupola-like top – Brana. The mountain is quite often visited, although the access is not quite easy and harmless. But we present it to more demanding and enterprising mountaineers as an introduction to a grand traverse of the ridges westwards as far as Skuta. On the way you also cross Turska gora, a broadly extended rise in the ridge, which otherwise doesn't have special validity as an independent goal. The tour is very demanding and strenuous, but is one of the finest in this range.

Grintovec, Skuta and Brana above Kamniška Bistrica

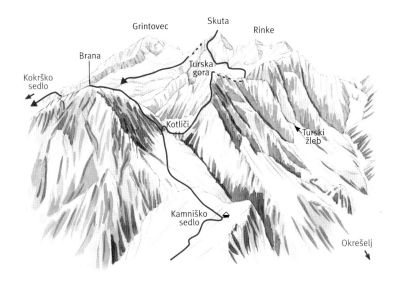

You must not be caught out by a storm on the ridge, so reliable weather is essential. The tour lasts two days, with the first stage to Kamniško sedlo serving as the overture, while the second day means hard work.

STARTING-POINT:
The path to Kamniško sedlo thrusts steeply up into the forest a few minutes above the mountain hut **Dom v Kamniški Bistrici**, 601 m.

DESCRIPTION:
Above a picturesque passage below big overhangs you cross a forest road, and then the gradient soon lessens. A half-hour's gentle walk towards the right follows, beyond a stony gully the path again starts to ascend more steeply through beech forest. Somewhat higher up you can quench your thirst in early summer, but in a drought period the spring dries up. The path continues through the forest to a fine resting-place in front of a little wooden hut with a bench. You notice in front of you a broad grassy plain surrounded by the high faces of Planjava (on the right) and Brana. Towards the saddle rises a fairly steep slope with a steady gradient; the unusual perspective makes the path seem never-ending. But up above you can regain your breath in the big, comfortably furnished mountain hut **Kamniška koča na Kamniškem sedlu,** 1864 m. If you're planning to do the whole tour, you need to stay the night here.

Brana rises to the west above the saddle and as the first goal is quite a good exercise for the morning warming-up session. The path at first winds gently through grass to the foot of the mountain. Here a path forks off to the right, dropping down to Okrešelj and further to Logarska dolina, whereas the path for Brana begins to climb over the northern slope with its rough scree. After half an hour you reach a fork, where you will later continue your tour westwards, but the lefthand path leads to the summit, immediately tackling steep rocks.

The climbing is not too demanding and exposed, however, and the iron security aids are helpful. Above, the gradient suddenly breaks off, revealing an extensive summit plateau in front of you. The summit of **Brana**, 2252 m, is on the left, only a few minutes away, marked by a metal cross. (If you decide on an ascent of Brana only, this is naturally a one-day tour, which together with the descent by the same way lasts about 7 h.)

At the fork to the north below the summit you now choose the westward route. The path soon leads into a realm of precipices, where you descend over broken, crumbly rocks by a well-secured section. The notch between Brana and Turska gora is called the **Kotliči** (Copper Pans), 1949 m. The name explains what your eyes can see: the surrounding terrain is rutted and pierced with holes, and coloured an unusual red (which betrays the presence of iron ore – in such an area beware of lightning!). Also the ridge towards the top of Turska gora is all crumbling and red, so that great caution is required, even though the exposed places are well secured. Here as well you often stare at the unusual natural "sculptures"; one even has the name Sod brez dna (Bottomless Barrel). The path keeps to the southern flank of the ridge, the difficulty diminishes towards the summit. From Brana to **Turska gora**, 2251 m, is an hour and a half's walk. The next in line is Skuta, the highest and most demanding of the tour. From Turska gora it seems quite near, in a predominating role with its pyramid-shaped eastern side. To the right of Skuta you notice the small group of four Rinkas, which this route avoids. On the southern side stretches the furrowed karst plateau of Mali podi (Small Plateau) and the path drops down from Turska gora westwards to its edge. Suddenly on the right yawns a dark gully, through which your gaze slips down to the head of the cwm Okrešelj above Logarska dolina. This is the couloir **Turski žleb**, snow-covered most of the year,

Brana, Turska gora, the Rinkas, Skuta, Grintovec and Kalška gora seen from Planjava

an unusually picturesque cleft in the monolithic northern faces of the mountain range. A demanding secured route from Okrešelj leads up through this (see the description on pp. 257-258). If for any reason you should need to shorten your tour while up at this point, it offers a quick (but not easy!) retreat from the high mountains. To Okrešelj takes 1.30 h, and from there you can climb up to Kamniško sedlo in 2 hours.

The route winds from the edge of Turski žleb westwards over karst terrain at the foot of the Rinkas. You notice a jagged ridge up above, which challenges rock-climbers and causes this path to switch to the southern side. Before encountering the rocks of Skuta's east face, you need to cross an extensive hollow with rough scree, and then ascend steeply in very pleasant climbing along a well-secured section. The route mostly follows the south-east ridge and is very panoramic. The last steps below the summit take you again over crumbling, red crags. The proud and mighty **Skuta**, 2532 m, is the third highest summit in the Kamnik-Savinja Alps and considerably outshines the two mountains you've come to know on the way. This is indeed the climax of the tour.

DESCENT:

It is best to descend to Cojzova koča on Kokrsko sedlo and then to Kamniška Bistrica (see the description in the previous section – Skuta). The path descends westwards over a slope of rough scree, avoiding the summit of Štruca on the right, and then drops down left onto the karst plateau of Veliki podi. It crosses it in a southerly direction, and then ascends steeply to the continuation of the southeast ridge of Grintovec immediately above **Kokrsko sedlo** (2 h from Skuta). If you're running short of daylight (or "fuel"), the mountain hut **Cojzova koča**, 1793 m, is at hand, otherwise you still have a good two hours' walk down into the valley by an undemanding but nevertheless steep path. In its entirety, the tour from Kamniško sedlo lasts approximately 10 h.

TIMES:

Kamniška Bistrica - Kamniško sedlo 3 h (overnight stay)
Kamniško sedlo - Brana 1 h
Brana - Turska gora 1.30 h
Turska gora - Skuta 2.30 h
(from Kamniško sedlo 5 h)
Skuta - Kokrsko sedlo 2 h
Kokrsko sedlo - Kamniška Bistrica 2 h
The entire circuit approx. 13 h

43

Planjava

A pleasant route to an expansive mountain

ALTITUDE: 2394 m
STARTING ALTITUDE: 601 m
HEIGHT DIFFERENCE: 1793 m

In the Kamnik-Savinja Alps Planjava is what Prisank is in the Julian Alps – the bulkiest, most massive mountain. Together with the slender Ojstrica – its opposite – it dominates the eastern half of this range. It rises directly to the east of the deeply cut Kamniško sedlo, which slices the main ridge in two, and from where most visitors ascend it. This expansive mountain is naturally very varied and can satisfy everyone. It offers rock-climbers as many as five independent faces. In the middle of one of the most frequented regions in the Slovene mountains you can enjoy solitude and primeval nature in the hidden valley of Repov kot at the southern foot of Planjava. The route described is the normal approach, representing a moderately demanding high-altitude tour. Exposed passages are well-secured.

Kamniško sedlo below Planjava; Krofička in the background

STARTING-POINT:

The starting-point is **Kamniška Bistrica**, 601 m.

DESCRIPTION:

The way to Kamniško sedlo has already been outlined for the ascent of Brana. You turn to face Planjava right in front of the mountain hut and the view is slightly disturbing. That's because Planjava here displays its steep, rocky appearance. But the experienced mountaineer will soon pick out a fine natural passage over grassy beds, which steeply divide the face towards the right. It is only some minutes' walk to the beginning of the rocks over rough scree. Here and there the ledge just mentioned is interrupted, but such places are reliably secured. Take care over the passage across a gully in the heart of the face, where a steep snow-field tends to lie far into the summer. Above, you observe the picturesque red towers that stand out from the west face. Above the gully the path ascends over a steep, slabbed slope onto the big ridge promontory **Sukalnik**, where the ground falls away to the extensive grassy slopes of Planjava's south side. Here you can look down into the deep valley of Repov kot, beyond which the pinnacles of the Zeleniške špice ridge are ranged in an exotic dance. The path to the summit of Planjava soon branches off from the horizontal route continuing towards the mountain hut Kocbekov dom on Korošica. The ground here is crumbly and partly grassy, and the path not too clear. However, the waymarks are reliable and you reach the top without any particular difficulties. A colossal precipice breaks away from under your feet. The north face of Planjava above the valley Logarska dolina is 1000 metres high!

DESCENT:

Returning the same way can be avoided by descending over Korošica and

The summit slopes of Planjava above Srebrno sedlo

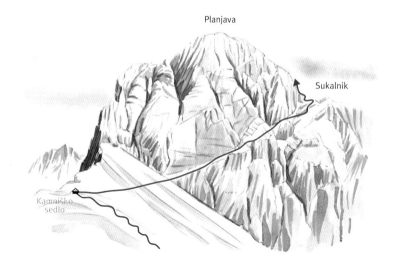

Planjava

Sukalnik

Kamniško sedlo

Presedljaj. This greatly lengthens the tour, but also enriches it. **Korošica** is an extensive basin to the east below Planjava, at the foot of Ojstrica. Here the mountain hut **Kocbekov dom**, 1803 m, is situated. From Planjava the path drops along the ridge towards the southeast, and then winds down steeply left and after an hour's walk brings you to Korošica. (Warning! – it is still nearly 4 h into the valley from here, so consider staying overnight in the hut.) The path leads on southwards. This pleasant walk over a soft carpet ends on the shallow saddle Prag (Threshold), where a path forks off left for the Savinja valley. The path for Kamniška Bistrica keeps to the original direction and begins to descend gradually over quite furrowed slopes. Here and there you cross some gullies. An hour and a half's walk from Korošica brings you to the saddle **Presedljaj**, 1610 m, where the south-lying group of Rzenik and Velika planina join the central mass of the range. Quite a demanding secured route heads in that direction but you need to turn onto the righthand path, which starts to fall steeply towards the southwest through a troughlike valley. Now you walk mostly through forest, occasionally coming out onto a panoramic promontory, where the dizzily steep face of Rzenik on the left draws most attention. The long steep gradient slowly diminishes, as you descend another hour and a half to the flat bottom of the **Bela** valley. You conclude the tour with a pleasant half-hour's walk on the level to the valley exit, where you join the main road 15 minutes away from the Dom v Kamniški Bistrici.

TIMES:

Kamniška Bistrica - Kamniško sedlo 3 h
Kamniško sedlo - Planjava 2 h
Planjava - Korošica 1 h
Korošica - Presedljaj 1 h
Presedljaj - Kamniška Bistrica 2-2.30 h

Jezersko

Jezersko is a really lovely alpine valley on the northwest side of the Kamnik-Savinja Alps. The glacier-shaped, trough-like valley is surrounded on all sides by a wreath of summits, through which the gorge of the River Kokra makes a way to the south. In the north the valley is fringed by the Karavanke ridge, along which the border runs. A road that links Gorenjska with Austrian Carinthia runs over the saddle Jezerski vrh, 1218 m. The valley is inhabited, but the people consider themselves Carinthians. The village here has the same name as the valley. The Kamnik-Savinja Alps present a serious, shady aspect with their wild faces, linked into one magnificent whole. The highest summits of this chain are lined up along the lofty ridge. From west to east these are Kočna, Grintovec, Dolgi hrbet (with its monolithic, vertical face this is the rock-climber's champion), Skuta and Rinka. The head of the valley at the foot of the giants is called Ravenska Kočna. On its left leans the furrowed Velika Baba, while right of the Kokra gorge rises Storžič. Even at a good distance you can tell that approaches to the summits in this region are not a simple joke. In this selection, only a round tour of Kočna and Grintovec will be described. For purely practical reasons this section will also include a description of the solitary Storžič. The road reaches Jezersko through the Kokra valley. There is a regular (though not frequent) bus service.

The northern faces of Skuta and Dolgi hrbet above Jezersko

44

Kočna-Grintovec

One of the finest routes above Jezersko

ALTITUDE: 2558 m
STARTING ALTITUDE: 1543 m
HEIGHT DIFFERENCE: 1015 m

The two highest summits of these Alps make up the righthand half of the majestic mountain wall above Jezersko. The chaotic, twin-summit Kočna is the exact opposite of the simply constructed pyramid of Grintovec. On a small terrace at the foot of their faces stands the friendly mountain hut Česka koča, which is the starting-point for the tour. This leads you along the secured route Kremžarjeva pot to Kočna, then along the ridge to Grintovec and further to the saddle Mlinarsko sedlo, and finally steeply back to the hut. An overnight stay is essential. (If you decide on ascending only one summit, the tour is practicable in one day.) It's a very demanding and strenuous tour, but one of the most beautiful in the Slovene mountains. But you must not tackle it too early in the summer, as you could be hindered by dangerous snow-fields.

Kočna seen from Grintovec, with the Julian Alps (left) and the Karavanke (right)

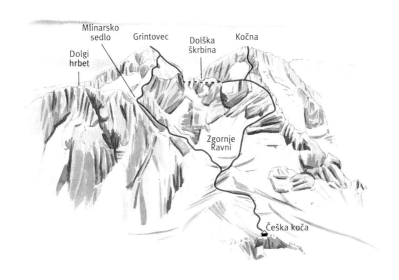

Mlinarsko sedlo · Grintovec · Dolška škrbina · Kočna · Dolgi hrbet · Zgornje Ravni · Češka koča

STARTING-POINT:

Two paths lead to **Češka koča**, 1543 m. The approach more worthy of a mountaineer is directly from the village of Zgornje Jezersko, 880 m. The way-marked route begins right in the village square, but driving along the road leading past the ski lift and the Makek farm will shorten the walking. The path winds towards the southeast mostly through forest, and the walk is pleasant and gradual. After a time the open area of Štularjeva planina interrupts the forest. Here you leave the slope above the Makekova Kočna valley and gaze at the glorious wreath of mountains above Ravenska Kočna. The pleasantly gentle path continues on to Češka koča. The other path is considerably shorter, leading from the bottom station of the load cableway in Ravenska Kočna, about 1100 m. The road brings you here from Zgornje Jezersko past the small lake Planšarsko jezero, 4 km. The path makes a considerable bend to the right and climbs to the hut in a good hour.

DESCRIPTION:

The route **Kremžarjeva pot** leads to Kočna along the southeast ridge, seen above the hut on the right. It is one of the finest secured climbing routes and represents a big challenge for the experienced mountaineer. Self-belaying is recommended. From Češka koča you ascend steeply into the cwm Zgornje Ravni, where the path for Mlinarsko sedlo branches off left (you will encounter this again in the afternoon). The climbing route begins right above the cwm, below a rocky spur, a protuberance of the northeast ridge. A good hour from the hut. At first the route climbs steeply onto the ridge itself, follows it in marvellous, exposed climbing for half an hour, and then continues over rocks left of the ridge. All the difficult and exposed places are well-secured. The last metres of climbing beneath the main ridge pass over steep slabs, and then your view skims over the expansive southern horizon. Soon the most picturesque place on the route has its turn as you crawl along a narrow little ledge under great overhangs as if through a shaft. Above, you must still climb a steep chimney (the hardest place), and then you soon step onto the pointed summit of Kočna, built of red rock.

The path to Grintovec leads more or less along the ridge, which has its deepest drop in the notch **Dolška škrbina**, 2317 m. You return along the Kremžar route to the fork a little below the renowned shaft, and then follow a well-secured path eastwards. This soon drops onto the southern side, later passing over the northern slope with its rough scree just beneath the summit of Grintovec. Some minutes before you stand upon this champion you pass the fork where you will later turn towards Mlinarsko sedlo. From Kočna to Grintovec takes a bare two hours of demanding climbing.

At the fork to the north below the summit you take the right path, descending along the northeast ridge. From the steep scree slope the path drops right into steep rocks, later running for a time along the ridge itself (fine, exposed climbing), and again to the right below it. Thus you reach the saddle **Mlinarsko sedlo**, 2334 m, which concludes the Grintovec massif. The last act of the tour once more takes place in the shady precipices of the north face, with the path zigzagging along natural passages. The steepness and exposure are quite considerable, yet the route is considerably easier than the Kremžar one. Special care is needed on some smooth ledges strewn with gravel. The route is well-secured. You descend over the face a good hour, and then take your farewell of steep rocks, iron pitons and ropes. The path winds over rough scree to the right and in the Zgornje Ravni basin half an hour above Češka koča this round tour comes full circle.

TIMES:

Jezersko - Češka koča 2 h

(from the bottom station of the load cableway 1h)

Češka koča - Kočna 3.30 h

Kočna - Grintovec 2 h

Grintovec - Češka koča 2.30-3 h

The entire tour 8-10 h

45

Storžič

The western border stone

ALTITUDE: 2132 m
STARTING ALTITUDE: c. 550 m, 1123 m
HEIGHT DIFFERENCE: c. 1580 m, 1009

Due to its solitary position and attractive appearance, Storžič is one of the most distinctive and noticeable mountains in Slovenia. Proudly it rises directly above the Gorenjska plain and catches everyone's eye from near and far. The southern side comprises extensive steep, grassy slopes with red rocks, while to the north the mountain is abruptly sliced off. Storžič is separated from the central chain of these Alps by the deep gorge of the River Kokra; this personality is completely independent of Kamnik and the Savinja, which gave the range its name. Naturally, such an appealing mountain is quite often visited, and so many paths lead to its summit that it's really hard to decide. Two strongly differing approaches will be described, so as to emphasize the varied character of Storžič. The summit is one of the most beautiful Slovene viewpoints.

The southern slopes of Storžič

A. THE SOUTHERN APPROACH

STARTING-POINT:
The easiest path to Storžič begins in the small village of **Mače**, c. 550 m, to the north above the larger settlement of Preddvor (c. 15 km from Kranj by road).

DESCRIPTION:
Above the village you walk for half an hour along a forest road beside the stream in the Suha valley, then the waymarks bear left onto a forested edge. On this pleasant, shady walk you cross the rise of Veliki vrh, 993 m, and then the path tackles the steep gradient in numerous zigzags. The trees recede only after a good hour's walk as you gain the open area of Kališče. Still another short gradient and then the large mountain hut **Dom na Kališču**, 1534 m, greets you on its rocky edge. The path continues northwards, rising gently towards the saddle Bašeljsko sedlo, 1630 m, at the foot of the summit section of Storžič. Here the view to the north opens up, and the route coming from this side, from Jezersko, will be described later. Now begins the finest, high-altitude part of the tour. The path twists across Storžič's open eastern slope and the views become ever broader. Mostly you walk over grassy slopes, full of brightly coloured flowers. Occasionally you must exert some effort over a rocky step, but otherwise the path is easy. Finally the abyss of the north face plunges beneath your feet as the summit is reached. If you wish to return to your starting-place, you must descend the same way.

TIMES:
Mače - Dom na Kališču 2.30 h
Dom na Kališču - Storžič 2 h

Storžič viewed from the north

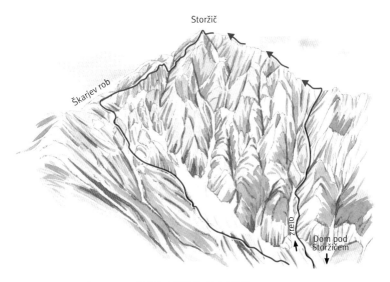

A. THE NORTHERN APPROACH

As is usually the case in the Slovene mountains, the northern approach to Storžič is also the steepest and most demanding. On this side a mighty face drops to the valley, torn by numerous gullies. Two demanding secured routes lead to the summit, which will be linked in a round tour.

STARTING-POINT:
The starting-point is the mountain hut **Dom pod Storžičem**, 1123 m, in a basin at the foot of the northwest face. It is reached by road from the small town of Tržič to the west below Storžič through the village of Lom (9 km, 1.45 h on foot along a way-marked shortcut). The ascent to Storžič is recommended along the route through Žrelo, and the descent along the somewhat easier north ridge, called Škarjev rob. On the whole the tour is moderately demanding, and the walking exceptionally steep.

DESCRIPTION:
Žrelo (Gullet) is the name of a steep gully, carved through the righthand side of the face. It is 20 minutes from the hut to the entry into the rocks. The entrance into Žrelo is indeed formed in a picturesque rocky gateway, but the path thrusts into the steep gradient right of the gully. Before you come to the first pitons, the roots of larches provide substitute holds. Then the route winds up the unrelentingly stiff gradient alternately along the gully or to the right of it. The more difficult places are found in the lower half of the gully and are well-secured. Even afterwards the gradient hardly eases and just below the summit you must still climb over a steep rock step. This brings you onto Storžič's west ridge, where a great swathe of Slovenia opens up in front of you. Compared to the way you've just come, the path on to the summit provides a pleasant walk along a ridge that isn't difficult at all. With every step the view grows richer.

Storžič attracts enthusiastic mountaineers in winter too

DESCENT:
The descent along the north ridge is not completely easy, and the brittle rock demands extra caution. From the top you descend into a gully of rough scree, which lower down continues over the entire face, but you cross out of it to the right in the direction of the overgrown north ridge. This is called **Škarjev rob,** and when you gain it, your difficulties are also over. The path drops along this edge, which is increasingly overgrown by dwarf pine, then bears left and slips into the forest. The round tour is completed just above Dom pod Storžičem.

TIMES:
Dom pod Storžičem - Žrelo - Storžič 3 h
Storžič - Škarjev rob - Dom pod Storžičem 2 h
The circular tour 5.30 h

Logarska dolina

What Vrata is in the Julian Alps, Logarska dolina is in the Kamnik-Savinja Alps. Renowned and much visited, characterized by many superlatives, it must be admitted that this is an extremely beautiful alpine valley. Logarska dolina is the northeast entrance into the heart of this mountain range. Along the flat bottom of the glacier carved valley flows the young River Savinja, which has its source in the fine waterfall **Rinka** above the head of the valley. Above the waterfall the broad cirque of **Okrešelj** lies surrounded by mighty rock faces. In the valley itself a few farmsteads are scattered, and rather more places catering for tourists. At the exit from Logarska dolina the Savinja flows through a long gorge; only here do you find compact settlements, the nearest being the village of **Solčava**. Above Logarska dolina true giants show their dark northern aspect, marked by alpine wildness. Between the precipitous faces of Krofička, Ojstrica, Planjava, Brana, Turska gora, Rinka and Mrzla gora (the summits are enumerated from left to right) some gully or bed has etched out a space where paths could be made. Mountaineering tours above Logarska dolina are mostly steep and demanding. Two friendly mountain huts, one or two hours' walk above the valley, serve as starting-points and will be presented in individual descriptions. A picturesque road winding along the gorge of the Savinja leads into Logarska dolina but there are few regular bus routes. The most beautiful access from central Slovenia in terms of landscape is the road Ljubljana-Kamnik-Črnivec pass-Gornji Grad-Solčava, but it is quicker to use the Ljubljana-Maribor motorway with the exit for Logarska dolina or the route via Jezersko and Pavličevo sedlo. During the summer tourist season it is necessary to pay on entrance to the valley.

Logarska dolina with the northern flanks of Ojstrica and Planjava

251

46

Ojstrica

A pointed summit to the east of the central chain

ALTITUDE: 2350 m
STARTING ALTITUDE: 837 m
HEIGHT DIFFERENCE: 1513 m

The central chain of the Kamnik-Savinja Alps is concluded in the east by an extremely fine and all-round distinctive mountain. Ojstrica is a very suitable name for it, being based on the adjective *oster*, which means 'sharp, pointed'. Ojstrica is truly well-honed, steep – and enticing. In many respects it actually overshadows Grintovec as the highest mountain. Naturally, it is one of the most frequented mountains, thanks also to its set of good and varied paths. Typically, Ojstrica presents its wildest and most inaccessible aspect towards the north and so is admired most by visitors to Logarska dolina. On this side is found its exceptionally steep and smooth north face, which rock-climbers evaluate as the finest in the whole range. Two paths lead to the summit from this valley, which will be linked to make an excellent round tour. Understandably, the ascent is by the more demanding Kopinškova pot and the descent by the easier route over Škarje. This

The north face of Ojstrica

Ojstrica   Lučka Baba   Planjava

Škrbina   Škarje

Rjavčki vrh

Zgornje jame

Klemenča jama

Logarska dolina

demanding tour can be executed in one day, but the friendly hut Koča na Klemenči jami offers a more pleasant way of carrying it out.

STARTING-POINT: You leave the asphalt road through the valley by the mountain hut **Dom planincev**, 837 m.

DESCRIPTION: The path is oriented eastwards and soon takes you up steeply through the forest. After an hour's walk the trees recede to reveal a wonderful alpine environment. Apparently near at hand, the vertiginous north face of Ojstrica rises into the sky, while **Koča na Klemenči jami**, 1208 m, stands in the middle of an extensive forest clearing. The next forested stage is covered in barely an hour and you enter the cwm of Zgornja jama, lying in the shadow of that great face. At a fork you choose the lefthand path, which climbs amidst gradually dwindling larches and dwarf pine. Now the terrain is getting steeper and ever more alpine. A stony gully runs out at the saddle **Škrbina**, 1800 m, where the climbing part of the tour begins. At this point the steep and solitary summit of Krofička, 2083 m, leans against Ojstrica, while on the other side your gaze slips down into the deep valley of Robanov kot, a sort of miniature Logarska dolina. From Škrbina the steep northeast ridge thrusts up towards Ojstrica's summit, and a bold, finely laid out but demanding secured route lies along it, known as **Kopinškova pot**. In actual fact, there is almost no ridge climbing as the route winds over steep rocks and patches of green left of the ridge; just here and there you can peep over some notch into the precipitous north face. The climbing is steep and strenuous yet the level of difficulty is moderate, with the exposed places being well-secured. The route doesn't follow the ridge right to the summit. About 150 m below the pointed peak it makes use of a broad ledge and you cross the upper part of the north face horizontally towards the right. If clear of snow, the ledge is easy but quite far into the summer you can be surprised by a dangerous snowfield here (an ice-axe is obligatory!). The abyss below yawns quite nearby and the 500-metre sheer drop can clearly send a shiver up your spine. The ledge comes to an end on the broken rocks of the northwest ridge, which soon leads you to the proud summit of Ojstrica, where an exceptionally rich panorama is waiting for you.

DESCENT: The easiest path to Ojstrica comes from the south, where at the foot of the summit pyramid lies the very broad alp **Korošica**, with the mountain hut **Kocbekov dom**, 1803 m. But this path will take you much further away from your starting-point, so the more direct descent over Škarje back into Logarska dolina will be described here. **Škarje** (Scissors), 2131 m, is the name of a notch to the west below Ojstrica. Above it are two pointed towers, hence the name. From the summit of Škarje you first drop straight down towards the south over friable rock, and at the first fork turn right, thus avoiding the towers of the main ridge. The path winds more or less horizontally over well-secured rocks, and then over grass and a gully of stones climbs to the previously mentioned notch, which separates the two massifs of Ojstrica and Planjava. (Here the opportunity to climb **Planjava** by its west ridge offers itself. The route is easier than the Kopinškova pot, though not entirely without difficulties. In between you cross the intermediate summit Lučka Baba, 2244 m. From Škarje to Planjava 1.30 h. From the latter you can descend to Kamniško sedlo (see pp. 240-242 and return via Okrešelj to Logarska dolina.)

From Škarje you drop onto the other side, first over a rocky gully, and then across heavy scree to a grassy saddle in front of the round head of Rjavčki vrh. You continue down to the right and soon reach the highest larches above the cwm Zgornja jama, where the circle is completed. You descend to Klemenča jama and on into the valley by a now familiar path.

TIMES:

Dom planincev - Koča na Klemenči jami 1h
Koča na Klemenči jami - Škrbina 2 h
Škrbina - Ojstrica (via Kopinškova pot) 2 h

The descent (over Škarje) 4 h
The whole tour 9-10 h

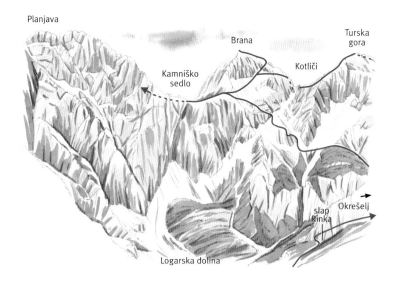

47

Planjava-Brana

Two giants approached from the north

ALTITUDE: 2394 m
STARTING ALTITUDE: 1385 m (837 m)
HEIGHT DIFFERENCE: 1009 m (1557 m)

From Logarska dolina Planjava presents itself as a mighty and massive mountain, closing in a considerable portion of the horizon. Its magnificent north face is no less than 1000 metres high! Its western neighbour, Brana, is less noticeable, but even so is one of the champions of the range. Between the two mountains the main ridge drops to Kamniško sedlo, the deepest cut in the main ridge and the easiest passage from the Savinja to the Kamnik side. This pair and the approaches to them have already been presented in the chapter on Kamniška Bistrica, but the paths from the north are equally popular and recommendable.

STARTING-POINT:
The starting-point is the cirque **Okrešelj** to the west above Logarska dolina,

The panorama with Ojstrica, Planjava, Brana and the Rinke from Olševa

where the mountain hut **Frischaufov dom**, 1385 m, stands. It is a lovely, much visited place in the heart of the mountains. At the bottom of the cirque a small grassy plain extends, fringed by larches. Above it are ranged magnificent faces and Okrešelj is the most important starting-point for climbing in the Savinja Alps. In fact, the climbing champion above Okrešelj is the face of Štajerska Rinka, appearing in the form of a mighty tower to the west. Left of the Rinka group you can with some difficulty pick out the dark shaft of Turski žleb, which you reach by the path described in the next section. If you wish to ascend Planjava or Brana, you must first reach Kamniško sedlo to the south above Okrešelj. Access to Okrešelj is easy, taking barely an hour along a comfortable path, which begins at the end of the road at the head of Logarska dolina. On the way you take a look at the famous Rinka waterfall.

DESCRIPTION:

The path to Kamniško sedlo is demanding. From Frischaufov dom you first push southwards through the forest to a small flat area at the foot of Turska gora. Then the path leads leftwards over grass and scree into the Brana massif, where after scarcely an hour's walk your way seems closed by a steep face. The path crosses it leftwards and is well-secured all the time. Above the rocks you step into a funnel-shaped basin, where snow can lie until late in the summer, in those conditions, the path is safely practicable only for an experienced mountaineer, equipped with an ice-axe. When clear of snow, this passage is not demanding. The route runs to the right and soon you step onto the panoramic, grassy ridge of Kamniško sedlo, where a wide view opens up towards the south. From Okrešelj 1.30 h. The big mountain hut Kamniška koča stands on the southern side of the saddle to your left.

If you're aiming for **Brana**, turn immediately right and in a bare hour you'll reach the summit. At first the way is easy but then some well-secured rocks, though not too steep, are waiting. From the end of the road into Logarska dolina to Brana is 3.30 h. Once again, there is a natural opportunity of continuing your tour to Turska gora with a descent through Turski žleb back to Okrešelj (see pp. 257-258). The round tour Okrešelj-Brana-Turska gora-Okrešelj lasts approximately 6 h and is very demanding.

The route to **Planjava** from Kamniško sedlo has already been described (see pp. 240-242).

DESCENT:

Besides returning by the same way, you can choose to descend towards the west along the ridge over Lučka Baba to the notch Škarje and down to the left past the hut Koča na Klemenči jami into Logarska dolina (see pp. 252-254).

TIMES:

Logarska dolina - Okrešelj 1 h
Okrešelj - Kamniško sedlo 1.30 h
Okrešelj - Brana 2.30 h
Kamniško sedlo - Planjava 2 h
The complete circuit 8-9 h

48

Turska gora

ALTITUDE: 2251 m
STARTING ALTITUDE: 1385 m
HEIGHT DIFFERENCE: 866 m

Turska gora is not one of the most important summits, but as a connecting link between its more excellent neighbours it is nevertheless indispensable and greatly visited. The northern approach from Okrešelj will be described above all on account of the interesting and wild passage through Turski žleb. This is a steep gully, squeezed between the faces of Turska gora and Rinka, which offers picturesque access to the "upper storey" of the Kamnik-Savinja Alps. The tour is very demanding.

STARTING-POINT:
The starting-point is **Frischaufov dom na Okrešlju,** 1385 m (1 h from Logarska dolina, by the path mentioned in the previous tour).

The north faces of the Rinkas viewed from Okrešelj

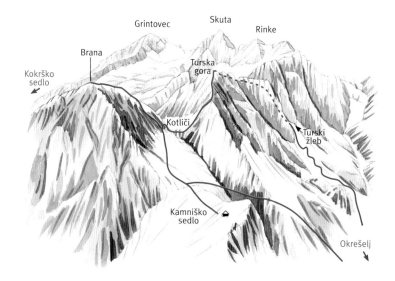

DESCRIPTION:

From here the path leads to the west. The pleasant walk along the gentle bottom of the cirque is followed by a steep ascent in numerous serpentine bends across a high scree, which narrows conically towards a narrow, dark cleft between perpendicular faces on the left above the head of the cirque. This is **Turski žleb**. From Okrešelj to its beginning lasts a bare hour. This shadowed couloir is snow-covered most of the year and is practicable only with suitable eqipment. Precisely for this reason a well-secured climbing route was built across the steep face on the right, which belongs to the Rinka massif. This runs parallel to the bottom of the gully, some metres above the bergschrund of the snow-field, steep and exposed all the time over the smooth faces. You step from piton to piton, beside the reliable steel rope. Equipment for self-belaying and a helmet are very recommendable. In this dark gully one doesn't feel particularly relaxed and above, on the edge of the karst plateau of Mali podi, where the sun shines again, everyone feels relieved. Climbing through Turski žleb lasts a bare hour. At the top you turn left and in half an hour, without any difficulty, you reach the summit.

DESCENT:

The shortest descent is naturally by the same route, but you can greatly enrich the tour by continuing to the east over Brana to Kamniško sedlo and then descend to Okrešelj.

TIMES:

Frischaufov dom - Turska gora 2.30 h
The circular tour via Brana 6 h

258

49

Raduha

On the other side of the deep gorge of the Savinja

ALTITUDE: 2062 m
STARTING ALTITUDE: 642 m
HEIGHT DIFFERENCE: 1420 m

Raduha is the eastern border stone of the mountain range. Although it exceeds 2000 metres and possesses just the right kind of north face, popular among rock-climbers, in a way it doesn't strictly belong to the high-altitude realm. This extensive mountain of soft forms fits better among the gentle backs of medium mountains, which stretch from here far to the east, right to the edge of the Pannonian Plain. Raduha is separated from the central chain of the Kamnik-Savinja Alps by the deep gorge of the River Savinja, which stresses even more its special place. The mountain is green and friendly, so it's no wonder that the highest farmhouse in Slovenia is situated on its flanks. If you tackle Raduha from its foot, you will find, nevertheless, that this is a high mountain. The approach is greatly shortened by any of the forest roads that

The north face of Raduha

reach far up its slopes. The more demanding northern approach, which has the character of a real alpine tour, will be described here.

STARTING-POINT:
The starting-point is **Solčava**, 642 m, the highest village in the Savinja valley, quite near the entrance to Logarska dolina.

DESCRIPTION:
Several paths lead to Raduha but this one begins in the gorge of the **Klobaša** stream, which flows into the Savinja just below Solčava. You must still walk half an hour along the road, and then the waymarked path branches off to the right. It winds through steep forest, interrupted every half hour by a solitary farm. The fine, robust homesteads stand on broad ridges with good views and constitute the indispensable feature of these parts, which already in a way tend towards Carinthia. The highest one, **Bukovnikova kmetija,** 1327 m, is the highest place in Slovenia where people live. The road you find yourself on here continues still further towards Raduha. A good half hour above the Bukovnik farm, the forest again retreats but instead of a farmhouse you now see the dwellings of the Grohat alp. Soon you come to the mountain hut **Koča na Grohatu,** 1460 m. (As far as the Bukovnik farm and still a little higher it is possible to drive along the road from Solčava over Podolševa and the Sleme saddle; 10 km. Raduha and Olševa can be connected into one tour.)
Raduha shows a steep face towards Grohat, which the Durce pass cuts into on the left. The path climbs gently in half an hour to a fork. The less experienced should choose the left path, which ascends across rough scree at the foot of the vertical face of Mala Raduha into a narrow, steep trough below the Durce pass. Just below this you need to climb a steep section beside a good iron

The view from the summit ridge of Raduha towards the Kamnik Alps with Ojstrica

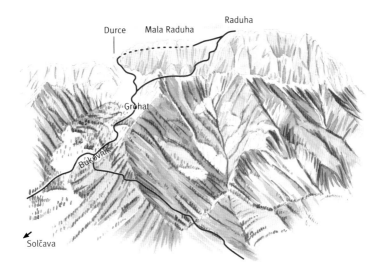

rope. Here you turn right, gently ascending over slopes covered in dwarf pine, you bypass Mala Raduha, and then reach the summit of Velika Raduha by an extremely panoramic ridge.

If at the fork half an hour above Grohat you select the righthand path, you must reckon with quite demanding climbing over the northwest face of Raduha. The path on the right crosses a steep edge, then runs almost horizontally among larches and dwarf pine at the foot of the face. Half an hour above the fork the path pushes upwards into rocks. First you climb along a steep gully, and then bear right over exposed but well-secured slabs. Above, the terrain is easier, only here and there you need to climb some rock step. You reach the summit ridge not far from the top of Raduha.

DIFFICULTY:
The route over the northwest face of Raduha is demanding.

DESCENT:
It is best to descend over the Durce pass.

TIMES:
Solčava - Koča na Grohatu 2.30 h
Koča na Grohatu - Raduha (over the Durce pass) 2 h
Koča na Grohatu - Raduha (over the northwest face) 1.30 h

Index

263

Maps

1 Triglav, 1:25.000. Ljubljana: Planinska zveza Slovenije, Inštitut za geodezijo in fotogrametrijo, 2001.
2 Triglavski narodni park, 1:50.000. Ljubljana: Planinska zveza Slovenije, Inštitut za geodezijo in fotogrametrijo, 2001.
3 Julijske Alpe, vzhodni del, 1:50.000. Ljubljana: Planinska zveza Slovenije, Inštitut za geodezijo in fotogrametrijo, 2000.
4 Julijske Alpe, zahodni del, 1:50.000. Ljubljana: Planinska zveza Slovenije, Inštitut za geodezijo in fotogrametrijo, 1999.
5 Kamniško-Savinjske Alpe, 1:50.000. Ljubljana: Planinska zveza Slovenije, Geodetski zavod Slovenije, 2000.
6 Grintovci, 1:25.000. Ljubljana: Planinska zveza Slovenije, Inštitut za geodezijo in fotogrametrijo, 1998.
7 Kranjska Gora z okolico, 1:25.000. Ljubljana: Planinska zveza Slovenije, Inštitut za geodezijo in fotogrametrijo, 1996.
8 Krnsko pogorje in Kobarid, 1:25.000. Ljubljana: Planinska zveza Slovenije, Inštitut za geodezijo in fotogrametrijo, 1992.
9 Karavanke, osrednji del, 1:50.000. Ljubljana: Planinska zveza Slovenije, Geodetski zavod Slovenije, 1999.

Authors of photographs

Skok Janez :	front cover, 6-7, 26, 32, 34, 36, 39, 46, 52, 70, 74-75, 80, 85, 90-91, 94, 97, 98, 103, 106, 108, 115, 116, 122, 125, 126, 128, 131, 134-135, 136, 139, 142, 145, 155, 158, 159, 160, 163, 164, 174, 175, 177, 182, 185, 189, 190, 203, 206, 211, 213,214-215, 217, 220, 223, 226, 228-229, 243, 244, 247, 248, 250, back cover
Bijuklič Mirko:	202
Česen Aleš:	238
Debevc Miha:	59, 102, 170, 178, 197, 200, 207, 234, 236, 241
Habjan Vladimir:	110, 192, 209
Janežič Peter:	18-19, 44-45, 54, 101, 107, 119, 251, 255
Kačičnik Matjaž:	157, 168, 186, 231, 257
Klemenc Stane:	30, 40, 65
Maher Igor:	62
Mihelič Jože:	2-3, 29, 42, 49, 68, 96, 113, 152-153
Modic Igor:	77, 88, 104, 105, 156, 167
Mrše Peter:	81, 171, 224
Pintarič Marko:	83, 180, 219
Podovšovnik Uroš:	260
Pivka Jurij:	259
Poljak Mario:	147
Prezelj Marko:	232, 240
Senegačnik Jurij:	56
Simić Marko:	172, 195
Strmšek Boris:	256
Zabukovec Blaž:	57

tourist board

LTO KRANJSKA GORA
tel: +386 (0) 4 58 85 020
fax: +386 (0) 4 58 85 021
e mail: info@kranjska-gora.si
www.kranjska-gora.si

tourist board

LTO BOHINJ
tel: +386 (0) 4 57 47 590
fax: +386 (0)4 57 47 591
e mail:lto@bohinj.si
www.bohinj.si

Juli

tourist board

LTO TURIZEM BLED
tel: +386(0) 4 578 05 00
fax: +386 (0) 4 578 05 01
e mail: info@dzt.bled.si
www.bled.si

tourist board

LTO SOTOČJE
tel: +386 (0) 5 38 00 480
fax: +386 (0) 5 38 00 483
e mail: info@lto-sotocje.si
www.lto-sotocje.si

Alps